Succeeding with Your
Master's Dissertation

Succeeding with Your Master's Dissertation

A step-by-step handbook

John Biggam

Open University Press

Open University Press
McGraw-Hill Education
McGraw-Hill House
Shoppenhangers Road
Maidenhead
Berkshire
England
SL6 2QL

email: enquiries@openup.co.uk
world wide web: www.openup.co.uk

and Two Penn Plaza, New York, NY 10121-2289, USA

First published 2008

A catalogue record of this book is available from the British Library

ISBN-10: 0 335 22719 8 (pb)   0 335 22720 1 (hb)
ISBN-13: 978 0 335 22719 8 (pb)   978 0 335 22720 4 (hb)

Library of Congress Cataloguing-in-Publication Data
CIP data applied for

Typeset by RefineCatch Limited, Bungay, Suffolk
Printed in the UK by Bell and Bain Ltd, Glasgow

Fictitious names of companies, products, people, characters and/or
data that may be used herein (in case studies or in examples) are not
intended to represent any real individual, company, product or event.

The **McGraw·Hill** Companies

This book is dedicated to:–

Three people, now deceased, all of whom left school in the days when it was unusual, if not exceptional, for those labelled 'working class' to continue with formal education beyond the age of 14: my father, Alexander, who did not have any formal qualifications; my mother, Margaret, who knew the value of them; and my father-in-law, William Macfarlane, who did not need any.

My wife, Kay, and my son, Jason.

The late Phil O'Donnell, of Motherwell F.C. and Celtic F.C. A gentleman and a role model to all students, regardless of field of study. *Non scholae sed vitae discimus.*

Contents

1

Introduction

A Master's dissertation: what is it? • *So, what skills do you need to succeed?* • *Watch your words!* • *How to use this book*

A *Master's* dissertation: what is it?

A professor was approached by one of her students, who enquired: 'Is it all right to put bullet points in an essay?' Another student queried: 'When you say you want journal articles, how many?' This tutor was disappointed that her students required their assessment criteria to be explained in such minutiae (Wojtas 2006: 2). What may appear trivial to a dissertation supervisor can be a source of concern to you, the student. A Master's dissertation involves the production of a substantial piece of work, normally consisting of about 15,000 words, and it is likely that this is the first time you have encountered such a work, in such depth; therefore, it is important that you understand fully what is required of a Master's student and, equally, how to get through the dissertation journey, from grasping an overview of the main phases of writing a dissertation (submitting your dissertation proposal, writing your research objectives, writing the Literature Review, etc.) to the finer points of completing the content of each phase. This book provides detailed guidance on how to complete your dissertation, thus meeting the needs of students eager for practical assistance in this commonplace, but challenging, mode of assessment.

Dissertations have always been a problematic area for students. Students registered for a *taught* Master's programme not only have to cope with their core subject areas, but they are also required, largely through independent study, and within tight time constraints, to complete a substantial dissertation project. Students registered for a Master's by *research*, although they have no taught element to contend with, often find the dissertation process equally stressful. For many Master's students, their venture into the world of the dissertation becomes nothing short of a guessing-game, where the tasks to be completed are difficult to comprehend, and where the final mark awarded for their efforts is even trickier to fathom. Students are aware that they have to write an *Introduction*, but they are not really sure how to go about it; they sort of know that they have to complete something called a *Literature Review*, but they are at a loss where to start or what it ought to contain, or what will get them good marks; the section on *Research Methods* (necessary if students are implementing their own practical research work to complement their Literature Review) seems so abstract to them, and concepts such as 'positivism' and 'phenomenology', so revered by their tutors, do not help matters; and so on.

There are many different types of Master's dissertations: some focusing on a review of literature relevant to your topic of study; others also requiring the implementation of practical research; some involving a presentation of the dissertation findings; others, still, obliging you to attend an oral examination. At the heart of each of these dissertations is the study of a particular subject, usually selected by you, the student.

How does a Master's qualification differ from an undergraduate qualification? The traditional view of a graduate degree qualification – such as a Bachelor of Arts (B.A.) in Business Studies – is that it is evidence that the holder of the degree has attained a level of *general* knowledge related to the subject area(s) named in the award (Hart 2006). For instance, a B.A. in History indicates that the holder has a general knowledge, at university level, of History, or specific aspects of history; similarly, a B.A. in Hospitality Management indicates that the holder has a general knowledge of hospitality management. A *Master's* qualification, by contrast, signifies that the holder has gone beyond the acquisition of general knowledge and has *advanced* specialized knowledge of a subject. Master's programmes come in various guises, with the more traditional and well-known Master's titles shown in Table 1.1.

Table 1.1 shows the more common type of Master's titles – MSc., MA, MLitt., and MPhil. – but they by no means exhaust the list of Master's titles found in university programmes. For example, Newcastle University in the UK offers a Master of Music (MMus.), while the University of Sydney in

Table 1.1 Traditional *Master's* programmes

Postgraduate title	Latin name	Abbreviation
Master of Science	*Magister Scientiae*	MSc.
Master of Arts	*Magister Artium*	MA
Master of Laws	*Legum Magister*	LL.M.
Master of Letters	*Magister Litterarum*	MLitt.
Master of Philosophy	*Magister Philosophiae*	MPhil.

Australia lists a Master of Design Science (*MDESSC.*) within its postgraduate portfolio, and the University of Nevada in the USA advertises a Master of Education (M.Ed.). The form of the title abbreviation is left to individual institutions, with some institutions italicizing the title abbreviation (e.g. *MDESSC.*), some placing a full stop after the abbreviation of Magister (e.g. M.Ed.), while others ignore full stops and italics altogether (e.g. MEd, MSc, MPhil, etc.).

Confusingly, an MSc. does not necessarily indicate that the topics studied are science-based, as many business schools within universities now offer MSc. programmes (e.g. MSc. in International Business). Equally confusing is the fact that not all Master's programmes are postgraduate programmes, where a related degree is the usual entrance qualification. For instance, the MA is traditionally viewed as an undergraduate degree in the UK, yet when offered in the USA it is normally offered as a postgraduate qualification. It is worth noting that universities in the UK and the USA sometimes use different terminology to refer to postgraduate programmes – UK universities stick to the term 'postgraduate' while universities in the USA commonly use the term 'graduate'. For example, the University of Chicago publicize their LL.M. as a *graduate* degree while the University of Cambridge present their LL.M. as a *postgraduate* degree, but both qualifications are advanced law degrees requiring a degree qualification for entry.

A critical element of any Master's programme, whether it is an advanced undergraduate degree (such as an MA in the UK) or a postgraduate programme proper (such as an MSc.), is the requirement to complete a *dissertation*. So, what is a dissertation? The Concise Oxford Dictionary (1998: 391) defines a dissertation as 'a detailed discourse on a subject, esp. one submitted in partial fulfilment of the requirements of a degree or diploma'. In effect, it appears to be a very long essay. In the context of a typical Master's programme, it is a focused 'essay', typically about 10,000–15,000 words in length (the MPhil. dissertation, often referred to as a *thesis*, is different in that the word length is easily in the range 30,000–50,000). A dissertation is more than an extended essay, though: it is an independent piece of work (by you, the student) to be completed in such a way as to satisfy the examiner(s) that you are a *competent researcher* with advanced knowledge on a specific topic, normally chosen by you, which relates to your Master's programme.

A *Master's* dissertation, as with Master's titles and programmes, can come in many shapes and sizes, varying from university to university, and even within different departments in the same university. The types of Master's dissertations available to you can include the straightforward Literature Review; or a work-based report, in which you explore a particular problem in an organization where you have worked, making practical recommendations based on your findings; or a laboratory-based dissertation, where you carry out experiments and then report on your results; or a dissertation which encompasses both a Literature Review and the collection and analysis of your own primary research data, providing you with the opportunity to compare theory (from your Literature Review) with practice (from your collected primary data, e.g. from interviews or questionnaires).

Your university should provide you with a Master's Handbook containing clear guidance on aspects of your dissertation. The Handbook will normally clarify the maximum length of your dissertation, dissertation format (line spacing, text type and size, style of referencing, page numbering, dissertation structure, etc.), expected minimum content for each major section of your dissertation (e.g. main areas to be covered in your chapter on Research Methods), the department's marking scheme, and details of your role and responsibilities.

Successful completion of a Master's dissertation, however, is more than adhering merely to university dissertation requirements and guidelines: you need competence in specific *dissertation-related skills* and a certain street savvy about the *rules of the game*.

So, what skills do you need to succeed?

Basically, to pass your Master's dissertation you need to show that you are a *competent researcher*. On the face of it, this is quite a difficult task, mainly because this is probably the first time that you have attempted an independent piece of research work of this magnitude. A competent researcher is someone who can, in the context of a Master's dissertation, exhibit proficiency in tackling the various phases normally found in the *Dissertation Life Cycle* (DLC), illustrated in Figure 1.1.

To complete the DLC successfully you require to show proficiency in skills specific to each stage of the cycle, i.e. you need to be able to do the following:

- Put forward a *credible research proposal* (Stage 1 of the DLC).
- *Evaluate literature*, from a variety of sources, pertinent to your research objectives (Stage 2).
- *Cite sources* – books, journals, web sources, conference proceedings, etc. – using a standard acceptable to the academic community, e.g. Harvard style of referencing, or American Psychological Association (APA) citation style, etc. (Stage 2).
- *Identify (and justify)* how you will collect (and analyse) your own research data (Stage 3).
- *Carry out your own empirical research* (Stage 4).
- *Discuss and analyse* your findings (Stage 5).
- *Wrap up your research work* (Stage 6).

Be aware that the DLC is rarely a straightforward linear process, where the journey from Stage 1 to Stage 7 is smooth and untroubled. More often than not, you will find yourself revisiting previous stages, usually as a result of

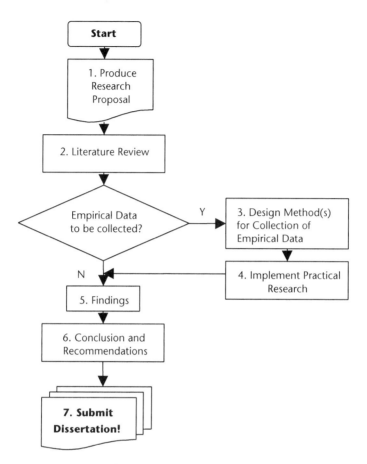

Figure 1.1 Dissertation Life Cycle (DLC)

discussions and advice from your supervisor or perhaps because you have found additional material that enhances aspects of your dissertation. The DLC is an iterative process, so get used to the idea that you will be looking over your shoulder to review and improve earlier parts of your dissertation. Also, there are other elements to a dissertation that are not listed as main phases of the DLC, but which nonetheless will be included in your final submission, such as an Abstract (sometimes referred to as the Synopsis), an Introduction, and a section listing your References (all of which are discussed in detail later).

As stated earlier, there are different *types* of Master's dissertations and they all involve research of one kind or another. You may be asked to carry out a review of literature pertinent to your research objectives. Or in addition to a review of literature you may be required to collect your own research data, to compare what you found out in your literature review against your own practical research findings (this is the more traditional dissertation). Alternatively, your dissertation may be framed in the form of a work-based report. Regardless of the type of dissertation that you are being asked to complete, the DLC still holds.

As well as skills pertinent to particular stages of the DLC – producing a credible research proposal, critically evaluating relevant literature, etc. – you will also require *generic* skills, i.e. skills that are useful regardless of the stage of the DLC in which you find yourself:

Generic skills

- *Time-management skills.* You need to be able to manage your time effectively. You do this by adopting two types of time-management perspectives: **macro-management** and **micro-management**. *Macro-management* requires that you manage your time in terms of the bigger dissertation picture, guessing intelligently how long you think it will take you to complete each chapter in your dissertation, dovetailing nicely into the required submission date. Pivotal to the macro-management of your time is the need to work backwards from your dissertation submission date to generate an effective time framework. *Micro-management* occurs when you work out the time it will take you to do the sub-sections that go to make up a particular chapter. For example, as a result of a macro approach to managing your time, you might decide that it will take you three weeks to write the introductory chapter to your dissertation and that, switching to micro mode, this chapter will have three parts to it and that you intend allocating one week to each part. Remember to allow time for the binding or presentation of your dissertation in accordance with your university's regulations. Apportioning time slots, in both macro and micro management mode, will give you a sense of awareness about what lies ahead and with that insight comes a sense of control over your dissertation.
- Linked to time-management skills are *organization skills.* You will have to organize a variety of dissertation-related activities: meetings with your supervisor, the overall structure of your dissertation, sub-sections within each chapter, your ideas and arguments, visits to the library, internet-based activities, reading material, cited sources, meetings with research subjects (e.g. people you might want to interview), and so on.
- *Self-discipline skills.* Keeping to your own timetable of activities will not prove easy. You will have other demands on your time, some predictable (e.g. parties, holidays, other assessments, part-time work, family commitments, etc.), others unpredictable (illness, relationship problems, family issues, etc.). Supervisors are realistic and accept that most students stray from their dissertation work from time to time, but the key to avoid

complete derailment is self-discipline, and that requires focus and an inner strength to keep going when things are getting on top of you. Time-management and sound organization will help you achieve a disciplined approach to your dissertation.

- *Communication skills*, both verbal and written. Communicating your ideas, arguments, rationale for choices, whether at meetings with your supervisor or in your submitted work, requires clarity of thought and expression. If you cannot say or write what you mean, then your work will be hindered. Sloppy grammar in written work is a particular concern highlighted by many supervisors. When communicating, in whatever form, keep it simple, keep it clear and keep it relevant. Cluttered waffle helps no one!

- Effective communication also requires good *listening skills*. It is important that you learn to listen to your supervisor when he gives you advice – he is not doing so for the good of his health. When your supervisor suggests that perhaps you should alter an aspect of your work in some way, he is telling you politely that it is deficient in some respect and that corrective action can be achieved by taking on board his counsel. In effect, he is telling you how to gain marks and avoid losing marks. He is marking your dissertation, so it makes sense that you heed his advice.

- *Presentational skills*. You may be required to present your work to examiners, in which case you ought to be aware of how to produce a skilful presentation, including use of technologies, voice projection, structure of content, audience engagement, etc. Presenting your work periodically to friends (and your supervisor) will provide you with invaluable experience in appreciating what works and what does not.

- *Social skills*. Getting on well with people – your supervisor, fellow students, research subjects, departmental secretary, etc. – will ease your dissertation journey.

- *Technical skills*. Internet searching skills, library skills, email and word processing skills are all essential aspects of dissertation work.

- *Independent learner skills*. This is the main difference between under-graduate degree work and Master's level work: the shift from *directed learning* to *independent learning*. Most dissertation handbooks highlight the importance of this requirement by including a separate section in the handbook on your responsibilities, emphasizing that it is *your* responsibility to identify a research topic, to put forward a research proposal, to plan and implement *your* dissertation activities and to be proactive in contacting your supervisor (i.e. to produce an independent piece of research). If you are a final-year undergraduate student considering applying to 'do' a Master's programme, then you need to appreciate that Master's work is very different from undergraduate work. Essentially, the difference is that at undergraduate level the learning primarily takes place through the lecturer (in the form of lectures, seminars, tutorials, laboratories, etc.) whereas at

Master's level the learning is mainly student-centred, i.e. there is a major shift of responsibility from the tutor to you, the student. This is no more evident than in the Master's dissertation, where the responsibility for selecting the research topic and writing the actual dissertation lies with the student; your supervisor acts as a guide, albeit an important one. Taking responsibility for your own work can be quite liberating, but it requires the development of new skills and confidence in your own abilities. By covering the Master's dissertation process in detail, from start to finish, this book provides the practical skills necessary to allow you to approach each stage of your dissertation with confidence.

Dissertation work can be a lonely process, so it is no bad thing to mitigate any sense of isolation by sharing your ideas about your work with your fellow students. This can be done more formally and constructively through something called *learner circles* (Biggam 2007a). This is where a group of students – a learner circle – get together, e.g. over coffee, to discuss their work-in-progress at regular intervals. They can also formally present their work to one other, using modern technology such as a data projector to display PowerPoint presentations, in which case they would need to borrow the data projector from their department and book a university room, all of which show initiative and engender a sense of togetherness. Learner circles are normally led by a supervisor, in effect, enacting group supervision, but they can be set up by students themselves, without the participation of supervisors. Akister *et al.* (2006) produced evidenced-based research showing that students who were supervised in groups were more positive when undertaking their dissertation and had a higher completion rate than students dependent on the more traditional one-to-one supervision model.

Finally, in addition to the aforementioned skills – specific and generic – there are certain personal *qualities* that are necessary prerequisites for the completion of a successful dissertation: *self-motivation*, *self-confidence*, and *self-centredness*. A lack of motivation, i.e. personal drivers (for example, in pursuit of a particular career path or intention to register for a higher degree), will reduce greatly the chances of you completing your dissertation. A Master's dissertation is the type of assessment that demands your time, concentration and enthusiasm over a lengthy period. A serious lack of genuine interest on your part will cause you to view every task as a tiresome activity, with the first real difficulty encountered probably resulting in the abandonment of your dissertation. On the other hand, if your motivation is strong, and you adopt a positive outlook, you can face every stage with enthusiastic curiosity, making the whole experience enjoyable and, ultimately, fruitful.

Have confidence in your own abilities. Occasional self-doubt is natural – everyone, staff and students, suffers from bouts of self-doubt. It is a natural human condition. In a Master's dissertation you are required to judge the work of other researchers (for example, within your review of literature) and to do so calls for a level of self-confidence to express your views on what these people are saying. One tutor recalls his student lamenting, 'Who am I to criticize this author when I am just a student and he has such an international reputation?' Your views are as valid as anyone else's (providing, of course, you back them up with supporting evidence!). You are on a Master's programme because the admission's tutor has confidence that you will complete your studies. Your supervisor is giving you the benefit of his time and expertise because he has confidence that you will produce a solid piece of research, providing that you follow his advice. Nothing pleases a supervisor more than when his students pass, and with flying colours at that! Others have faith in your abilities, so have faith in yourself.

There will be occasions during your dissertation journey when others – friends, family members, boyfriends/girlfriends, partners, spouses, etc. – will make demands upon your time. On such occasions you need to remind yourself that your priority is your dissertation – if you respond to every request for help from those around you then you will have difficulty in concentrating on your work. Self-centredness is a quality that will serve you well during your dissertation. From the outset, inform those close to you that you are serious about completing your dissertation, that it is a priority for you, and that you will require understanding and patience from others as you devote your time and energies to give of your best. A book worth reading on how to make the best of your dissertation time is Roberts (2007), *Getting the Most out of the Research Experience.*

Figure 1.2 summarizes the combined skills – specific and generic – and personal qualities that you need to complete a winning dissertation.

What of the *rules of the game*? Although this is your first time attempting a Master's dissertation, your supervisor has probably seen hundreds of dissertation students pass through his door. Through experience, he has learned how to assess the type of dissertation student he is supervising. With each meeting, email communication, telephone conversation, work-in-progress submitted, he will form an accumulative picture of your abilities. The rules of the game refer to not only the university's *formal* rules and regulations in terms of your submitted dissertation (word count, page format, style of referencing, etc.) but also to the *informal*, unwritten processes and behaviour that constitute your dissertation journey, such as how you conduct yourself at meetings with your supervisor, the impression you give when you email your tutor, the quality of your work-in-progress, and so on. For example, if at meetings with your supervisor you ask no questions or spend your time complaining that you cannot find any material on your chosen subject area (a common student complaint!), then you are ignoring the informal rules of the game: if you want to be viewed as a 'good' student, then behave like one (ask questions, discuss enthusiastically the work that you have researched, show initiative, etc.).

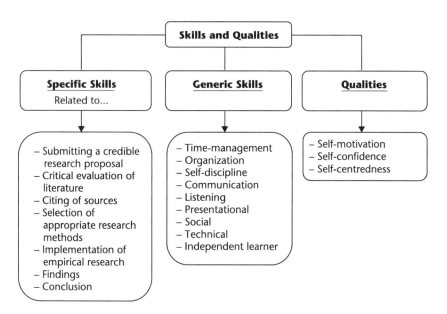

Figure 1.2 Skills and qualities needed to succeed

Watch your words!

Your dissertation handbook will stipulate the maximum number of words that your submitted dissertation must not succeed, for example it might state that 'The word limit for your dissertation must not exceed 15,000 words'. Or your dissertation guidelines may include a word limit with a leeway of +/– 10 per cent, meaning that you can be 10 per cent over the recommended word limit or 10 per cent under the recommended word limit, without suffering any penalty.

It is important that you adhere to the stated dissertation word-length for your Master's dissertation, for a number of reasons. The first, and obvious reason, is that you may lose marks for ignoring your institution's guidelines. If your dissertation was to be written in no more than, say, 10,000 words, and you write 14,000 words then you may be penalized before your marker actually starts to read your dissertation! The actual penalty incurred depends on your institution's rules and regulations, but it is not uncommon to lose 5–10 per cent of your overall marks. On the other hand, your institution may ignore your transgression, provided the extra words add value to your dissertation. One tutor in a university was known to stop reading (and marking!) a dissertation after the allocated words had been reached! Incidentally, if you have exceeded the recommended number of words but your institution's handbook makes no mention of a possible penalty for such a breach, then you may be in a position to argue that you should not be penalized because the lack of a stated penalty implied to you that none would be given or that the recommended word-length was not to be taken too seriously.

When you start your dissertation you will have no idea whether or not you will exceed your allocated dissertation word-length. It is only when you are knee-deep in the write-up that you will begin to get an inkling of how quickly you might be eating up your available words. For instance, suppose that you have just finished writing your Literature Review and that it took you 8,000 words to do so. However, from sample dissertations borrowed from the university library, you noticed that the number of words used for that particular section was typically in the region of 3,500. As a result of this comparison, you might reasonably conclude that you are in danger of exceeding your overall word-length. This issue reflects how well you have *micro-managed* your activities: the tasks that you have to do (e.g. write your dissertation Introduction, Literature Review, Research Methods chapter, collect data, etc.), the time you expect each of these tasks to take (e.g. one week for the Introduction, six weeks to write the Literature Review, etc.), as well as the number of words that you anticipate each dissertation chapter/section to use up (e.g. 800 words for the Introduction, 3,500 words for the Literature Review, etc.).

Another reason why exceeding the recommended word-length may be unwise is that you may be guilty of *padding*. Sticking to an expected word-length is evidence that you can say something in a given number of words. If you go over the word-length, then you may be indicating an inability to write succinctly. Padding occurs when you include irrelevant material in your dissertation, just for the sake of 'beefing up' your dissertation. It is easy to spot and, at best, will not gain you extra marks: more often than not, it will lose you marks, because it is an unnecessary distraction, interfering with the focus and substance of your dissertation. It is a great temptation to include material that you have read, even if it is not *really* relevant, just because you have gone to the trouble of finding and reading it! Have the courage to reject what is not essential to your dissertation's research objectives.

What do you do if you suspect that you are going over the recommended dissertation word-length? First of all, remove any padding, i.e. excise unnecessary material. If you still consider that you need extra words to play with, then ask permission to exceed the word-length. Write to your supervisor, giving the following information:

1 your request to exceed the recommended word-length;
2 the (new) word-length that you need to complete your dissertation;
3 the reason(s) for needing the extra words.

Point three above is important. It is insufficient to write, for example, that you need an extra 3,000 words over and above the recommended limit because that is how many words it has taken you, or will take you, to complete your dissertation. It is likely that your supervisor will write back to you, advising that you are in the same boat as other students and that you need to reduce your word-length accordingly. On the other hand, if you were to explain, for example, that your data collection was extensive and that to do it justice you require the extra words to capture the richness of your empirical work – then you would be better placed to secure permission to exceed the word-length without penalty. You need to think about the position of your supervisor when you make a request to go over the word-length: if he allows one student, *without good reason*, to exceed the word-length, then he must make the same opportunity available to all his students, which makes the idea of a word-length meaningless. Hence the need for a valid reason to go beyond the declared word-limit.

Finally, it is good practice when you have finished your dissertation to include the word-count near the start of your dissertation, somewhere between the cover page and your introductory chapter (check your Dissertation Handbook for guidance). All word-processing software has a facility for a word-count. Remember to exclude appendices from your word-count, as they are not normally included.

How to use this book

Writing a Master's dissertation is not easy: if it were, then it would not be worth doing. Consequently, there are so many areas where you can fall down. Fortunately, there are things that you can do to minimize the chances of mediocrity – or worse, failure – and improve the opportunities to secure impressive marks. This book takes you patiently through the stages of a dissertation – the Dissertation Life Cycle – explaining how to gain (and lose!) marks at each stage of the marking scheme, as well as exploring a worrying feature in many dissertations: plagiarism (Biggam 2007b). The topics to be covered include: submitting your research proposal; writing the introductory chapter to your dissertation; clarifying your research objectives; how to reference and review literature; describing and justifying your research methods; developing a framework for analysing your empirical research; producing a solid conclusion to your work; writing a competent abstract; presenting your work; and the importance of good grammar. Throughout, detailed sample answers, together with relevant practical examples, will be used to illustrate good and bad practice. As you approach each stage of your dissertation, use this book for comprehensive guidance on good and bad practice.

A common mistake by students

In each chapter, common mistakes made by students with regard to dissertation writing will be highlighted. For instance, if it is necessary to warn you about bad practice related to referencing literature, then this study will go on to indicate errors that are commonly made by students when they try and reference works that they have read. For example, a common mistake by students is not to take the advice of their dissertation supervisor, although one student, after listening attentively to his tutor explaining the technique of writing a Literature Review, and ending his advice with the words 'blah blah blah', took his tutor's advice too literally. When he submitted his Literature Review it contained only the words 'blah blah blah'!

To get a good start on your dissertation it is necessary to be well prepared for what lies ahead, otherwise 'a great deal of time can be wasted and goodwill dissipated by inadequate preparation' (Bell 1993: 1). To prepare properly you will need to appreciate the phases that your work will go through, from outlining your research objectives to concluding your dissertation, and know how to address each of these phases. This book will take you through each phase in detail. By the end of this book you should understand the parts that go to make up a dissertation, what makes a good dissertation and, just as importantly, why students often fail to secure easy marks. Writing a dissertation need not be a guessing-game. Writing a dissertation that will achieve pass marks or – even better – excellent marks is as much a technique as it is an art. The aim of this book is to lay bare the techniques that you need to undertake a dissertation, in effect, to equip you with the knowledge and skills to produce a highly competent piece of work. There is truth in the old adage *knowledge is power*; in your case, knowledge equates to marks.

Summary of key points

- An undergraduate degree is evidence that the holder has a *general knowledge* of the named subject area; a Master's degree is normally a postgraduate qualification, indicating that the holder has *advanced knowledge* of the named subject area.
- Master's programmes come in many guises (*taught* Master's, Master's by *research*, with a variety of titles – M.Litt., MSc., MPhil., MMus., etc. – and different assessment requirements).
- The Master's dissertation is a long *research-based* essay, typically 10,000–15,000 words in length. There are a variety of types of Master's dissertations (work-based dissertations, laboratory-based dissertations, literature review-based dissertation, literature review and empirically-based dissertations, etc.).

- The Dissertation Life Cycle (DLC) highlights the conventional stages of the dissertation journey: produce a research proposal, write a Literature Review, design appropriate research methods, implement empirical research, analyse the findings, conclude the research, and submit the completed work.
- To complete a Master's dissertation, you require a combination of generic skills (time-management, organizational, self-discipline, communication, listening, presentational, social, technical, independent learner skills) and personal qualities (self-motivation, self-confidence, and self-centredness), as well as skills specific to dissertation-writing (submitting a realistic research proposal, writing a Literature Review, proper citing of sources, etc.).
- Take cognizance of the maximum word-length for your dissertation. If you anticipate exceeding the word-limit, then request permission from your supervisor, giving your reason(s).

2

Preparing for your dissertation

Putting together your research proposal • Producing a dissertation template • Supervisor meetings

Putting together your research proposal

Research focus and overall research aim

The first thing you need to do is to get a research proposal together. This is where you write down, and present to your potential supervisor, your proposed area of study. A good research proposal will: (a) provide some background information on the area that you are interested in; (b) explain the rationale behind why you want to focus on a particular aspect of this subject (you need to convince your supervisor that this is an area worthy of study); (c) identify the overall aim of your research (i.e. what you are trying to achieve); (d) specify the individual objectives required to help you achieve your overall research aim; (e) outline how you will carry out your research (your research methods); (f) provide an estimate of how long you think you will take to complete the various parts of your dissertation; and (g) list the literature that you have referred to in producing your proposal (i.e. include a short References section – refer to Chapter 4, The Literature Review, Section 4.2, Referencing, to understand how to cite sources and construct a Reference list.) Your institution may have a slightly different format for constructing a research proposal, but it will essentially contain the aforementioned elements.

The main task in your research proposal is to clarify whatever it is that you propose to research. It is not as easy as it sounds. First of all you need to pick a subject that interests you; then, you have to focus on some aspect of that subject which you think is worth researching (though you should be aware that some institutions will decide themselves your topic and focus of research, particularly in the hard sciences); finally, you need to communicate these ideas in writing.

Suppose that you are a Master's student interested in choosing e-Learning as the subject of your dissertation. However, you cannot do a dissertation on the general subject of e-Learning: your proposal must be *focused* on a particular aspect of e-Learning. If you were keen to investigate how academic staff are being prepared to cope with the challenge of e-Learning in the university environment, then that would qualify as an example of a focused project. On the other hand, if you were interested in 'studying computer security', then that would be too vague for a research proposal; changing that to 'a study of online banking breaches and their impact on customer confidence' would form a much more focused area of study. The trick to achieving 'research focus' is first of all to think of a subject area in general terms (e-Learning, computer security, drugs, domestic abuse, absent management, etc.) and then to home in on a particular aspect of that subject. Even then, you cannot simply pluck your research focus out of thin air. You need to do some background reading to determine if it is a topic worthy of study (e.g. published reports and articles may highlight the need for more research in your chosen field and so provide evidence to support your research proposal).

Let us revisit the student keen on doing her Master's dissertation on e-Learning. She wisely decides that this is too general and unwieldy an area for study and so reduces her field of interest to an investigation of how academic staff are being prepared to cope with the challenge of e-Learning in the university environment. She now has focus which will not only save her time and energy but also please her supervisor and make life easier for him when he comes to offer guidance throughout the duration of her research. Nonetheless, one of the questions that her supervisor will ask is 'Why do you want to study that area?' or 'What evidence is there that it is an area worthy of study?' This is where your background reading comes in to play: you show him that you have done some initial reading and lay before him your rationale for your proposal. For instance – staying with the e-Learning example – it could be that there are conflicting reports on the progress of e-Learning in universities, with some literature enthusiastically predicting exponential growth in e-Learning as a means of teaching students, with staff embracing e-Learning with open arms; while other literature casts doubt on such views, complaining that evidence of staff opinions and experiences of e-Learning are anecdotal in nature (perhaps universities are blowing their own trumpets!) and that proper research needs to be instigated to find out how staff are indeed being prepared to meet this new technological challenge.

Next, you need to clarify your *overall research aim* and the *specific objectives* that you require to meet in order to achieve your overall research aim. Your overall research aim will be a general statement. It tends to derive from your focus of study. In the e-Learning example, where the research focus is to investigate how academic staff are being prepared to cope with the challenge of e-Learning in the university environment, the research aim could be expressed as follows:

Research Focus: To investigate how academic staff are being prepared to
⎜   cope with the challenge of e-Learning in the university
↓   environment.
Research Aim: The overall aim of this research is to advance an understanding of the impact of e-Learning in the university
environment in relation to academic staff training
preparation.

An easy way to arrive at your overall research aim is to break the process down into simple steps (Figure 2.1), starting with Step 1 where you think up one word to identify your research area of interest (e.g. 'e-security'). In Step 2, you include other words to give a clearer idea of your research focus (e.g. 'e-security', 'breaches', 'customer confidence', 'online banking'). Then you connect these words to form a sentence (e.g. 'This is a study of e-security breaches and their impact on customer confidence in the area of online banking').

Finally, in Step 3, you incorporate the phrase 'overall aim' (abbreviated to 'aim' if you want) to produce your formal research aim:

> The overall aim of this research is to explore the impact of e-security breaches on customer confidence related to online banking.

Suppose that you change your mind and opt instead to write a dissertation on how to achieve a top mark in employment aptitude tests in the banking industry (though somewhere in your dissertation you will need to define what you mean by a 'top mark'). To arrive at your overall research aim you repeat the same process as before, this time concentrating on your new topic (Figure 2.2).

Once again, think of your research area in terms of one word or label (e.g. 'Employment aptitude tests'); add other words that help clarify your research focus (e.g. 'Top marks', 'What it takes'; 'Banking industry'); and write this as a sentence (e.g. 'This is a study of what it takes to achieve a top mark in employment aptitude tests in the banking industry'). Finally, convert this into a formal research statement:

> The overall aim of this research is to elucidate the elements that determine a top mark in employment aptitude tests set by the banking industry.

Figure 2.1 Writing your overall research aim

If you follow this process, it will allow you to arrive, with confidence, at your written research aim. For easy reference it is now summarized below:

Step 1 Think of your research area in terms of *one* word or label.
Step 2 *Add* other words to help clarify the context/focus of your research.
Step 3 *Connect* these words to form a sentence.
Step 4 *Convert* this sentence into a formal research statement, 'The overall aim of this research . . .'

Professional researchers often prefer to formulate their overall research aim as a *research question*. Rather than writing that your overall research aim is to

Figure 2.2 Another example of how to arrive at your research aim

elucidate the elements that determine a top mark in employment aptitude tests set by the banking industry', you could instead articulate your research task in the following terms: 'Central to this research is the need to answer the question, *what are the elements that determine a top mark in employment aptitude tests set by the banking industry?'* In this way, you may find your research task to be more focused and driven, in the pursuit of an answer.

The next sub-section will explain how to achieve your (overall) research aim by breaking down your research aim into specific, achievable *research objectives*.

Research objectives and keywords

You now have to decide what you need to do in order to realize your overall research aim. This means that you have to list your individual objectives, or mini-aims. Listed below are objectives for the aforementioned e-Learning dissertation (which we will develop and use for reference throughout this book to illustrate dissertation issues):

Specifically, within the context of higher education, the objectives of this research are to:

1   *Identify* the forces driving e-Learning and the barriers to the successful delivery of e-Learning programmes.
2   *Evaluate critically* models and frameworks relevant to supporting academic staff in coping with e-Learning.
3   *Explore* staff stakeholder views and practices related to e-Learning preparation, including drivers and barriers to e-Learning.
4   *Formulate* recommendations on staff preparation issues.

The words in italic are what are called keywords. They indicate the depth of study to be carried out. There are a whole host of keywords that are available for student use, such as *identify, assess, evaluate, explore, outline, discuss, analyse,* etc. These are verbs used to indicate the type of study activity linked with each objective. For instance, *identify* normally suggests a straightforward academic undertaking, one not requiring much in the way of intellectual discussion and debate. In the above example, the student would use the first objective to set the scene by ascertaining the forces driving e-Learning and barriers to the successful delivery of e-Learning (even then, the student would link the drivers and barriers to the focus of the research study, i.e. staff preparation for e-Learning).

It is important that for your big objectives you incorporate keywords that indicate in-depth academic study. Keywords such as *evaluate critically, assess, explore, investigate, examine,* all imply an appropriate level of intellectual activity suitable for a Master's dissertation. Hence, objectives 2 and 3 use the keywords *evaluate critically* and *explore* to indicate to the supervisor that these objectives will form the main part of the student's research. Objective 4 uses quite a neutral keyword – *formulate* – implying that as a result of the research the student will make certain recommendations.

Students tend to have difficulty in expressing their overall research aim and related individual objectives. It is not unknown for students to be still grappling with their objectives long after their dissertation has begun. At a first supervisor meeting, one student presented her objectives in the following general format:

1 Identify . . .
2 Identify . . .
3 Identify . . .
4 Identify . . .
5 Identify . . .
6 Identify . . .
7 Identify . . .

By including the keyword *identify* for each objective, she was suggesting that her work would be superficial in nature, lacking in depth. Normally, using *identify* is acceptable for an early objective (e.g. to provide background information) but try and steer clear of using such a keyword in other objectives (although there are exceptions, for example, it may be that you wish to identify the causes of cancer in a particular study and that such a task is widely recognized as a significant achievement in itself; in which case the use of *identify* would be an acceptable keyword). Furthermore, she had too many objectives, which would have had the effect of either making her work appear piecemeal or unnecessarily increasing her workload. Four or five objectives are typical. Another student did not specifically list his research objectives, but instead, in a woolly and long-winded paragraph, referred obliquely to about 10 issues that he wanted to tackle! This was far too many issues; and, in any case, he ought to have clearly itemized his individual research objectives.

If your objectives are not in a convenient format, e.g. in the form of a numbered list, then you are making the reader work hard to understand what your research is about and, furthermore, you are not making it easier for your marker, or yourself for that matter, to ascertain if, at the end of your dissertation, you have completed your initial objectives. In addition, if you do not enumerate and clarify your research objectives then at a later stage in your dissertation you may find yourself straying from what you set out to study. Play safe and make life easy for everybody: by all means explain your research objectives, but write them down in a numbered list.

Students who are unaware of how to list their research objectives tend to use vague terms – such as 'do' or 'study' or 'look at' or 'learn about' – that shed inadequate light on the level or type of research study to be undertaken. Using such fuzzy terms will make it difficult for you – and your marker – to determine, at the final submission of your work, if you have met your initial research objectives (e.g. how does your supervisor assess whether or not you have 'looked at' your area of study?).

In general, a good approach to listing objectives is to use a simple keyword for the first objective (such as *identify*, *classify*, *outline*, *discuss*, etc.) to provide the background to your subject area; for the other objectives (excluding the last one) use keywords that suggest in-depth research work (such as *explore, evaluate critically, assess critically, examine, analyse, determine,* etc.); and for the final objective use a keyword that links easily to a concluding activity (such as *formulate, produce, develop, recommend, propose, advance,* etc.). If you have converted your overall aim into a specific research question to which you seek an answer, then you may also decide to similarly reshape your individual research objectives into sub-questions, the answers to which will help you meet your main research question.

Research methods

A research proposal should contain background information on your subject of interest, leading you to justify why you want to study this subject (with reference to appropriate literature for supporting evidence), as well as identifying your overall aim and specific objectives; in addition, it should also include information on how you intend to do your research. The latter is referred to as your *research method(s).* For your research proposal it is necessary to outline how you will research your chosen field of study. Two ways in which Master's dissertation students are normally expected to implement their research work are as follows:

1 Through a Literature Review.
2 By collecting empirical data.

The Literature Review is where you seek out literature from a number of sources (journals, books, conference proceedings, etc.) pertinent to your research interests, with a view to showing that you are well read in the area and that you can evaluate critically the worth and relevance of sources germane to your research. You are not required to implement a full Literature Review within the context of your research proposal: rather, all you need do at this stage is provide some background information and rationale to support your proposal. It is only once you start your dissertation proper, presumably after your proposal has been accepted, that you will be required to complete a substantial review of literature. Nonetheless, this background work will make use of references to appropriate literature sources. Two or three pages are usually sufficient for this background study, but to be sure you need to read your institution's research proposal requirements.

For the section on research methods you will need to indicate the types of literature that you will be making reference to in your full study. You do this in two ways: by referring to general kinds of literature sources, such as books, journals, conference proceedings, reports, etc.; and by giving some examples of the literature that will be relevant to your research. So, if your research area was related to computer security you might make the following statement:

This study will make use of a number of literature sources, including reference to pertinent books, journals, reports, conference proceedings and Government publications. Examples of these include: periodical surveys such as the DTI Information Security Breaches Survey and the CSI/FBI Computer Security Breaches Survey; the *Journal of Information Warfare*; and proceedings of the European Conference on Information Warfare.

If your research does not depend solely on a Literature Review, i.e. it is not based purely on theory, but you also intend collecting your own data to supplement your Literature Review findings – which is the normal position for a Master's dissertation – then you must state the research approach you anticipate adopting to accomplish your practical work. For example, if you know that you will be implementing an experiment of some sort, then say so. Similarly, if you expect to explore a specific type of organization (e.g. a university), then once again state this. You also ought to articulate how you expect to collect your data (questionnaires, interviews, etc.). Chapter 5 entitled 'Research Methods' explores the different research strategies and methods of data collection in depth.

Setting a timescale

It is standard practice to include an estimate of how long you anticipate each stage of your research to take. By doing so, you will begin to appreciate what lies in store for you in terms of how long you will roughly need to devote to each task. To do this, you write down the distinct phases of your dissertation and opposite each phase enter the number of weeks or months you expect the corresponding activity to last. For example, an MSc. dissertation to be completed, say, over a 4-month period (16 weeks) between June and September may have the following timescale (Table 2.1). Of course, this is assuming that you are writing up your dissertation as you go along. Your timings may differ because your dissertation may be longer or shorter in duration; nevertheless the principle is the same.

Table 2.1 Project timescales (4-month Master's dissertation)

Dissertation activity	Duration (in weeks)	Month
Clarify aims/objectives	2	June
Literature Review	4	June–July
Research methods	2	July
Data collection	3	Aug.
Findings	3	Aug.–Sep.
Conclusion	2	Sep.

Some of the dissertation activities will overlap and so the picture is not as straightforward as depicted in Table 2.1. For example, it appears that the bulk of the Literature Review chapter is expected to be completed in four weeks (if you have the timescale as shown in Table 2.1) but the reality is that you will still be referring to relevant literature throughout the life of the dissertation. Also, Table 2.1 does not take into account variations in holiday periods and this has to be borne in mind when you develop your own timescales. Furthermore, it is rare that you will adhere rigidly to your initial projected timescales. It is not a fault; it is just that life rarely follows our intentions to the letter. As Rabbie Burns said, the best laid plans of mice and men often go wrong. Bear that in mind when you plan your activities and incorporate free weeks to accommodate the unexpected (such as flu, tiredness, other project deadlines, domestic situations, etc.). Nonetheless, setting down a plan of dissertation activities, including timescales, helps you gain an overview of what lies ahead and provides you with an appreciation of how much time you have to play with for each of your dissertation elements (clarifying your research objectives, writing your literature review, etc.).

If you use a chart, such as a bar chart, to display your timescale then this will add a professional look to your presentation. Figure 2.3 shows the projected timescales for another Master's dissertation, but in the form of a bar chart. Other charts could be used with similar success: you are not restricted to using a bar chart. For example, a Gantt chart is a good way to display your research tasks graphically. A Gantt chart is a special type of bar chart, where the bars represent the duration of each task and are placed in the chart to show the sequence of tasks as well as potential overlap. Figure 2.4 is an example of a Gantt chart.

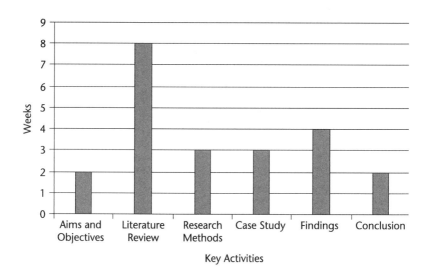

Figure 2.3 Projected dissertation timescales (in weeks)

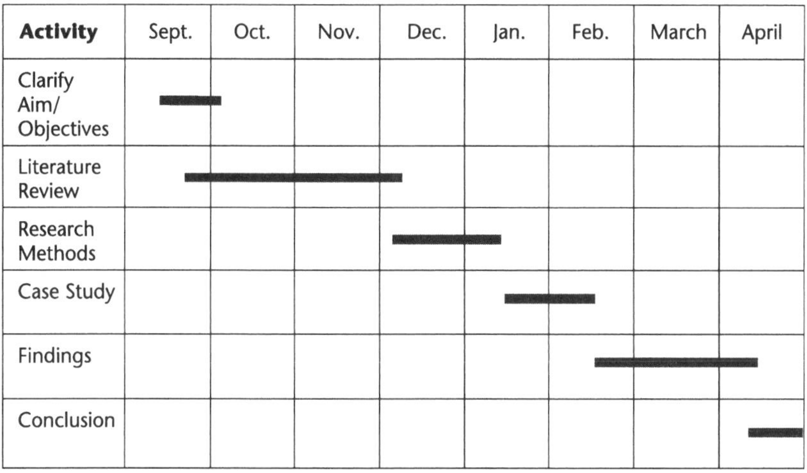

Activity	Sept.	Oct.	Nov.	Dec.	Jan.	Feb.	March	April
Clarify Aim/ Objectives	▬▬							
Literature Review		▬▬▬▬▬▬						
Research Methods				▬▬▬				
Case Study					▬▬			
Findings						▬▬▬▬		
Conclusion								▬

Figure 2.4 Gantt chart showing dissertation timescale

You must take every opportunity, however small, to show off your work in the best light. Using charts to display information is one way to make your work look good and gain easy marks. Your supervisor will appreciate your efforts and will already begin to see you as a 'good' student.

Producing a dissertation template

Once your research proposal has been approved, and before you start your research work, it is recommended that you create a dissertation template (DT). A DT is where you create your cover pages for each of the main sections that you expect your research project to contain. A DT will typically have the cover pages shown in Figure 2.5, although the headings and arrangement of sections may change depending on the guidelines set out in your dissertation handbook.

Most of the pages will be empty pages, that is they will contain just a heading or two. Importantly, though, they will give you a sense of direction and discipline. Indeed, depending on your project, and if you want to divide the pages further, you could have as many as 20 'empty' pages which you have created in the first day of your dissertation! Psychologically, this should give you a boost. Put these pages inside a folder, labelled 'Dissertation', and complete each sub-section in detail as you advance through your project. On a practical level, it will make it easier for you and your supervisor to get, at a few glances, an instant appreciation of how your dissertation is progressing.

Figure 2.5 A dissertation template

Supervisor meetings

If you understand how to take advantage of meetings with your supervisor, then you will be better placed to advance work on your dissertation. On the other hand, if you fail to appreciate how to exploit supervisor meetings then you may hinder the development of your research. Dissertation supervisors will recognize the following scene (something you want to avoid!). A student attends his first meeting with his supervisor and when the student is asked by his supervisor to clarify his research objectives, the reply is somewhat hesitant, vague, and lacking in any meaningful detail, ending with the student requesting ideas from his supervisor. This scenario is typical of a first meeting between supervisors and students. Too often students arrive at their first supervisor meeting with no clear idea of what they want to study. This sets a bad first impression. Although your supervisor can help shape your initial ideas, it is not for him to think up your ideas in the first place or to produce your detailed research objectives.

Unfortunately, there are times when naive (or exasperated!) staff do provide struggling students with specific dissertation topics, even to the extent of practically writing their dissertation title, overall aim and related objectives. As a student, you may find this approach very helpful and to your liking, but be warned. If you have not thought up the specific focus of your research, but left that to your supervisor, then it is unlikely that you will understand fully what you are supposed to be researching, in which case you and your supervisor may just be creating problems further down the (dissertation) line. Also, if you leave your supervisor to develop your research ideas, then he may emerge with a research proposal that fails to fire you with enthusiasm or ignite your imagination. Students who actually enjoy their work, and take pride in what they are doing, are more likely to gain good marks. It is much better to form your own research proposal: in that way you will engage in a project that interests you and which you understand, both of which, in turn, form an excellent basis for your dissertation journey. For those reasons, most staff tend to leave the initial topic selection entirely up to the student. Of course, that does not mean that you can pick any topic and expect it to be worthy of study.

So, when you arrive for your first meeting with your supervisor, *come prepared* and *armed with questions*. Be able to state quite clearly your area of study, overall aim and related objectives, including a rationale for studying your chosen topic. Also, present your supervisor with a working title for your dissertation (this can change as your work progresses):

> The title of my dissertation is xxxx and my overall aim is to study . . . with a view to getting a deeper understanding of. . . . The reason I want to study this area is because preliminary literature review findings indicate . . . For example, Burns in his report published in 2007, titled . . . argues that there is a need . . .

Example:

> The title of my dissertation is 'A Study of Algorithms to Facilitate Software Testing in a Mobile Environment' and my overall aim is to study the appropriateness and effectiveness of current software-testing paradigms to such environments, with a view to identifying deficiencies and developing an improved algorithm to meet the needs of mobile computing software developers. The reason I want to study this area is that new technologies are being produced at an alarming rate, becoming smaller and personalized (e.g. iPods, PDAs, notebooks, advanced mobile phones, etc.), and as this is taking place there is an increasing need to ensure that those who are developing new mobile technologies do so using relevant and effective testing algorithms, otherwise the security of the products may be compromised. A number of researchers have expressed concern about this very issue . . .

Your supervisor will be looking at your initial proposal in terms of: (a) Does the intended research have focus?; (b) Are the objectives clear?; and (c) Are the objectives achievable in the timescale? Ask your supervisor what he thinks of your dissertation topic (after all, he will be marking it): 'Is my research topic worthy of study?'; 'Are my objectives clear to you?'; 'Do you think I will be able to do them in the time available, in other words, is my proposal realistic?'

For future meetings with your supervisor, adopt a similar approach: *show him your work-to-date* and *ask questions*. If you have created a dissertation template (as described in the previous sub-section), then you can build up incrementally your work, permitting your supervisor to assess, quickly and conveniently, your progress. Unfortunately, from experience, most students tend to arrive at meetings, sit there, and expect their supervisor to tell them what to do next.

Prior to each meeting, email your supervisor your work-in-progress. Avoid sending irritatingly mysterious emails, where you do not identify who you are, or emails that assume a casual level of intimacy that is inappropriate, both of which were evident in the email in Figure 2.6 sent by a student to his supervisor.

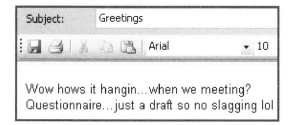

Figure 2.6 An inappropriate email

At the meetings, try to avoid going through the motions of a question-and-answer session, where your supervisor asks you a question, you answer, and so on: two monologues do not constitute a dialogue. These meetings are not interviews, so do not view them as such. Your supervisor is not trying to interrogate you. He wants to know how your work is progressing and to pinpoint areas where you might need help, and this requires both parties to *engage in communication*. The worse thing that you can do is just sit there blankly and expect your supervisor to talk all the time: one-way 'discussions' are rarely productive. Volunteer to summarize your work and then seek advice on issues that concern you. Stay clear of this howler, however: 'I can't find anything on this subject!' Every year there is always one student who arrives at a first meeting and says: 'I can't find anything on this subject' and when the supervisor types in the student's dissertation topic into Google, in the student's presence, literally hundreds of relevant documents appear instantaneously onto the screen. Declaring 'I can't find anything on this subject!' just shows laziness on your part and a lack of serious intent about your dissertation. Establishing a working relationship with your supervisor requires a genuine attempt to engage with the dissertation process.

Meetings with your supervisor should be looked upon as an opportunity to gauge your supervisor's opinion about your work and to seek corrective action when things are going wrong. Every meeting with your supervisor, if handled properly, could be saving you marks that you would otherwise have lost. And remember this: students who rarely turn up for meetings, rarely pass. Phillips and Pugh (2007: 15) emphasize, 'Good communication and rapport between students and their supervisors are the most important elements of supervision.' The only way you can start to achieve a decent rapport with your supervisor, and communicate dissertation issues, is if you arrive at meetings prepared.

One other thing. If you cannot make a meeting with your supervisor, then email him explaining the reason for your non-attendance and make another appointment. That is only good manners.

Summary of key points

- A dissertation research proposal contains details of your overall research aim, the individual research objectives deemed necessary to achieve your main research aim, your background reading, including the justification and value of your proposed research, the research methods needed to implement your research, expected timescales, and a list of sources used.
- To write your overall research aim, think of your research subject in terms of one word, add other words to clarify your research focus, connect them to form a sentence, and convert the sentence into a formal research aim. You can, if you wish, then re-write your formal research aim as a research question.

- In addition to your overall research aim, you must list the individual research objectives which you believe will, when added together, fulfil your principal research aim. Start each of your research aims using a keyword (e.g. *identify*, *assess*, *explore*, etc.), i.e. a verb to suggest type and depth of study related to each research objective. You can, as with your main research aim, formulate your individual research objectives in the form of specific research questions.
- You will also need to outline, in your research proposal, your research methods, i.e. how you intend going about carrying out your research, e.g. review of relevant literature and/or collection and analysis of empirical data.
- Include in your research proposal a timescale of how long you expect to take to complete each of your main research tasks. You can illustrate your time-scale using either a simple table or, more interestingly, a chart (e.g. a bar chart or a Gantt chart).
- A Dissertation Template (DT) is a useful way of structuring your research tasks, gaining a quick overview of your progress, and providing a sense of direction and discipline. Create a folder to house your DT and complete it accumulatively, bringing it with you to meetings with your dissertation supervisor.
- Meetings with your supervisor should be constructive, which in turn requires you to come prepared with ideas, draft/completed versions of your work, and questions.

3

The dissertation Introduction

*The general structure of the Introduction • Background • Research focus
(revisited) • Overall research aim and individual research objectives
• Value of your research • A further suggestion*

The general structure of the Introduction

The Introduction to your dissertation ought to do a number of things:

- Provide preliminary background information (to place your study in context).
- Clarify your focus of study.
- Specify your overall research aim and individual objectives.
- Point out the value of your research.

Accordingly, you could structure your introductory chapter as follows:

1. **Introduction**

    1.1 Background
    1.2 Research Focus
    1.3 Overall Research Aim and Individual Research Objectives
    1.4 Value of this Research

If you find it more convenient it is perfectly acceptable to subsume sub-section
1.4 within 1.2 and/or 1.3, as is evident in the sample Introduction chapter in

Appendix A. This chapter will now go through and explain each of the above elements of the dissertation Introduction. Much of what is written in Chapter 2, 'Preparing for your Dissertation', applies to this chapter and, consequently, students often take the bulk of their initial research proposal, with some alteration as a result of tutor feedback, and use it to form the basis of their dissertation Introduction. Nevertheless, this chapter will take you carefully through each component of a dissertation Introduction, showing examples of good (and bad) practice to illustrate salient points. At the end of this chapter you should be in an excellent position to write the introduction to your own dissertation.

Background

It is generally bad practice to dive in and immediately identify the focus of your study. Why? Because your tutor (and external marker) will want to know what led you to study your specific research area. He will want to know why your research is worth doing: in other words, who will benefit from your work and why? This usually means identifying a gap in existing research or revealing a problem that needs addressing, with a belief that your research will benefit those interested in filling this gap or confronting this problem. Perhaps you are looking at a topic from a different angle or maybe recent reports indicate that there is a call for research in your particular area of interest. It is not enough justification to say that you are researching a particular area because you find it interesting: you need to go further and explain the rationale for your research in terms of a *need* for your research.

So, where can you get information that tells you about research in your field of interest that needs addressing? There are a number of sources that can help you: conference proceedings, journal papers, published reports, media headlines, the Internet, as well as issues raised in your lectures/seminars. Let us suppose that, like most students starting out on their dissertation, you have no concrete idea of what you want to research, but you know that you would like to do something on, say, computer Spam (unsolicited emails), and that is as far as you have got. The first thing you should do is find out about Spam: what it is, how it works, and the problems it causes. In that way you will start to become knowledgeable on the subject. Get hold of a recent *conference proceeding* on computer security and unearth current issues related to Spam; read trade magazines, e.g. *Computing* or *Computer Weekly*, and scan for Spam-related articles; and access the Internet for up-to-date articles. Ideas for dissertation focus will not appear out of thin air: you need to do some basic groundwork.

A common mistake by students

A common mistake by students is to pay scant attention to background reading. As mentioned earlier, students at the start of their dissertation can sometimes be seen shaking their head whilst exclaiming to their supervisor that they 'cannot find anything' on their dissertation topic, e-Learning, for example, or e-security. The conversation usually goes something like this:

'Hi, Dr Biggam.'

'John, call me John.'

'Well, eh, John, it's just that I can't find anything on e-security.'

'OK, if I remember correctly, Bob, you are supposed to be looking at e-security and Spam. Specifically why, despite technological advances in e-security, computer users are still getting inundated with Spam. Is that correct?'

'Yes.'

'And you say you cannot find anything on e-security and spam? Zilts, Nada, Nothing?'

At this point the supervisor turns to his computer, accesses the Internet and types the words 'E-security and Spam' into his search engine, and lo and behold, before their very eyes the screen magically fills up with a multitude of references. 'Isn't technology wonderful!', announces the supervisor.

Do not depend on your supervisor finding your background reading for you, because you may end up adopting this lazy approach throughout the duration of your dissertation. You might think it is a great idea to find such a 'helpful' supervisor, but there is a major flaw with this approach. When you finally submit your work and it is marked by your tutor, you will lose marks for showing a lack of independence. Therefore, if you are interested in not just merely passing your dissertation, but gaining good marks, then avoid the habit of depending on your supervisor for material. That is not to say that your supervisor cannot advise you on the relevance of your material or attempt to guide you in the right direction by, on occasion, referring you to pertinent articles/reports, etc. To avoid confusion over the degree of help that is expected, supervisors need to set parameters and enforce them quickly.

Back to the Google example. One could go on to say to the student that he can become more focused in his use of Google (or whatever search engine he uses). For example, to get access to Spam statistics, type in 'Spam Statistics'; to access Spam reports, type in 'Spam Reports'. You can put the year after your request to help find up-to-date material, e.g. 'E-security and Spam reports 2007'. Similarly, you can endeavour to understand why Spam is on the increase by typing in 'Spam failings' or 'Spam failures' or some variation on the same theme. Unfortunately, search engines, although enormously useful, can produce too much information, much of which may not be relevant. If you want to confine your search to complete documents, then type 'pdf' at the end of your query, for example 'E-security and Spam 2007 pdf'. PDF stands for Portable Document Format, i.e. a document that is read by Adobe Acrobat. PDF documents in your subject area have the advantage that they are usually complete documents and so tend to be well written and contain references to other literature/websites that will further aid your research.

Another Google facility – one used by academics – is Google Scholar. It is, in effect, a mini search engine, but one devoted to retrieving scholarly documents. Access it by typing 'Google Scholar' in the Google search engine or by clicking on the Google Scholar option which is available on the Google search engine. *Emerald* is another online facility used by academics (http://emeraldinsight.com), a source that you may find useful. You will require a username and password to access the articles stored in Emerald (Figure 3.1). Most academic institutions have access to Emerald – ask your supervisor about your institution's username/password.

The Internet is a great place to get a quick feel for your subject area, and to utilize otherwise expensive reports for free, but it is important that you access other sources: visit your university library and check out respected academic journals relevant to your work; use your department's resources; exploit your supervisor's knowledge of articles/books appropriate to your dissertation topic; have a coffee in your local bookstore and browse their bookshelves. In other words, the Internet is all fine and dandy, but good research involves using a variety of sources to acquire a balanced and credible picture of whatever it is you are studying.

Once you get a feel for your subject, and you know what you specifically want to research and why, you can then start to write the *Background* part of

Figure 3.1

Republished with permission from Emerald Group Publishing Limited.

your Introduction. You do this first of all by gently introducing the reader to your research area in general. That is to say, if your research focus was on, for example, the need to study the type of people who spread viruses on the Web, you do not start your Introduction by stating: 'There is a need to study the type of people who spread viruses on the Internet. This dissertation will do that by . . .' Instead, it is better to begin by smoothly introducing the reader to the idea of e-security threats: 'E-security is of growing concern for those who use the Internet (DTI 2006). These threats can range from Denial of Service (DOS) attacks, Web vandalism, Spam, viruses to fraudulent use of emails.' Note that the first sentence contains a reference to literature (in this case, the Department of Trade and Industry, i.e. DTI). Let the reader know, as early as possible, that you are well read in the area, and there is no better time to do that than in the first paragraph of your dissertation.

Let us now return to the e-Learning example, identified in the previous chapter. The overall aim of that dissertation topic was to 'advance an understanding of the impact of e-Learning in the university environment in relation to academic staff training preparation'. A sample Introduction is included in Appendix A (note that a separate sub-section explaining the value of the proposed research has not been created: instead the case for the importance of the study has been subsumed in the sample sub-sections 1.2 Research focus and 1.3 Overall research aim and individual research objectives). This sample Introduction consists of three main parts: 1.1 Background; 1.2 Research focus and 1.3 Overall research aim and individual research objectives. For now we will concentrate on the sample Background. Read this section now.

Note the structure of this Background: the specific focus of the research is not identified in the Background (that is done in the section following, labelled 1.2 Research focus). Instead, the reader is eased into the chosen subject area – academic staff and e-Learning in the university environment – through a general discussion of traditional teaching and learning, followed by reference to the drive for e-Learning in the university environment, leading to a changing role for academic staff, and ending with the need for staff to be prepared to cope with this change. By setting the scene and placing the research in context, the author prepares the reader for a greater understanding of his research focus.

A common mistake by students

If students do not write *too little* on their background section, then paradoxically another common mistake by students is to go to the other extreme and spend *too much* time on background information. Normally, one or two pages should suffice. You want to arrive at your research focus quite quickly, but not before you provide some basic information that allows the reader to appreciate your research in context. You need to remember that this is an Introduction you are talking about here, so you do not want to spend too much time on

> background information, otherwise the reader will start to wonder what your research is supposed to be about. The length of your Background will depend on the number of words that you have to play with in your dissertation.

The sample Background in Appendix A has some other good points that need emphasizing. In the very first paragraph there is a reference to other literature:

> Aristotle's lectures, preserved in the writings of Plato, are examples of such an approach, where the student is educated on particular topics through the mechanism of illuminating conversations – *dialogues* – between tutor and student (Taylor 1955).

By doing so, you are letting the reader know that you understand good academic practice: you are supporting your ideas with reference to other authors and you are showing that you know how to reference (in this case, using the author/date system, or Harvard system of referencing – referencing will be covered in Chapter 4, The Literature Review). Second, in the sample Background section there is a mix of references (indirect references, direct quotes, as well as pictures of web sites to illustrate points), making it interesting for the reader. Examples of these different ways to present information are extracted from the sample Background sub-section and illustrated below:

1 *Indirect referencing*:
   Aristotle's lectures, preserved in the writings of Plato . . . between tutor and student (Taylor 1955).
2 *Direct referencing*:
   Haywood *et al.* (2004) believe that most students . . .
3 *Direct referencing with quotation embedded in sentence*:
   There is also much interest from universities to exploit ICT in distance learning, with Moe and Blodget (2000) emphasising that 'the next big killer application for the Internet is going to be education'.
4 *Direct referencing with separate indented quotation*:
   In the UK, the Dearing Report (1997) foresaw benefits of using ICT in higher education:

   > . . . we believe that the innovative application of . . . C&IT holds out much promise for improving the quality, flexibility and effectiveness of higher education. The potential benefits will extend to, and affect the practice of, learning and teaching and research. (13.1)

5 *Multiple indirect referencing*:
   Online learning, networked learning, distributed learning, flexible learning, virtual learning, are some of the terms used to describe learning that uses technology as a vehicle for educational delivery (Salmon, 1998; Jung, 2000; Rosenberg, 2001; Collis and Moonen, 2001).

It is in the next sub-section – Research focus, in the sample Introduction – where you reveal the actual focus of your research, which includes the rationale for your research together with the specifics of what you intend doing. At this stage, you have made your job easier by placing your research within some sort of context.

Research focus (revisited)

Two things your tutor will want to know: (1) the focus of your research; and (2) the rationale for your study. It is important that you clarify the area(s) you intend researching and that you also explain why you want to do this research.

Reference will be made to the sub-section Research focus in the sample Introduction in Appendix A, to make some pertinent points on how to elucidate the focus of your research, so read it now.

The sample 'Research Focus' sub-section in Appendix A starts by linking back to the Background sub-section ('There is some confusion about the benefits of e-Learning'). Try and imitate this approach because it lets your discussion flow and keeps the reader on track (as well as yourself!).

A common mistake by students

A common mistake by students is to begin each sub-section as if it were unrelated to the previous sub-section: this can disrupt the flow of your dissertation and, more importantly, cause you to stray from your main thesis. When tutors read a student's dissertation, and a new chapter begins with no apparent link to the previous chapter, or sub-section, then they will be asking themselves one or two questions, such as 'How does this follow from the previous section?' or 'Is the student going off at a tangent?'

Very quickly in the sample Research Focus the topic is turned to the student's area of interest, which is, preparing university staff for e-Learning: 'E-Learning commentators are also warning that academic staff in universities require to be prepared to cope with e-Learning, to make the shift from *sage on the stage* to *guide on the side.*'

As stated, the sample Research focus sub-section starts by linking back to the Background sub-section ('There is some confusion about the benefits of e-Learning'). The same paragraph then goes on to provide some examples of this confusion about the benefits of e-Learning by referring to other literature, thereby convincing the tutor who will be marking the dissertation that the writer is a well-read researcher, and not someone who makes statements without providing supporting evidence.

A common mistake by students

A common mistake by students when first introducing their chosen field of study, is to provide one or two sentences on their dissertation topic and think that they have provided enough justification on why their topic is worthy of study. No! You must convince the reader that you have a 'worthy area of study': (1) by referring to other literature; and (2) by persuading the reader of the need for your study. While completing (1) and (2), you also tailor your examples and discussion to reflect the individual objectives that are of interest to you (you do not want them to be a surprise to the reader, when you finally clarify them at the end of your introductory chapter).

The second paragraph in the sample Research focus sub-section – ('E-Learning commentators are also warning that academic staff in universities require to be prepared to cope with e-Learning, to make the shift from *sage on the stage* to *guide on the side*') – introduces what will be the main focus of study for the student's dissertation, i.e. preparing university staff for e-Learning. Once again, the writer has taken the opportunity to refer to other authors, either through direct quotations or via simple author/date referencing.

The third paragraph – ('Clearly, academic staff support is crucial for the success of e-Learning, and a major factor in gaining academic support is to prepare them to be able to meet the challenge of e-Learning (Bates 2000; Epic 2002; Gerrard 2002).') – explains why research in the area of staff preparation for e-Learning is important, with the author using phrases that deliberately make it clear that he is attempting to justify his research ('Critical to the value and logic of the research in this study . . .'; '. . . is therefore an area worthy of study'; 'The importance of research in this field of e-Learning . . .'), referring to literature to support his argument ('Vermeer (2000) complains of too little research of staff experiences in e-Learning and that much commentary is anecdotal in nature'; 'Coppola *et al.* (2001: 96) urge that "there is a critical need for study of faculty experiences" ').

Once you have justified why your research, in general, is worth doing, you can then focus on how you will achieve your overall research aim, that is, you can then discuss the rationale behind your individual research objectives. The main argument behind your individual research objectives, whatever they are, tends to be that by achieving them you will achieve your overall research aim. To remind you, the sample research objectives are:

Specifically, within the context of higher education, the objectives of this research are to:

1   *Identify* the forces driving e-Learning and the barriers to the successful delivery of e-Learning programmes.
2   *Evaluate critically* models and frameworks relevant to supporting academic staff in coping with e-Learning.
3   *Explore* staff stakeholder views and practices related to e-Learning preparation, including drivers and barriers to e-Learning.
4   *Formulate* recommendations on staff preparation issues.

However, these objectives need to be revealed gradually, in an evolutionary way. Thus, you do not start your Research focus sub-section by blatantly stating your overall research aim and your associated individual objectives: that is too crude an approach. It is much better to allow your overall aim and specific objectives to appear as a result of academic discussion. The remainder of the sample Research focus sub-section in Appendix A does this very thing: it breaks down the overall research aim into individual object-ives, while justifying the need for these specific areas of study. Note that the terms 'overall research aim' and 'specific research objectives' are not actually used in the sample Research focus sub-section: this is a matter of choice. If you wish, you can use the Research focus sub-section to clarify your overall research area, justify it, and identify the specific research areas that you will be studying, and not worry too much about labels. It is in the next sub-section of the Introductory chapter – Overall research aim and individual research objectives – where you finally nail down for the reader your specific research focus, using the terms 'overall research aim' and 'individual research objectives'.

Overall research aim and individual research objectives

This sub-section should be relatively easy for students. It is in the previous sub-section of your introductory chapter, i.e. Research focus, where you ought to have explained to your tutor what you intend to study and why. This sub-section merely summarizes your area of study, without the need to justify why (because you should have done this earlier), capturing a succinct summary that can be used for future reference by both your supervisor and yourself. Reference will be made to the sample 'Overall research aim and individual research objectives' sub-section in Appendix A, so read it now.

   The sample sub-section begins by re-stating the overall aim of the student's research ('The overall aim of this research is to advance an understanding of the impact of e-Learning in the university environment in relation to academic staff training preparation'). Try and adopt this practice. You do not need to justify your overall aim again, but make an effort to restate why the individual objectives are important, as is done in the sample chapter ('However, in order to understand staff preparation issues it is felt necessary to gain an insight into the forces driving e-Learning and to explore the barriers to the implementation of e-Learning programmes'; 'Further, this research will assess existing guidelines supporting staff and student needs . . .'). Also, take the opportunity to throw some light on how you will carry out your research, for example through a literature review and, perhaps, the collection of empirical data ('In turn, two main research vehicles will be exploited to facilitate this study: an in-depth review of relevant literature and the collection and analysis of empirical data'). There is no need at this stage to explain in detail how you will gather and analyse your empirical data: you can simply refer the reader to your later section on research methods ('The section entitled Research Methods contains the details of both the research strategy and the data collection techniques to be used to obtain empirical data'). You should, however, provide *outline information,* such as your general research strategy (e.g. case study), research subjects (e.g. university staff) and data collection technique(s) (e.g. interviews), but the precise details of your research choices are left to your Research Methods chapter.

In this part of your introduction you must state unequivocally, using simple terse statements, the specific research objectives that you intend meeting in order to achieve your overall research aim, as in the sample chapter:

Specifically, within the context of higher education, the objectives of this research are to:

1 *Identify* the forces driving e-Learning and the barriers to the successful delivery of e-Learning programmes.
2 *Evaluate critically* models and frameworks relevant to supporting academic staff in coping with e-Learning.
3 *Explore* staff stakeholder views and practices related to e-Learning preparation, including drivers and barriers to e-Learning.
4 *Formulate* recommendations on staff preparation issues.

If you want to lose marks, then make sure that your objectives are inappropriate, unfocused, vague, and unrealistic. You can do this by ensuring that you include objectives that have little to do with your stated aim, are too general in nature, include fuzzy keywords (such as 'look at'), and are unrealistic (i.e. are over-ambitious). On the other hand, to achieve good marks in this area you need to list objectives that are:

• appropriate (i.e. clearly related to what you want to study);

- focused (i.e. each objective is distinct and incrementally aids in achieving your overall research aim);
- clear (i.e. avoids ambiguity and includes snappy, meaningful keywords);
- achievable (i.e. is realistic, given the timescale available to complete the dissertation).

Initially you will be marked on the appropriateness of these objectives and perceived focus (or lack thereof), including how realistic they are. When you finally submit your dissertation you will also be marked on whether or not you have achieved your research objectives. So think carefully about your individual research objectives. In effect, when you list your specific research objectives, you are really saying to your supervisor: 'This is what I am going to do in this dissertation, so mark me on these objectives'.

Some advice

- Start each objective with a key word ('Identify', 'Assess', 'Evaluate', 'Explore', 'Examine', 'Investigate', 'Determine', 'Review', etc.). This will help you focus. Appendix J contains a list of keywords that you may find useful.
- The first individual objective tends to be a simple one, such as 'Identify' or 'Clarify', to help set the scene in your research study ('identify security issues', 'clarify the causes of smoking', etc.) prior to in-depth research in the main body of your work.
- The other keywords ought to indicate depth of study ('Evaluate critically', 'Explore', etc.) because the associated objectives will form the main part of your research. In the above example, 'evaluate critically' and 'explore' are used in objectives 2 and 3 respectively, where objective 2 will involve an extensive review of relevant literature, while objective 3 refers to the collection of empirical data.
- Do not have too many objectives: one or two is too few; six tends to be too many. Have one objective that sets the scene (e.g. to define a subject under study), another that will form the bulk of the literature review, another still that will refer to the empirical study (i.e. collection of raw data, e.g. interviews), and a final objective related to making recommendations. That makes four objectives. If you feel it necessary to include an additional objective, this tends to occur in objective 2, where you have the opportunity to indicate two major areas of study in the Literature Review (e.g. 'review the e-learning initiatives *and* their effectiveness in the workplace', 'assessing e-security threats *and* countermeasures', etc.). There is no definitive rule in the number of objectives allowed, but having too few is just as problematic as having too many, with the former leading to vagueness and the latter resulting in piecemeal research.

What follows is a fine example, from a student's dissertation, of a crisply written overall research aim and associated research objectives:

The aim of this dissertation is to gain an understanding of how Cybercrime is effecting the online business community, with a view to offering guidance on the way forward. The following objectives have been identified of paramount importance in helping to achieve the aforementioned aim:

- *Clarification* of what is meant by the term *Cybercrime*.
- *Exploration* of the vulnerability of business organizations to Cybercrime.
- *Critical assessment* of the effectiveness of current preventative measures.
- *Implementation* of a case study of Cybercrime on an online business.
- *Recommendations* to the business community, through a generic online security framework, on how to combat Cybercrime.

The above objectives are clear and logical and there is a developmental flow to the student's proposed research. The student went on to justify the need for each of the objectives and offered some insight into the areas that she would be looking at: 'The first objective is necessary because the term Cybercrime can be misleading . . . Objectives 2 and 3 will form the core of the Literature Review and will involve the study of areas such as . . . Objective 4, the collection and analysis of empirical data, will allow the researcher the opportunity to study, in depth, one organization . . . Finally, as a result of the Literature Review findings and an analysis of the case study, recommendations . . .'.

Your tutor may request that you pose your research in the form of specific research questions. This is easy to do. First of all write down your overall research aim, then the individual objectives you think you need to meet in order to satisfy this overall aim (as suggested above). Next, convert your overall research aim into a research question (see p. 16). Finally, convert your individual objectives into sub-questions. For example, the sample objectives in Appendix A are:

Specifically, within the context of higher education, the objectives of this research are to:

1   *Identify* the forces driving e-Learning and the barriers to the successful delivery of e-Learning programmes.
2   *Evaluate critically* models and frameworks relevant to supporting academic staff in coping with e-Learning.
3   *Explore* staff stakeholder views and practices related to e-Learning preparation, including drivers and barriers to e-Learning.
4   *Formulate* recommendations on staff preparation issues.

These objectives, converted into questions, now become:

Specifically, within the context of higher education, the objectives of this research are to answer the following questions:

1   What are the forces driving e-Learning and the barriers to the successful delivery of e-Learning programmes?
2   What models and frameworks are available to support academic staff in coping with e-Learning and how helpful are they?
3   What are staff stakeholder views and practices related to e-Learning preparation, including drivers and barriers to e-Learning?
4   As a result of these research questions, recommendations on staff preparation issues will be formulated.

Notice that objective 4 was not rewritten as a question, but simply added as an output. Also, you can mix and match how you wish to write your overall research aim and corresponding research objectives. For example, you can state your overall research aim, not as a question, but as a simple research task ('The purpose of this research is to investigate . . .') and then shape your individual research objectives into questions, the answers to which you reckon will facilitate your main research aim. Or you could do the reverse: write your overall research aim as a research question to be pursued ('The main question that this research will attempt to answer is . . .') and then list the individual research tasks you consider need to be completed to produce an answer to your substantive research question ('Objective 1 will identify the forces driving e-Learning and the barriers to the successful delivery of e-Learning programmes; Objective 2 will evaluate critically models and frameworks relevant to supporting academic staff in coping with e-Learning . . .', etc.). Alternatively, you can decide to dispense with the matter of research questions altogether and simply list your intended overall research aim and individual research objectives. To play safe on which approach to adopt, consult your dissertation supervisor. Different institutions, and different departments in the same institution, can often adopt different practices.

One last piece of advice: include expected timescales for each objective, using a bar chart or a Gantt chart (or whatever pictorial means you feel comfortable with). Even a basic table will suffice. The way to create your pictorial representation is to list, not the objectives, but the parts that will form the substance of your dissertation (Introduction, Literature Review, Research Methods, Discussion, Conclusion and Recommendations) and the time that you expect each activity to take, in terms of either weeks or months. It is not important that your expected timescales prove accurate, merely that you recognize the need for strategic planning, that you have an awareness of the big picture and how each of the tasks needed to complete this picture connect, and that you have made a reasonable estimate on how long you expect to complete the main parts of your dissertation.

Of course, you do not pluck your timescales out of thin air: have an intelligent guess at how long you think each task will take you, taking into account time for illness (e.g. common flu), holidays, unexpected emergencies, other work, days when you might be tired, etc. In other words, do not expect your timescale to run like clockwork – it will not.

A common mistake by students

A common mistake by students is not to start their dissertation when they are supposed to, but to leave it as late as possible, citing other commitments but always promising that after such-and-such they will concentrate almost exclusively on their dissertation. It is not uncommon for students still to be struggling with their Literature Review (and, on occasion, still rewriting their individual objectives!) when they ought to have completed their chapter on research methods. Too often, when students are submitting their final dissertation they complain that they wish they had more time. If only they had listened to their supervisor's advice in the first place!

You could, if you find it more convenient, merge the two sub-sections Research focus and overall research aim and individual research objectives into one section: Research focus. There is nothing wrong with that approach, but if you do that, then remember to combine the main elements of each sub-section, i.e. an explanation of the research area that you intend exploring followed by the identification of your specific research objectives.

Value of your research

Initially, in the Research focus sub-section of your Introduction you ought to justify why you are doing your research, but it can also be a good idea to have a separate sub-section, entitled 'Value of This Research' or 'Importance of This Research' or 'Research Worth' or 'Added Value', where you make it crystal clear to the reader – i.e. those who will be judging the merit, or otherwise, of your efforts – how your work will add value to your field of study.

A common mistake by students

It really is not difficult to address this concept of 'added value', but unfortunately a common mistake by students is to omit any blatant reference to the importance of what they are doing and instead, at best, merely hint at the worth of their dissertation. **BE BOLD**. Either have a paragraph or two, or have a complete sub-section (i.e. 'Value of This Research') where you state, unequivocally, the worth of your work.

In what ways could your work *add value*? It could be that the domain you have picked to research is lacking in critical investigation. Or you are looking at a subject area from a different angle. Or your chosen research area is topical and urgent (e.g. important medical issues or current computer security problems). You need to state why you think your research is important and worth doing (think in terms of who will benefit from your work and in what ways it will shed light on specific research issues). State quite categorically why your research study is important: 'This research is important for a number of reasons . . .' or 'This research adds value to current research in a variety of ways . . .'.

You can break down the importance of your research into two areas: first, why your Literature Review is important, and, second, why your empirical research is important. When explaining the importance of your Literature Review, refer to your individual research objectives and how the Literature Review will help meet them. But also explain the *overall* importance of your Literature Review (perhaps it provides a coherent perspective on a subject area that has previously received scant attention, producing a deeper intellectual understanding; or it meets an urgent need to address a topical subject, e.g. medical research or computer security issues). Next, and still on the importance of your Literature Review, explain the value of your specific sub-sections (e.g. barriers to e-Learning). In other words, explain why you need to do a Literature Review, the areas that you intend reviewing, and the benefits to the research community and others (e.g. business community) of this academic research.

Whereas students sometimes find it difficult to justify a Literature Review (and so tend not to), they find it is much easier to justify the worth of empirical research. It may be that your particular empirical research activity is unique and will provide a valuable insight into a problem area (although your research does not need to be unique to be of value). It may be that your empirical research will complement the work of others. Or that there is a call for practical research in your area (from other researchers complaining about the paucity of research in your chosen field). You can also argue in terms of the value of comparing and contrasting theory (i.e. your Literature Review) with practice (i.e. your empirical work). Where possible, show evidence of support for your empirical research, such as:

> The importance of research in this field of e-Learning becomes even more apparent when other researchers mourn the lack of research in this area. Vermeer (2000: 329) complains of too little research of staff experiences in e-Learning and that much commentary is anecdotal in nature, mainly coming from 'the enthusiasm of the recently converted', while Coppola *et al.* (2001: 96) urge that 'there is a critical need for study of faculty experiences'; and as far afield as New Zealand there is a national priority for 'more research into the effectiveness and theoretical base of e-learning' as a result of practitioners 'finding their progress restricted by the lack of available research into e-Learning' (Ministry of Education 2004: 1).

If you wish, you can summarize how your work, with reference to your research objectives, will contribute to the research community:

> This research work will contribute to the development to the discipline of e-Learning in a number of important ways: first, by providing a critical review of issues pertinent to the implementation of e-Learning (what is driving e-Learning and what can act as a barrier); second, by critically examining existing models and frameworks to support academic staff; third, by obtaining the views of a variety of staff stakeholders on existing practices in e-Learning, a rich picture of e-Learning can emerge, allowing a meaningful comparison between theory and practice, from which an improved understanding of e-Learning issues in higher education can be derived, particularly with regard to academic staff training and support in preparing for e-Learning.

In essence, pointing out the value or importance of your intended research will aid in explaining to the reader why you have chosen to research a particular topic.

A further suggestion

Remember, within each chapter of your dissertation you should take every opportunity to gain marks. Another way to enhance your dissertation Introduction is by tagging on, at the end of your Introduction, an outline of each chapter in your dissertation. You can do this by typing up the headings for each chapter, and then, once the dissertation is complete, fill in basic information outlining the areas covered in each of the chapters. If the Introduction of your dissertation had as its structure the sub-sections 1.1 Background; 1.2 Research focus; and 1.3 Summary of overall research aim and individual research objectives, then the sub-section Outline structure would be labelled 1.4 Outline structure. At this stage you can type up the headings for sub-section 1.4, which are just your chapter headings, for example:

1.4 Outline Structure

Chapter 1 Introduction
Chapter 2 Issues and Review of Related Literature
Chapter 3 Research Methods
Chapter 4 Case Study Results: Academic Staff; Elite Staff
Chapter 5 Conclusion
Chapter 6 References

As you complete each chapter, you are then in a position to write down the main areas that were covered in that chapter. Note that you are not summarizing the content of each chapter in your Outline Structure. You are merely providing the reader with a statement of the main topics addressed:

Chapter 1 Introduction

This chapter provides the reader with **background** information on the impact of e-Learning on the traditional paradigm for teaching and learning in the university environment, including an illustration of some drivers and barriers, and the need for an understanding on how staff are being prepared for e-Learning, to make the switch from *sage on the stage* to *guide on the side*. The **focus** of this research is discussed and justified and the **overall research aim and individual research objectives** are identified.

In this example, the main things that were discussed in the sample Introduction chapter in Appendix A have been highlighted: *background* information, research *focus* and the *overall research aim and individual research objectives*. These were easily obtained from the subheadings in the sample chapter. Similarly, once you have completed your Literature Review, go back to your introductory chapter – Chapter 1 Introduction – and complete the relevant part of your outline structure. Once again, do this by identifying the key topics in your Literature Review, i.e. just take the subheadings that you created for your Literature Review chapter and lift them to form the basis of your outline structure:

1.4 Outline Structure

Chapter 1 Introduction

This chapter provides the reader with **background** information on the impact of e-Learning on the traditional paradigm for teaching and learning in the university environment, including an illustration of some drivers and barriers, and the need for an understanding on how staff are being prepared for e-Learning, to make the switch from *sage on the stage* to *guide on the side*. The **focus** of this research is discussed and justified and the **overall research aim and individual research objectives** are identified.

Chapter 2 Issues and Review of Related Literature

This chapter **defines** the term e-Learning, discusses **distance learning** (a driver for e-Learning), clarifies the **drivers** for e-Learning (including major reports, strategic forces, and the benefits of e-Learning to different stakeholders), explores **barriers** to e-Learning, evaluates **guidelines and models** on e-Learning support infrastructures in relation to providing support for academic staff preparation and **justifies the need for empirical data** on academic staff preparation issues.

Chapter 3 Research Methods

Chapter 4 Case Study Results: Academic Staff; Elite Staff

Chapter 5 Conclusion

Chapter 6 References

Every time you finish a chapter in your dissertation, return to your introduction to complete the relevant part of your outline structure. Appendix B contains a completed example of an outline structure. Not only is an outline structure helpful to the reader, importantly it can also get you extra marks. It is not difficult to do, and is another step towards convincing your tutor that you are a top student.

Summary of key points

- The introductory chapter to your dissertation should be structured so as to present the following information: background; research focus; overall research aim and individual research objectives; and the value of your intended research.
- The Background sub-section to your Introduction should place your research area in context, referring to relevant literature sources using a variety of direct and indirect referencing techniques.
- The Research Focus sub-section of your Introduction can be combined with the Background sub-section, or placed in a separate sub-section. It describes the subject of your research.
- The Overall Aim and Individual Research Objectives sub-section of your Introduction clarifies your research focus in simple terms, where your main research aim is identified and the specific research objectives needed to complete your main aim are enumerated. Both your overall aim and your individual research objectives can be transformed into research questions.

In this sub-section provide an overview of the research methods that you will use to do your research and remember to estimate the length of time to complete your major research tasks.

- Next, a sub-section, or a paragraph or two placed in previous sub-sections, should be created, explaining the value of your research, i.e. why you think your research is worth doing (think in terms of the beneficiaries of your work).
- Finally, create an outline structure, which you complete accumulatively as your progress through your dissertation. The outline structure highlights the main sub-sections contained in each of your chapters.

4

The Literature Review

Focus on your research objectives • Referencing • Description vs critical evaluation • Learning theory and your dissertation • Structuring your Literature Review

Focus on your research objectives

What advice can one give about writing a Literature Review? It would certainly help if you understood the point of a Literature Review. You carry out a review of literature to find out who is saying what about the things you are interested in, specifically your research objectives, and to show your tutor that you have read widely, and in depth, and that you have the necessary skills to both interpret and evaluate such literature, or as Haywood and Wragg (1982: 2) put it: a review of literature should demonstrate that 'the writer has studied existing work in the field with insight'.

Once again, let us revisit the sample research objectives listed in Appendix A, but this time with an eye on the Literature Review:

Specifically, within the context of higher education, the objectives of this research are to:

1 *Identify* the forces driving e-Learning and the barriers to the successful delivery of e-Learning programmes.
2 *Evaluate critically* models and frameworks relevant to supporting academic staff in coping with e-Learning.
3 *Explore* staff stakeholder views and practices related to e-Learning preparation, including drivers and barriers to e-Learning.
4 *Formulate* recommendations on staff preparation issues.

In terms of the Literature Review, for the first objective above we would find out who is saying what about the 'forces driving e-Learning and the barriers to the successful delivery of e-Learning programmes'. Similarly, we would look at relevant literature to evaluate e-Learning frameworks (objective 2), thus placing ourselves in a good position at the end of our dissertation to argue that objective 2 above was also achieved. Objective 3 could be implemented through a case study and objective 4 is derived as a result of our findings from objectives 1, 2 and 3.

When writing the Literature Review, it is very easy for students to drift from their main research objectives to find themselves immersed in writing about peripheral aspects of their topic that are extraneous to their research. A simple but clever way to avoid this pitfall is to create sub-sections/headings in your Literature Review chapter that link directly to your specific research objectives. This makes it is difficult to stray from what you are supposed to be writing about. For example, for the research objectives above to be covered in the Literature Review (i.e. objectives 1 and 2), you could create the chapter sub-headings shown in Figure 4.1. In this way, you are forcing yourself to concentrate on looking at literature germane to your stated objectives and thus minimizing the danger of sleepwalking into wasteful and unrelated discussion.

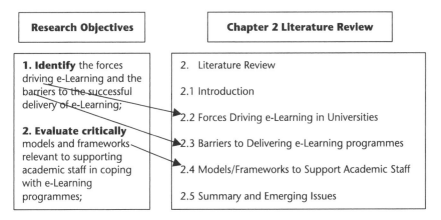

Figure 4.1 Mapping research objectives to chapter sub-sections

But what of the *content* of a Literature Review? What passes for a good Literature Review? A *good* Literature Review is characterized by the following features:

- It lays out what research has been done by others *relevant to your research aim/objectives* (why waste your time discussing irrelevant stuff?).
- It presents the work of others in a *clear, interesting* and *progressive manner* (to build up a coherent/logical picture).
- It provides evidence of *in-depth critical evaluation* (i.e. to show that YOU can give an opinion and support it with argument/evidence).

- It highlights *pertinent/emerging issues* (otherwise what is the point of your Literature Review?).
- It *cites a variety of relevant sources properly* (to show that you are well read and scholarly in your approach).

Below are examiner comments, complementing aspects of various student Literature Reviews, comments that you want to see written on your marked dissertation:

- '*Highly focused* Literature Review . . .'
- 'Clear evidence of *critical evaluation* . . .'
- '*Logical* structure . . . *eliciting* main issues . . .'
- 'Well done! An excellent *in-depth* review of *relevant* literature, supported by *properly cited* sources . . .'

Conversely, a *bad* Literature Review exhibits too many of the following (bad) practices:

- Irrelevant rambling (i.e. what we call '*student drift*');
- Ideas presented in no particular order (and so difficult to follow thread of student discussion);
- Too descriptive (with no/little attempt to give an opinion, much less support it with reasoned argument);
- Ends abruptly, devoid of any clarification of main findings;
- Limited sources used (mainly websites), coupled with inconsistent referencing styles.

The following are other excerpts from actual examiner comments, highlighting deficiencies in student Literature Reviews (comments you hope do not appear in your marked work!):

- 'Poor standard of referencing.'
- 'Too descriptive in nature.'
- 'No evidence of critical evaluation.'
- 'Lacks focus.'
- 'Limited use of sources.'
- 'Superficial discussions.'

From the examiner's perspective, she is looking at your review of literature to see if it is relevant to your research focus, that it illustrates a spread and depth to your reading, and that it shows evidence of *critical evaluation*. Make sure that you refer to a wide variety of sources, such as respected journals, books, conference proceedings, reports, credible websites, etc. to demonstrate to your examiner(s) that you are well read in your dissertation topic and that you have a sound grasp of the theory associated with your research area. Too many students focus on uncritical website sources, displaying a lack of breadth of material relevant to their study, resulting in a one-dimensional perspective.

Common problems that students encounter when they first start to write their Literature Review are that they are not sure: (1) where to find literature; (2) how to reference the literature properly; (3) how to review the literature; and (4) how to structure their Literature Review chapter. The first problem – where to find the literature – is easy to address, because the answer is: 'Go and look for it!' There is no royal road to learning, and the material will not just appear in front of you as if by magic: you have to go and look for it. By all means type keywords into your Internet browser (use Google Scholar) but also visit the university library, look at past dissertations, read relevant journals, get hold of recently published conference proceedings related to your topic, and follow up the references supplied in your lecture and seminar hand-outs. The material you need will not appear all at once, rather you will discover that one source will lead to another, one author directing you to another, one article referring to another article that may be of use to you, and so on. Collecting literature sources is an accumulative process that requires patience and perseverance in equal measure.

Seeking out and unearthing literature sources is also an investigative skill. One could compare such a task as akin to the work of a detective: you start with certain questions which you need answers to (i.e. your research objectives), search for clues to find answers to those questions/issues (in this case, the clues are to be found, initially anyway, in literature sources), you discard that which is irrelevant to your work (i.e. unrelated to your research objectives), follow up leads to other sources (i.e. references made by other authors to work that they have read), construct a case based on evidence (i.e. address your specific research objectives based, in the first instance, on your literature findings) and finally lay down the facts as you see them (i.e. present the results of your Literature Review, highlighting your main findings and the implications of your work).

In terms of your structure, it is good practice at the start of your Literature Review to remind the reader (i.e. your tutor/marker) of your research objectives and the areas that you intend covering in your Literature Review. By doing this you will be helping yourself to achieve focus, which is so important in a Literature Review. It is not uncommon for students, half way through their Literature Review, to forget about their initial objectives and to wander into other areas which, although interesting, are irrelevant to their work (and are taking up valuable space in their dissertation).

Appendix C contains a fitting example of an introductory section to a Literature Review (for a postgraduate dissertation). It re-lists the research objectives and indicates which objectives will be tackled within the Literature Review, as well as reiterating the value of the Literature Review topics, and so places the relative importance of the Literature Review within the context of the dissertation.

A common mistake by students

A common mistake by students is to, without warning, immediately start discussing literature that they have read, leaving the reader to work out how it relates to the student's research objectives. Try and avoid such impatience: spell out carefully to the reader the topics that you intend covering. It keeps you on the right track and lets the reader know what to expect.

This chapter will now concentrate on how to reference your sources, how to evaluate critically the literature that you deem relevant to your dissertation topic, and how to structure your Literature Review chapter. Whoever will be marking your dissertation will be examining it for evidence of your competence in these skills.

Referencing

Part of the rationale for completing a Literature Review is to show that you have read widely in your subject area and that your choice of literature is pertinent to your research. You are also being tested that you know how to evaluate the literature that you read – more of that later. Accordingly, an essential skill that needs to be evident in your Literature Review is that of referencing, i.e. how you refer to your sources of evidence in the body of your text and at the end of your dissertation (where you will create a separate chapter called References, wherein you will collate all the sources cited in the body of your text). One needs to be clear on this matter – when you refer to other authors in your Literature Review you are also required to record the details of your sources (author's name, date of publication, title of publication, etc.) in a References section at the back of your dissertation.

Too many students neglect to compile their sources as they proceed, and then get into an unnecessary panic at the end when they cannot find all their references. As you refer to a secondary source (book, journal, website article, etc.) in your review of literature, get into the habit of writing down the source details (author's name, date of publication, page numbers, etc.). That will make your job of compiling a References section much easier.

You really ought to get full marks for your referencing because it is not difficult. Remember, this sub-section is your Literature Review, so if you are not sure how to reference sources, either in the corpus of your dissertation or in your References section, then you will lose silly marks. Let us first deal with the art of referencing in the body of your text.

There are many styles of referencing, but the Harvard style is one of the more commonly used styles, primarily because it is clear and concise, and so will be used for demonstration purposes in the examples throughout this book. Avoid adopting any old style of referencing – universities are normally quite strict in their regulations about such matters. The Harvard style is often referred to as the author/date style, for what will become obvious reasons. There are a variety of ways that you can reference sources in the body of your text. In the first instance, you can quote a source. If the quotation is not too large then you can include it in a sentence, as follows:

Ryan (2001: 10) warns that universities 'must provide professional development to support the academic development of their staff'.

Note that the author has been identified in two ways: first, by name; and, second, by giving the year of the publication from which the partial quotation appears (hence the Harvard style is referred to as the author/date system).

The quotation is included in parentheses and the page number of where in the cited publication the text appears (in this case, page 10) is indicated opposite the year of publication: 'Ryan (2001: 10)'. You should be aware that there are variations of the Harvard style of referencing. For example, one could also have recorded Ryan's publication details as follows:

Ryan (2001, p.10). . .

Thus using a comma rather than a colon to separate the year of publication from the page number, and also prefacing the page number with the abbreviation 'p.'. Both forms of referencing are correct, but whichever one you use, then be consistent throughout your dissertation.

If the quotation is large, and by that one means it takes up three or more lines, then you ought to place it in a paragraph in its own right and indent it (to show that it is a quotation and not just another paragraph). Here is an example of referencing where the quotation requires a separate, indented, paragraph:

This point is made by the Australian National Training Authority (2003: 16) when, in a report for their Flexible Learning Framework, they try and identify what they mean by e-Learning (in their case, in relation to vocational training):

'e-Learning is a broader concept (than online learning), encompassing a wide set of applications and processes which use all available electronic media to deliver vocational education and training more flexibly. The term "e-Learning" is now used in the Framework to capture the general intent to support a broad range of electronic media (Internet, intranets, extranets, satellite broadcast, audio/video tape, interactive TV and CD-ROM) . . .'

Some writers would have used the same convention above but not bothered to include the quotation marks, arguing that the indentation itself, together with the citation, makes it clear that the block of text is a quotation. This is a reasonable argument and in fact it is normal practice to remove quotation marks in a long extract. The quotation marks are optional, but some academics like to include them. To play safe, consult your dissertation supervisor to ascertain his preference.

If you are quoting a source, then you need to enter the page, or pages, where the quotation was taken. You can do this in the body of your text, either when you cite the author – e.g. Burns (2005: 4) believes that 'e-Learning is not without its problems' – or, if it is a large quotation with its own separate paragraph, at the end of the quotation. Alternatively, you can identify the page number, not in the body of the text, but when you list all your references at the end of your dissertation, in a separate chapter, as shown below:

References

Park, C. (2003). 'In other (people's) words: plagiarism by university students – literature and lessons', *Assessment and Evaluation in Higher Education*, 28(5): 471–488.

Phillips, E. M. and Pugh, D. S. (2007). *How to Get a Ph.D.: A Handbook for Students and their Supervisors*, Berkshire: Open University Press, p. 15.

Proudfoot, R., Thompson, A. and Kastan, D. S. (2001) (Eds.). *The Arden Shakespeare Complete Works*, London: Thomson Learning, p. 520.

Riddell, P. and Webster, P. (2006). 'Support for Labour at lowest level since 1992', *The Times*, 9 May, p. 2.

When recording *journal* details in your References chapter, you can enter the information as in the 'Park, C. (2003)' example:

. . . *Assessment and Evaluation in Higher Education*, 28(5): 471–488.

Or you can decide to use abbreviated words ('vol.', 'no.', 'pp.'):

. . . *Assessment and Evaluation in Higher Education*, vol. 28, no. 5, pp. 471–488.

However you decide to document your journal references, make sure that you stick to the same style when listing other journal sources. Incidentally, a single 'p.' is used to refer to a specific page (e.g. p. 3), whereas 'pp.' indicates a range of pages (e.g. pp. 14–28).

If, when quoting a source, you decide to identify the page number in the References chapter, as above, rather than in the body of your text, then you may encounter a problem when you use several quotations from the same source. For example, if three quotations were derived from Proudfoot *et al.* (2001), then we could have three separate page numbers to identify, but where would you put them? You cannot put them all beside the same source in your

References chapter, because you would not know which page number was referring to which quotation, as in:

References

Proudfoot, R., Thompson, A., and Kastan, D. S. (2001) (Eds.). *The Arden Shakespeare Complete Works*, London: Thomson Learning, p. 5, p. 201, p. 520.

In such circumstances, you place the page numbers in the body of the text. That is why most students tend to simplify things and place the page numbers, for all quotations, in the body of their text.

There are times when you are citing sources where you can include page numbers in the body of your document *and* in your References section at the back of your dissertation. For example, suppose that in your Literature Review you have introduced a quotation and decide to follow common practice by citing the page number beside the author's name, as in:

Peeke (1984: 24) asserts that 'to be a successful researcher can demand a lessening commitment to the task of teaching'.

If the source for this quotation was a journal, then when you are completing your References section, you need to record where the whole article (not just the quotation) is placed in the journal:

Peeke, G. (1984). 'Teacher as researcher', *Educational Research*, 26(1): 24–26.

You can also see that when you have a long quotation, that it has its own paragraph, is indented, surrounded with quotation marks (optional), *italicized*, and the font size can be reduced (optional). This means that it is easy for your marker to recognize these paragraphs as large quotations and not to confuse them with 'normal' paragraphs. It also makes the text look more interesting.

You do not need to quote every source that you reference; in fact, it can get boring for the reader and it also takes up a lot of your word count, so be judicial in your use of quotations. To cite an author, or authors, without quoting them is easy enough to do, examples of which are:

Example 1
Laurillard (2001) argues that e-Learning requires new skills to deal with a new pedagogy.

Example 2
Academic staff support is crucial to the success of e-Learning (Bates 2000; Epic 2002; Gerrard 2004).

Example 3
Biggam (2004a, 2004b; 2005) queries the need for student examinations.

In the first example, you simply refer to the author and date of publication. When there are two or more references to be cited, as in example two, then list them chronologically in parentheses and separate the authors using a semi-colon, e.g. '(Weng 2003; Bourdon 2004; Turner 2005)'. If an author has more than one publication in the same year, as in example 3, then refer to the first one as 'a' and the second one as 'b', and so on, e.g. 'Thomson (2003a, 2003b) holds consistently to the view that referencing is a dying art'.

There may be occasions in your Literature Review when the source that you are citing has more than one author. If the source was identified as having two authors, then refer to them as follows: Beatty and Jefferson (2006). In the body of your text, if there are more than two authors for the source that you wish to reference, it is convention to cite the first author and refer to the others using the Latin abbreviation '*et al.*', which means 'and others'. For example, 'Hogarth *et al.* (2004)' indicates that there are at least three authors responsible for this source. The '*et al.*' is actually an abbreviation of '*et alii, et alia*, etc.', hence the full stop after '*al*' to indicate that the Latin phrase is itself an abbreviation. When you list all your references at the end of your dissertation, in your References section, make sure that you replace the '*et al.*' part of your citations with the actual author names. It is not a crime if you forget, but it does show your tutor that you are careful about recording all your sources. Your supervisor may not be bothered either way, but it is good academic practice.

Ibid.: another Latin term. To avoid citing the same source, again and again, you can use the Latin word *ibid.* (= *ibidem*), which stands for 'in the same place', to indicate that you are referring to the *previously* cited source, as shown in the text below:

Barlow and Hogarth (2007) argue that mobile technologies are detrimental to the educational development of university students. Perceptions of the advantages of interconnectivity are often exaggerated. Even the simple skill of handwriting has been replaced by ungrammatical abbreviations (*ibid.*).

Yet another Latin term: *op. cit.* (= *opere citato*), which means 'from the work cited'. You use *op. cit.* to indicate that you are referring to a source that you have already cited (somewhere) in your dissertation. *Op. cit.* is different from *ibid.* in that *ibid.* refers only to the last source cited (as in the above example) whereas *op. cit.* refers to a source cited *somewhere* previously in your dissertation, i.e. it need not be the last source cited in your discussion. For example:

Biggam and Murphy (2007) recommend a strategic approach to tackling plagiarism in universities. Other academics adopt a similar position (Thomson 2003; Edwards 2005; Smith 2006). Differences of opinion surface, however, when it comes to deciding upon appropriate levels of punishment for transgressors. Some researchers argue for leniency, claiming that students are victims themselves. Biggam and Murphy (*op. cit.*) refute this line of argument.

Viz. and *Inter alia*. *Viz.* is an abbreviation of the Latin word *videlicet* (itself a combination of two Latin words, *videre* 'to see' + *licet* 'it is permissible') and its meaning is captured in the terms 'in other words', 'that is to say', and 'namely'. It is used to introduce examples and lists ('namely') or to interpret meaning ('in other words', 'that is to say'). Examples of its use are:

Example 1
Robert had a number of complaints that he wished to raise with his boss, *viz.*: his lack of promotion; his unreasonable working hours; and his workload.

Example 2
Stevenson (2007) underlined the importance of education, *viz.* that a learned society is better placed to cope with life's challenges.

Example 3
Fotheringham's main point, *viz.* that good teachers were born and not made, was much disputed.

Annoyingly, students often use the term viz-a-viz, through comical ignorance, as a synonym for *viz.* Viz-a-viz is not a valid term, in any language, and has no meaning. Vis-à-vis (pronounced vee-a-vee, not veez-a-veez), on the other hand, is a valid term: it is French and means 'face-to-face' which is used when comparing two things (facing each other). The term, therefore, is translated to mean 'compared to' or 'with respect to' or 'in relation to', as in 'Eastern Philosophy vis-à-vis Western Philosophy' or 'Boys vis-à-vis Girls are a troublesome lot'. A looser interpretation of 'with respect to' allows the term vis-à-vis to be linked closely with the word 'namely' as used in the Latin abbreviation *viz.*, for example: 'Questions about the human condition vis-à-vis love, jealousy, anger, pity, etc. remain as yet unanswered'.

Inter alia is a Latin term meaning 'among other things'. Examples of its use are:

Example 1
The supervisor advised his dissertation students, *inter alia*, to improve their grammar.

Example 2
Thomson (2004) believed that personal fulfilment depended on, *inter alia*, financial security.

Example 3
The judge said, *inter alia*, that the time to bring the case to court had elapsed.

Occasionally you might come across a source that you wish to quote, but you spot a mistake in the source text (either grammatical or mis-spelling): it is not your place to correct the linguistic error but what you can do is quote verbatim and place *sic* in square brackets (i.e. [*sic*]) to indicate that you are aware of the error and it is not your error. 'Sic' is Latin (surprise, surprise!) and stands for 'thus, so, as it stands'. It always appears in square brackets, is normally italicized, and has no full stop because it is a full word in its own right. For example, suppose that you wish to quote the following sentence, written in 1982 by someone called Grearson:

The age of consumerism is well and trully integrated into today's society.

You notice that the word 'trully' is a mis-spelling and should read 'truly' instead. Rather than correcting the mistake, you can place [*sic*] after the mis-spelling, to show that you are aware of the error:

Grearson (1982: 10) captured the essence of Thatcher's Britain when he observed that the 'age of consumerism is well and trully [*sic*] integrated into today's society'.

You would take the same approach if you were to notice a *grammatical* error in a sentence that you wished to quote. Suppose someone called Thomson (1996) writes that 'To have the opportunity to carefully observe people at work is a fruitful activity.' There is a grammatical error in the sentence, occurring in the text 'to carefully observe', where an infinitive has been split (split infinitives are discussed on p. 186). A grammatically correct, if somewhat inelegant, version would be: 'To have the opportunity *to observe carefully* people at work is a fruitful activity.' It is not your job, however, to repair grammatically-challenged sources: just quote the source and place '[*sic*]' where the error appears, as follows.

Thomson (1996: 21) recognises the importance of observation as a research activity: 'To have the opportunity to carefully observe [*sic*] people at work is a fruitful activity.'

Nevertheless, it is permissible to use square brackets to insert a word or phrase that makes clear to the reader what a quotation is referring to, as in:

Stevenson claims that sexism is rife in the modern world: 'too often they [females] are treated as second class citizens.'

You are not altering the source text in any way: all that you are doing is attempting to clarify meaning. Be careful, though, that you do not abuse this facility as it can be very irritating to the reader, particularly if the missing information is trivial and probably known to the intended audience:

The manager was impressed with his team, commenting that '[Henrik] Larsson was brilliant again. The way he tackled [players] and ran back [to aid his team-mates] was awesome. We can't wait for the new [football] season to start again!'

There will be times when you are reading a source (book, journal article, etc.) and the author of the book/journal/article that you are reading cites another source, a source that you yourself want to cite. For example, suppose that you have in front of you a book written in 2007 by someone called Barlow. Suppose further that Barlow refers to a journal article written in 2004 by someone called MacFarlane – and that you also wish to refer to MacFarlane. You do so as follows:

MacFarlane (2004, cited in Barlow, 2007) holds the view that . . .
Or
One view expressed forcefully holds that . . . (MacFarlane, 2004, cited in Barlow, 2007) . . .

When you cite sources in the body of your text you are only identifying the author(s) and year of publication. Somewhere in your dissertation you need to list all your references and write down the full details of your sources. You can include a Bibliography instead of a References chapter, but it does not make sense to do both. A References chapter is a list of all the sources that you have cited explicitly in the body of your dissertation; whereas a Bibliography lists all the sources that you have referred to explicitly in the body of your text *and* also every source that you have read, but not included in the body of your text. It is simpler to stick to creating a References chapter only, but check with your supervisor.

Your References chapter, which tends to appear after your Conclusion chapter and before any Appendices that you have included, is an alphabetical list of your sources, for example:

REFERENCES

Adelman, C., Jenkins, D. and Kemmis, S. (1977). 'Re-thinking case study: notes from the second Cambridge conference', *Cambridge Journal of Education*, 6: 139–150.

Albrink, W. (2001). 'From Knowledge Transfer to Knowledge Management', in *Proceedings of 7th International Conference on Technology Supported Learning & Training*, Online Educa Berlin, November, p. 5.

Aldridge, S. and Rowley, J. (2001). 'Conducting a withdrawal survey', *Quarterly in Higher Education*, 7(1): 55–63.

Alexander, S. (2001). 'E-Learning developments and experiences', *Education and Training*, 43(5): 240–248.

Alstyne, V., Brynjolfsson, E. and Madnick, S. (1995). 'Why not one big database? Principles of data ownership', *Decision Support Systems*, 15: 267–284.

You need to be aware that there are different conventions for listing different types of sources, such as books, journals, conference proceedings, and websites. The format for referencing each of these sources is given below. In the demonstrations below, the generic format for the specific type of source is first given, followed by examples. Note that for book referencing, the title of the book is *italicized*, whereas for a journal it is the name of the journal that is in *italics*. Note below that the convention is to insert a full stop (.) after the author's name and year (e.g. 'Dreyfuss, H. L. (2001).'); however some publishers omit this convention, preferring to implement their own house style.

Book

Author's surname, initials (year). *Title of book*, Place of publication: Publisher. Examples:

Dreyfus, H.L. (2001). *On the Internet*, London: Routledge.
Davenport, T.H. and Prusak, L. (1998). *Working Knowledge*, Boston: Harvard Business School Press 4.

Journal

Author's surname, initials (year). 'Title of article', *Name of Journal*, volume number (issue number): page(s). Example:

Burns, E. (1994). 'Information Assets, Technology and Organisation', *Management Science*, 40(12): 645–662.

Tearle, P., Dillon, P. and Davies, N. (1999). 'Use of information technology by English university teachers. Developments and trends at the time of the National Inquiry into Higher Education', *Journal of Further and Higher Education*, 23(1): 5–15.

Newspaper

Author's surname, initials (year). 'Title of article', *Name of Newspaper*, page(s).

In other words, same format as for a journal citing, but without the need to provide an issue number. Example:

Riddell, P. and Webster, P. (2006). 'Support for Labour at lowest level since 1992', *The Times*, 9 May, p. 2.

Where the author is not known:

The Indian Agra News (2007). 'Carbon footprints and economic globalisation', 18th April, p. 4.

Conference Proceedings

Author's surname, initials (year). 'Title of article', *Name of Conference Proceedings*, Place conference was held, page(s), include website address if taken from a website and indicate date when last accessed. Example:

Conole, G., Oliver, M., Isroff, K. and Ravenscroft, A. (2004). 'Addressing Methodological Issues in e-Learning Research', in *Proceedings of the Networked Learning Conference 2004*, Sheffield. Available at: www.sef.ac.uk/nlc/Proceedings/Symposa4.htm. Last accessed: 2nd October 2004.

Website

Author's name, initials (year). 'Title of article' [online]. Available at: indicate website address. Last accessed: date. Example:

Brender, A. (2004). 'Speakers Promote Distance Education to Audiences in Asia' [online]. Available at: www.chronicle.com. Last accessed: 12th November 2004.

For a website you might find that you have little information to write down, or that the article you once read is no longer there. Do not panic: the trick is to write down as much as you can. If there is no author for the web article/source, then record the name of the website instead, e.g. The eLearning Centre (2005). 'eLearning is taking giant steps!' [online], etc.

Thesis

Author's name, initials (year). *Title of thesis*, Title of award, Institution: Place.

Fictitious examples follow:

Aitken, R. (2008). *Exploring the Role of Laughter in the Workplace*, PhD thesis, Inverclyde University: Glasgow.

Or if it is an unpublished dissertation (e.g. an undergraduate dissertation):

Anderson, T. (2008). *Forecasting Economic Growth: Lessons from Abroad*, 3rd year Dissertation, BA Economics, Inverclyde University: Glasgow.

Lectures/Seminars

Lecture's name, initials, (year of lecture, seminar). *Title of lecture/seminar* [Information about lecture/seminar]. Date of lecture/seminar.

Biggam, J. (2008). *E-security in the Digital Age* [Lecture given to MSc E-Business students, Division of Business Information Management, Inverclyde University]. 3rd February.

If the lecture/seminar material is available on a virtual learning environment (e.g. Blackboard) then you can append this information before the date above (Available: website details).

To record the example where Barlow, in her book written in 2007, cites a journal article written by MacFarlane in 2004, and where you have also referred to MacFarlane in the body of your text (as described earlier), then you can note this information in your References section by first of all citing MacFarlane's journal article in the normal way, adding the phrase 'cited in' (or 'in'), then citing Barlow's book in the normal way, as follows:

> MacFarlane, K. (2004). 'Alternative Approach to Cognitive Learning', *Organisational Learning*, 10(2): 23–45, cited in Barlow (2007). *Learning Again*, Milton Keynes: Open University Press, p. 634.

> Suppose that you have read a book titled *Classic and Cavalier: Essays on Jonson and the Sons of Ben* and that is made up of chapters written by different authors and that you want to reference one of the chapters, written by Martin Elsky. You reference the chapter first, then indicate the general book details, as shown in the example below:

> Elsky, M. (1982). 'Words, Things, and Names: Jonson's Poetry and Philosophical Grammar', in *Classic and Cavalier: Essays on Jonson and the Sons of Ben*, ed. by Summers, C. J. and Pebworth, T.-L., Pittsburg: University of Pittsburg Press, pp. 31–44.

> Remember, you can omit the 'pp.' if you wish, when indicating the chapter's page numbers.

Citing sources is a laborious, mechanical process but it is a necessary part of being viewed as a competent researcher. The upside is that there are easy marks up for grabs.

Description vs critical evaluation

Related to referencing is the matter of how to make use of quotations, and the wider issue of differentiating between *describing* the work of other researchers and *critically evaluating* their efforts.

A common mistake by students

A common mistake by students is to quote a source out of the blue, without any warning. A typical example of this, extracted from a student's dissertation, is 'Software Piracy can be defined as the unauthorised copying, reproduction, use, manufacture or distribution of software products (Source: Microsoft)'. What is wrong with that quotation? A number of things. In the first place the actual referencing is poor: the Harvard style of referencing (author/date system) has not been applied properly – it should have read '(Microsoft, 2004)' (or ('Microsoft, 2004)') instead of '(Source: Microsoft)'. However, the main problem with the quotation is that it forms a sentence on its own, with nothing before that sentence to prepare the reader for a quotation, and no comment on the quotation itself. In other words, the quotation appears out of the blue, with no warning beforehand and no explanation afterwards.

It is important that you let the reader know when you are about to quote someone. If you are embedding a quotation in your sentence, then you can do so like this:

Thomson (2005: 345) has a cynical view of e-Learning: 'it is a big con'.

Or, if the quotation is long (3+ lines), then introduce the quotation to the reader as shown in the following example.

The Dearing Report (1997) foresaw benefits of using ICT in higher education:

'we believe that the innovative application of . . . C&IT holds out much prom-ise for improving the quality, flexibility and effectiveness of higher education. The potential benefits will extend to, and affect the practice of, learning and teaching and research' (Dearing Report 1997: 13.1).

Too often students use quotations, long and short, that either form a complete sentence on their own (or take up complete paragraphs) without making any effort to introduce the quotations, or explain them, which they then compound with poor referencing. You will have succeeded only in showing your supervisor that you can neither reference nor make appropriate use of quotations. By all means quote sources, but do so in a constructive manner.

Just as bad is the overuse of quotations. If the Literature Review part of your dissertation is full of other people's words, then you are leaving little or no room for your own voice to come through. Supervisors want to know, *inter alia*, your thoughts on the literature that you are reading, so use quotations judiciously and as supporting material for *your* discussion. It is YOUR dissertation, so let YOUR voice come through.

What separates a good student from an average/poor student in the Literature Review is that the former will illustrate *critical evaluation* in their work, while the latter concentrates on merely *describing* what they have read. Here are examples of typical (negative) comments from supervisors, related to the Literature Review:

- Too descriptive!
- Completely devoid of critical thinking.
- Superficial discussion with little in the way of critical thought.
- Interesting thesis let down by uncritical acceptance of relevant literature.
- Referencing is shoddy and further complicated by thin assessment of important issues.
- Student concentrates on describing issues to the detriment of reasoned argument.

What is the difference between *critical evaluation* and *description*? Imagine that you have started your Literature Review, its focus is on e-Learning, and that you have decided that one of the first things that you will do in your Literature Review will be to define e-Learning. You write the following piece of text:

> Charles Clarke, the Education Secretary, in a foreword to a consultation document on e-Learning (Department for Education and Skills 2003a: 1), defined e-Learning in the following simplistic terms: 'If someone is learning in a way that uses information and communication technologies, they are using e-Learning.' According to this definition, using the Internet as a vehicle for learning would qualify as e-Learning.

The aforementioned piece of text has some admirable qualities, *viz.*: it is clear, the referencing has been applied properly, and the quotation used has been embedded successfully in the body of the text. Also, the student has provided a basic description, through an example, of what he believes to be Charles Clarke's view of what counts as e-Learning. This piece of text would achieve pass marks. However, it is better to go beyond merely describing what someone else thinks: to get decent marks you have to show you can offer critical evaluation – what Haywood and Wragg (1982) call 'insight' – of other people's views. That does not mean to say that you review the work of others from a negative perspective, though on occasion that may be appropriate, but simply that you offer your own point of view and support it with reasoned argument. For example, if the student had written the following piece of text instead, then he would have achieved more marks, because he is using his critical faculties:

Charles Clarke, the Education Secretary, in a foreword to a consultation document on e-Learning (Department for Education and Skills 2003a: 1), defined e-Learning in the following simplistic terms: 'If someone is learning in a way that uses information and communication technologies, they are using e-Learning.' According to this definition, using the Internet as a vehicle for learning would qualify as e-Learning. **Unfortunately, the definition, although having the benefit of brevity, suffers from a lack of clarity. For example, it is difficult to think of an example of technology-enabled learning that would be excluded from this definition, i.e. it is all-inclusive and therefore unhelpful in understanding what counts as e-Learning (and what does not).**

The first two sentences are the same as the previous text. The added text (from 'Unfortunately, the definition . . .' onwards) shows that the student knows how to review the work of others in a critical way. It is irrelevant whether or not your supervisor agrees with your opinion: what your supervisor wants to see from you is that you have an opinion on the literature that you are reading and that you can support your opinion. To move towards achieving top marks for your Literature Review, adopt the following technique:

(a) Describe what you are reading (to show that you can interpret what others write).
(b) Offer your views on what you have read.
(c) Support your views (illustrate *critical evaluation*).

Here is another example that ticks all three boxes above. The use of square brackets indicates where points (a), (b) and (c) occur ([a], [b], and [c] would obviously not appear in the original text):

There are a number of definitions that equate e-Learning with Internet-based learning. For example, Rodney Thomas, Founder and Chief Executive Officer of academyinternet, a UK-based company offering e-Learning solutions to Universities and the business community, [a] associates e-Learning with Internet-based learning (2001: 2):

'Today's learning communities gather in the virtual space provided by the Internet – communicating at the speed of thought, on a global scale. E-Learning is the most effective, efficient means ever invented for people to get the knowledge they need, at the time when they need it most, wherever they happen to be.' (Foreword to company publication)

However, [b] to restrict e-Learning to Internet-based learning could lead to anomalies in deciding what is accepted as e-Learning. For example, [c] if a university has two groups of students studying a module, with one set learning at home through the Internet, and the other set of students learning on-campus, with both sets of students using identical 'e-Learning' software, then it would be inconsistent to classify one type of learning as e-Learning, and the other not, just because it is not Internet-based. To underline this point, WebCT's course authoring software is used over the Internet and on-campus, with 80% of its software used on-campus (Bates 2001), indicating that e-Learning can appear in either pure e-Learning environments and also be part of a traditional teaching and learning setting.

A word of warning: do not overdo the critical evaluation. That is, you do not need to evaluate critically every piece of literature that you read, or interpret and assess the worth of every quotation that you use. To do so would create unnecessary work for yourself, significantly hinder progress in your dissertation, and make turgid reading for your supervisor. There are times when you describe things and there are other times when you decide to go further and delve critically into perceived wisdom. That judgement is for you to make, but essentially you display critical evaluation when you are involved in tackling issues that are central to your dissertation.

A word of caution about how you use words when referring to the work of other researchers. If you write, 'Gillingham (2006) *discovered* that . . .', then you are viewing his work in a *positive* light, agreeing with his position. Alternatively, if you were to write 'Gillingham (2006) *alleges* that . . .', then you are viewing his work in a negative light, casting doubt on his opinion. On the other hand, if you write 'Gillingham (2006) *concludes* that . . .', then you are adopting a neutral stance. The verbs you use – *discovered, alleges, concludes,* etc. – can reveal to the reader what you really think about the literature that you are reading, so use them carefully. There is nothing wrong, *per se,* in using positive verbs to show that you are supportive of someone else's ideas, if that is the perception that you want to convey to your reader; similarly, there is nothing wrong in using negative verbs, such as 'claims', 'distorts', 'confuses', etc. if that is your intention. More often than not, though, when students describe the sources that they have read they tend to re-use the same two or three verbs, again and again, such as the neutral 'Thomson (2004) *states* that . . .' or the telepathic 'Thomson (2004) *thinks* that . . .' or, worse, the lazy 'Thomson (2004) *says* that . . .' Table 4.1 gives a snapshot of the wide variety of verbs that are available for your use.

Table 4.1 Snapshot of useful verbs

Accepts	Asserts	Compares	Convinces	Determines
Acknowledges	Assumes	Compiles	Cultivates	Develops
Acquiesces	Attempts	Complains	Dabbles	Digresses
Adduces	Bombasts	Concludes	Debates	Dilutes
Admits	Bores	Concocts	Debunks	Disagrees
Adopts	Builds	Concurs	Declares	Discloses
Advances	Cajoles	Confirms	Deduces	Discovers
Advises	Calculates	Confuses	Defends	Discusses
Advocates	Captures	Considers	Delves	Dismisses
Agrees	Cautions	Conspires	Demonstrates	Dispels
Alludes	Challenges	Constructs	Denounces	Dispenses
Appears	Clarifies	Contemplates	Denies	Displays
Argues	Clings	Contends	Derides	Disputes
Arrives	Clutches	Contrives	Derives	Dissents
Articulates	Comments	Conveys	Desists	

Appendix I contains a comprehensive list of verbs from which you can per-use and select verbs that reflect what you want to write, which in turn ought to go some way to preventing you from repeating the same tired old verbs *ad nauseam*.

An appropriate use of verbs will help towards achieving a readable, coherent and persuasive Literature Review. In terms of critical evaluation, what you want to see written on your marked dissertation are the following effusive comments:

- Excellent. Student not only describes pertinent issues but engages the reader with reasoned argument. Well done!
- An impressive Literature Review. Relevant sources used + clear evidence of critical evaluation. Keep up the good work!
- Student knows how to interpret the work of others and offer her own opinion, supported by clear and logical argument. Highly commendable.
- At last your own voice is shining through! And what a voice! Enjoyed reading this work. Focused, thoughtful and worthy of publication. Superb stuff.

If you follow the advice given, then you should be well placed to achieve such fulsome remarks!

In a final attempt to get the importance of critical evaluation across to you, we will look at a theory of learning developed in the middle of the last century by Bloom (1956) but one which still has credibility today. You will see that the elements in his learning theory are used, if not directly, then indirectly by your supervisors when they judge the worth of your submitted dissertation. Understand Bloom's theory – and how it relates to your dissertation – and you will be in an excellent position to exploit the elements in his theory when you write up your work. In the meantime, if you want further guidance on how to improve your basic essay-writing skills, then read the following study guide: Greetham, B. (2001). *How to Write Better Essays*, New York: Palgrave Study Guides.

Learning theory and your dissertation

There is more than one way to learn how to do things. Learning a martial art, for example, can be done through reading books, watching videos, listening to friends talk about martial arts and, of course, through actual participation. Likewise, in the world of education there are different ways that students can learn. Benjamin Bloom (1956) identified three broad ways in which students learn. These involve the use of:

1 Cognitive skills (development of mental skills to acquire knowledge).
2 Affective skills (development of feelings, emotions and attitudes).
3 Psychomotor skills (development of manual and physical skills).

Learning about a martial art, for instance, will incorporate all three types of learning: understanding the theory of martial art techniques entails the application and development of *cognitive* skills; attitudes towards aspects of your chosen martial art requires the application and development of *affective* skills; and *psychomotor* skills are applied and developed when you practise the physical techniques 'on the mat'. There is a symbiotic, circular relationship between the use of the aforementioned skills and their actual development: as you apply them, you develop them, and as you develop them you are better able to apply them. For example, if you are learning how to perform a turning kick in Tae Kwon Do, a Korean martial art, then as your instructor explains the kick to you, you will make use of your cognitive skills – mental skills – to try and understand what he is saying. You can apply your new-found knowledge of the turning kick when you try to perform the technique (using psychomotor skills). As a result of your physical attempt at executing the kick, you can reflect on your performance, relating theory to practice, which means that you develop your cognitive and psychomotor skills each time you apply the technique and reflect on your progress. This is called *learning*, and it is an active process. It requires your involvement – sitting in a lecture theatre, half asleep, is *not* learning! This theory about learning is all very well, but how does it relate to succeeding with your dissertation?

In the context of your dissertation, it is your cognitive skills that you are being marked on. You need to show your marker that you have them, and that you have them at a variety of levels. Bloom categorized the different layers of cognitive learning (as he saw them), which is referred to collectively as Bloom's taxonomy of learning and illustrated in the learning pyramid in Figure 4.2.

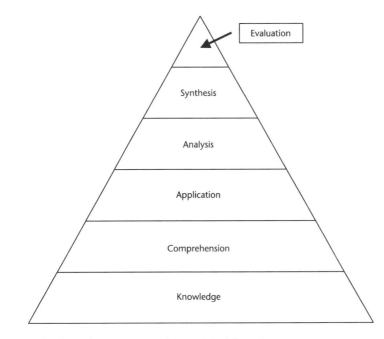

Figure 4.2 Bloom's taxonomy of (cognitive) learning

Let us relate this to your dissertation. When your dissertation marker goes through your dissertation, he is looking for evidence of your higher-level cognitive skills (such as *analysis, synthesis* and *evaluation*). If you stick to low-level cognitive skills (such as *knowledge* and basic *comprehension*), you will get low marks. If you exhibit higher-level cognitive skills, then you will secure high marks.

Table 4.2 shows examples of evidence for each of these cognitive skills in your Literature Review.

Bloom's categories of learning have been updated, with some of the elements retained, others moved position or merged or apparently removed (Figure 4.3). This new version by Anderson and Krathwohl (2001) replaces the low-level cognitive skill *Knowledge* with *Remembering* (to emphasize that this skill is just all about showing memory skills); *Comprehension* is replaced with *Understanding* (but basically means the same thing); *Synthesis* is removed (although it is embedded in the new top-level skill, *Create*); a new skill, *Create* is included (although it does not necessarily mean that you create your own

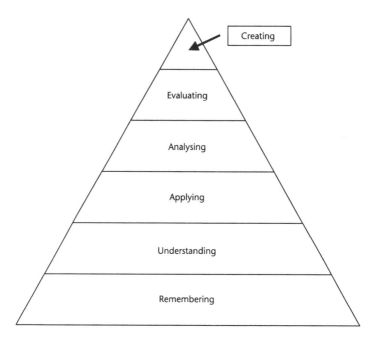

Figure 4.3 Updated version of Bloom's taxonomy of (cognitive) learning

ideas, or theories, as such, but more commonly that you bring together your thoughts into a coherent whole).

Do not worry about the subtle differences between the two models of learning: they both amount to roughly the same thing, even if the labels are different here and there. The key message you need to get from these models is that sticking to low-level cognitive skills in your Literature Review will get you low marks, whereas providing clear evidence of high-level skills will get you high marks. Of course, you will need to show some memory skills (e.g. quoting the work of researchers or recalling someone's idea) but you must take the opportunity to illustrate that you have high-level cognitive skills, by applying theory (through examples), analysing what you have read, collating your thoughts (synthesis), giving your opinion and backing it up with evidence and argument; all painting a rich picture of a critical, comprehensive and coherent review of literature relevant to your research objectives. The cognitive skills that you display in your review of literature should also be replicated throughout the other major stages of the dissertation life cycle, *viz.*: your Research Methods, Findings, and Conclusion and Recommendations.

Table 4.2 Sample evidence of cognitive skills in your dissertation

Cognitive skill	Evidence (in your Literature Review)
1 Knowledge	Repeating what you have heard in a lecture. Writing down simple facts and figures. Quoting other authors. So, basic memory skills, but no evidence that you understand what you write about.
2 Comprehension	Paraphrasing what you have heard (in a lecture) or read. Summarizing material in your own words, illustrating simple comprehension skills.
3 Application	Taking someone's idea, or view, or theory, and giving a practical example to show that you can apply this idea or view or theory. In other words, you can relate theory to the real world.
4 Analysis	Breaking down arguments into constituent parts, dissecting an author's logic, identifying key issues in reports, surveys, articles, etc.
5 Synthesis	Bringing together strands of your argument and discussion, voiced at different stages of your dissertation, to create a coherent message to the reader.
6 Evaluation	Evaluating critically the work of other authors, combining a variety of cognitive skills above, presenting evidence of your ability to understand what you are reading, giving opinions and justifying them.

Structuring your Literature Review

At the end of your Literature Review you want to be in a position where you have clarified what has emerged from your reading in terms of the issues as they relate to your research focus and in terms of the need for your empirical study (if you intend doing one).

To help you achieve the twin objectives above, you need first of all to structure your Literature Review in a logical way. To do this, create sub-sections in your Literature Review chapter that reflect the topics that you think you need to cover to meet your specific research objectives. By creating sub-section headings that link to your research objectives you are ensuring that your work will be focused.

A common mistake by students

A common mistake by students is to stray from their intended research focus. Too often supervisors witness muddled dissertations that meander aimlessly and fail to keep the reader focused on the student's initial research objectives. Avoid that mistake by setting out to create sub-section headings that are tailored to correlate to your research objectives.

Consider the sample e-Learning research objectives below:

Specifically, within the context of higher education, the objectives of this research are to:

1   *Identify* the forces driving e-Learning and the barriers to the successful delivery of e-Learning programmes.
2   *Evaluate critically* models and frameworks relevant to supporting academic staff in coping with e-Learning.
3   *Explore* staff stakeholder views and practices related to e-Learning preparation, including drivers and barriers to e-Learning.
4   *Formulate* recommendations on staff preparation issues.

The first two objectives would be tackled in the Literature Review chapter, while objective 3 would be implemented through the collection and analysis of empirical data (e.g. case study). Looking at objective 1, e-Learning drivers could form one sub-section and e-Learning barriers another sub-section. Right away you have three sub-sections to your Literature Review chapter (remember to start with an *introductory* sub-section, where you will let the reader know the topics that you are going to discuss and how they relate to your research objectives – see the example in Appendix C as an illustration of good practice). If your Literature Review chapter was numbered Chapter 2 (Chapter 1 being your dissertation introduction), then these three sub-sections would be numbered as follows:

2.1 Introduction

2.2 The Drive for e-Learning in Higher Education

2.3 Barriers to e-Learning

Given that the sample research objectives focus on preparing staff for e-Learning, then it makes sense to include something abut the need to prepare staff for e-Learning in one of the sub-section headings, which could now read:

2.1 Introduction

2.2 The Drive for e-Learning in Higher Education

2.3 Barriers to e-Learning and the Need to Prepare Academic Staff

or

2.1 Introduction

2.2 The Drive for e-Learning in Higher Education

2.3 Barriers to e-Learning

2.4 The Need to Prepare Academic Staff for e-Learning

Next, look at what sub-sections could be created from your second objective (*'Evaluate critically* models and frameworks relevant to supporting academic staff in coping with e-Learning'). An appropriate sub-section appears in 2.4 below: a sub-section could be formed related to models and frameworks to help academic staff prepare for e-Learning:

2.1 Introduction

2.2 The Drive for e-Learning in Higher Education

2.3 Barriers to e-Learning and the Need to Prepare Academic Staff

2.4 Guidelines and Models on e-Learning Support Infrastructures

By adopting the approach of linking your sub-section headings to your research objectives you are ensuring that your work will be very focused (= good marks), reducing the opportunity for irrelevant waffle and student drift.

Finally, you need to conclude your Literature Review by highlighting emerging issues, so make your final section heading about emerging issues (or key issues or pertinent issues, etc.):

2.1 Introduction

2.2 The Drive for e-Learning in Higher Education

2.3 Barriers to e-Learning and the Need to Prepare Academic Staff

2.4 Guidelines and Models on e-Learning Support Infrastructures

2.5 Emerging Issues

If your dissertation involves the implementation of *empirical research* (normally required for postgraduate dissertations), then amend your concluding sub-section heading to deal with this aspect:

2.1 Introduction

2.2 The Drive for e-Learning in Higher Education

    2.3 Barriers to e-Learning and the Need to Prepare Academic Staff

    2.4 Guidelines and Models on e-Learning Support Infrastructures

    2.5 Emerging Issues and the Need for Empirical Research

Sometimes it is fitting, after the introduction to your Literature Review, to attempt to define the area that you are studying. The example above concerns e-Learning, so a heading 'Defining e-Learning' could be inserted:

    2.1 Introduction

    2.2 Defining e-Learning

    2.3 The Drive for e-Learning in Higher Education

    2.4 Barriers to e-Learning and the Need to Prepare Academic Staff

    2.5 Guidelines and Models on e-Learning Support Infrastructures

    2.6 Emerging Issues and the Need for Empirical Research

If your topic was, say, 'accessibility and website design', then you may wish to have a sub-section on what you mean by 'accessibility'. Similarly, if your research is focused on 'modernism and its impact on contemporary art' then a good starting point could be a sub-section on defining what you mean by 'modernism' (and/or 'contemporary art').

  Now you have a very structured, focused and logical approach to your Literature Review, one that ought to prevent Literature Review 'drift'. Of course, as you complete your individual sub-sections it is likely that you will also create sub-sections within sub-sections. For instance in sub-section 2.3 above – The Drive for e-Learning in Higher Education – an appropriate collection of further section headings could be:

    2.3 The Drive for e-Learning in Higher Education

        2.3.1 An Early Impetus: The Dearing Report

        2.3.2 Strategic Forces Driving e-Learning

        2.3.3 Benefits of e-Learning

One thing to bear in mind when you create such sub-divisions – if you are not writing very much within each sub-section, then your Literature Review will appear superficial and so lacking depth. One student (who rarely turned up for pre-arranged meetings) had about 20 sub-section headings in a draft Literature Review submission, with each of the 20 sub-sections containing only two or three sentences. In such a scenario you need to remove a number of your headings and merge others. Here is an example of one student's attempt at a sub-section, in entirety, within her Literature Review:

2.2 Research Aim

The aim of this research is to investigate current approaches to the development of business information systems (IS) within the public sector in terms of their cost-effectiveness.

As you can see, she has very little to say. Remember, in your Literature Review you are trying to show your supervisor that you are well read and can evaluate critically the work of others, and you can only do that if you have given yourself enough space under each sub-section to engage in meaningful discussion. Of course, deficient structuring is not confined to the Literature Review. Another student, in her chapter on research methods, had the following structure (an extract is shown for illustration purposes, but most of her chapter was peppered similarly with headings under which appeared only one or two sentences):

3.2 Research Philosophy

3.2.1 Phenomenology
[Two sentences on phenomenology]

3.2.2 Positivism
[One sentence on positivism]

3.2.3 Research Philosophy
[Two sentences on research philosophy]. Etc.

How should you conclude your Literature Review? If you followed the advice on how to create sub-section headings, then it should be an easy matter to conclude your Literature Review. In your Literature Review conclusion you are doing two things: highlighting the issues that have emerged from your reading; and so providing a justification for any empirical work that you want to do. Appendix D contains a sample conclusion for a Literature Review, based on the e-Learning example used throughout this book.

What is good about this sample conclusion that you might wish to replicate when concluding your own Literature Review? First of all, it summarizes the findings from the Literature Review ('The study of relevant e-Learning literature . . .'). Your Literature Review might be quite large and complex, so by providing a précis you will help the reader to understand your work. A summary is also a useful aide-mémoire for you in that it ought to help you to stay focused and so avoid the potential for 'drift'. When you summarize your Literature Review findings, make sure that you emphasize what you consider to be the salient points ('The review of literature stressed the need . . .'). You do not need to go over the arguments again because that takes up valuable words: just point out what you found out in the literature vis-à-vis your research objectives. If your research involves the collection and analysis of empirical data, then you ought to explain, in your Literature Review conclusion, the necessity for such empirical research, e.g. perhaps the literature that you looked at expressed concern about the lack of empirical research in your field of study or perhaps current studies are incomplete in some way ('A crucial issue for the development of e-Learning . . .'). Finally, make some sort of reference to your next chapter – Research Methods – so as to provide a link for the reader ('The next stage of this research will detail the Research Methods to be used . . .'). By providing a summary, highlight of main points, need for empirical research (if you are implementing empirical research) and a link to the next chapter, the conclusion to your Literature Review ought to add to the quality of your dissertation. Depending on the word-length of your dissertation, your summary may be shorter, or longer, in length than the sample summary given in Appendix D.

Summary of key points

- Write a brief introduction to your Literature Review, reminding the reader of your research objectives, the topics that you will cover in your Literature Review and how they relate to your research objectives.
- The art of referencing sources is an important part of writing an accomplished Literature Review. The Harvard system of referencing – the author/date system – is popular with staff and students alike.
- The use of Latin terms can add an intellectual flavour to your dissertation, provided they are applied correctly. In the context of a Literature Review, useful Latin terms include: *et al.*, *ibid.*, *op. cit.*, *viz.*, *inter alia*, and [*sic*].
- Use quotations to support your writing and not as a substitute for your own words. Remember to introduce quotations properly and, when you consider it appropriate, offer comment on them.
- Describing the work of others is a basic undergraduate skill; Master's students are expected to go beyond mere description and engage in critical evaluation. Critical evaluation = description (of something) + your views (on that 'something') + reasons for holding your views.
- Appendix I contains a rich variety of verbs ('accepts', 'captures', 'expresses', 'speculates', etc.) to help you describe the work of other authors.
- Learning involves the development of cognitive skills (mental skills), affective skills (feelings, emotions) and psychomotor skills (physical skills).
- To achieve good marks you need to exhibit higher-level cognitive skills in your writing: *analysis*, *synthesis* and *evaluation* (in Bloom's taxonomy of learning) or *analysing*, *evaluating*, *creating* (in Anderson and Krathwohl's updated model).
- To avoid drifting away from your research focus, create sub-headings in your Literature Review that link explicitly to your research objectives.
- Conclude your Literature Review with a summary of your main findings (related to your research objectives) and have a link to your Research Methods chapter.

5

Research methods

What's it all about? • Research strategy • Data collection • Framework for data analysis • Limitations and potential problems

What's it all about?

What is the point of a chapter on research methods? If you intend collecting your own data, i.e. implementing your own empirical research, then you need to tell the reader how you propose to go about this process. Your results will not be trusted if you fail to inform the reader how you did your research. Tales abound of students who fail because they neither provide information on their research subjects – *who, when, where, why* – nor include, for example, their questionnaires (leaving their tutors to guess the questions they allegedly asked and to try and work out why the questions were being asked). Research studies that lack crucial information on the research methods used, and why the research was implemented, are worse than useless and cannot be trusted. The trick, therefore, is to give the reader clear and unambiguous information on these issues, so much so that, if the reader wishes, they could easily replicate your studies. Consequently, the information that you will give to the reader (your tutor/marker) on your research methods will be highly structured and detailed, reflecting the meticulous nature of research work (Gill and Johnson 1997).

You will still need a chapter on research methods even if you have no plans to gather your own raw data but depend purely on secondary data, e.g. a Literature Review, for your findings. In which case, you will clarify where you will get your literature (books, journal articles, government reports, Internet), emphasizing literature that will be of particular relevance to your research objectives and taking care to justify your choice of secondary sources. However, the typical scenario in a Master's dissertation is for students to complete a Literature Review *and* to collect and analyse their own data. This chapter will focus on the latter scenario, where you are expected, in addition to producing a Literature Review, to collect and analyse your own empirical data. Accordingly, the research methods chapter that you write relates to how you will collect and analyse your empirical data.

Too many students seem to be struck by *vagueitis* – a reluctance to reveal what they are doing in their own research – with the result that their chapter on research methods is often the worse aspect of their research project. In fact, it is the research methods chapter, more than any other chapter, that differentiates the top student from the average/poor student: the top student knows his stuff and is not afraid to provide crystal clear information on the research he is undertaking, including the rationale for his chosen approach; whereas the average/poor student makes it only too obvious that he does not understand this chapter and merely peppers his efforts with unexplained terminology and confusing, and often contradictory, statements.

Surveys often appear in the popular press and monthly magazines: 'A survey shows that 1 million people take drugs!'; '50% of people use email every day'; etc. Unfortunately, these surveys are rarely implemented by professional researchers and tend to be paid for by commercial interest groups, thereby tainting the trustworthiness of the results. Details about the research methods adopted – other than '1,000 sampled' – are usually minimal, with little information on how people were selected, the context in which the questions were asked, or the actual questionnaire used, etc. As such, these surveys often lack academic credibility. So do not be influenced by 'research' that is carried out by special interest groups on behalf of the popular press or magazines. Good, solid research requires a much more methodical and transparent approach, one that meets the high standards set by the academic community. The quality press, unlike the popular press, are more likely to adhere to such standards when reporting on surveys (although that is not always the case!) by making use of professional research bodies, such as Populus, and adopting a transparent approach as shown in the excerpt appended to an article by Riddell and Webster (2006: 2) with the title 'Support for Labour [a political party in the UK] at lowest level since 1992':

> Populus interviewed a random sample of 1,509 adults over 18 by telephone between May 5 and May 7. Interviews were conducted across the country and the results have been weighted to be representative of all adults. Populus is a member of the British Polling Council and abides by its rules.
>
> For details go to www.populuslimited.com.

There are a number of strands to a research methods chapter, typically including the following sub-sections:

- Introduction
- Research strategy
- Data collection
- Framework for data analysis
- Limitations and potential problems.

Table 5.1 highlights the sort of questions that your dissertation marker will be thinking about as he goes through your research methods.

Table 5.1 Marker's view of your chapter on research methods

Research methods	Questions to be addressed
Introduction	*What* specific *research objective* does your empirical research relate to? *Why* are you collecting your own data? Is there any indication on how you are going to *structure* your chapter?
Research strategy	*What* is your overall research strategy? (Case study, survey, experimental, historical, action research, grounded theory, ethnographic research, or what?) *Why* have you chosen that research strategy? *How* do you intend sampling your target population? *Why* have you chosen that sampling approach?
Data collection	*How* do you propose to collect your data? (Questionnaires, interviews, observation, organizational reports, etc.?) *Why* have you chosen to collect your data that way?
Framework for data analysis	Once you have collected your data, what are you going to do with it? In other words, *how* are you going to analyse your findings?
Limitations and potential problems	Do you see any *limitations or problems* with your practical research? (E.g. limitations in your chosen strategy or problems getting access to your research subjects?) Have you faced the twin issues of *validity* and *reliability*? (I.e. are the research choices you made *appropriate* and can your work be *trusted*?)

As you can see, there are a lot of *what* and *why* questions – and that is the key to completing a strong research methods chapter. State with absolute clarity *what* approaches you are adopting – for your overall research strategy, specific data collection techniques, means of analysing your data – and *why* you are doing things that way. It is the combination of *what* and *why* that will gain you good marks: ignoring one will cost you dear! Ignoring both will cost you your dissertation!!

Hopefully you now have the hang of writing an Introduction to a chapter, so introducing your research methods chapter should be quite straightforward.

First of all, remind your tutor of your specific research objectives. Next, refer to the research objective(s) that relate to your research methods chapter: 'A valuable aspect of this research relates to Objective 3: the opportunity to study e-Learning strategy and implementation in practice . . .'. Then, remind the reader of the need for your own research work, with reference back to your Literature Review: 'Chapter 2 – Issues and Review of Related Literature – identified a gap in existing research in that there was ample evidence on the need for . . .'. Include the potential benefits of your intended research: 'Objective 3 takes this research one step further . . . By comparing theory with practice the research will gain a fuller . . .'. Finally, outline the topics that you will cover in your research methods chapter: 'This section – Research Methods – will provide the details of the research strategy adopted to address the research issues identified above, together with the means of collecting data for analysis, including . . .'. Appendix E – Sample Research Methods – begins with a sample introduction to a research methods chapter, but your chapter may be shorter, or longer, depending on how many words that you have to play with and what you want to say.

Let us now look at the other parts that usually go to make up the research methods chapter, starting with your research strategy.

Research strategy

Introduction

Most students tend to score less than average marks for this section, principally because they either do not understand what is meant by a research strategy or they fail to explain why they are using a particular research strategy, or because they select a strategy that is wholly inappropriate for their research.

A common mistake by students

A common mistake by students is to spend the bulk of their time discussing research strategies in general, with scant attention given to the one that they have chosen and, crucially, why.

What is a research strategy? Quite simply, it is where you describe *how* you intend implementing your own research study, i.e. the strategy that you intend adopting to complete your empirical study. For instance, suppose that you were alarmed at the number of MSc. students who gained poor marks for their dissertation submissions and you wanted to find out why this was so. To begin with, you could carry out a Literature Review to find out what other researchers had to say about the subject. Suppose further that the findings from your Literature Review revealed that there was a need for empirical data, rather than anecdotal evidence; or that there were a number of empirical studies but that they concentrated on staff views rather than the views of students, and it is the latter group that you want to question. You decide to do your own practical research work to help address this deficiency. To do this, however, you need to work out your overall approach to implementing your research, i.e. your research strategy.

Rather than invent your own research strategy, there are numerous ones from which you can choose, including case studies, surveys, ethnography, and action research, to name but a few. It makes sense to use a tried and tested research strategy because it ought to have academic credibility, although that does not stop academics themselves arguing the merits of one approach over another. What you have to do is to select the approach that best suits *your* research. Related to the student dissertation example above, you could select one MSc. programme in one university – i.e. implement a case study – and interview a sample of students who had failed their dissertation to ascertain their views on why they think they failed.

For the moment, it is time to digress and outline some of the research strategies that are available to researchers, and to you, when carrying out empirical research. A *case study* is a study of one example of a particular type (e.g. Oxford University is one example of a particular type of university, i.e. ancient universities; similarly, Ryanair is one example of one airline, a budget airline). Cohen and Manion (1995: 106) describe a case study thus:

> The case study researcher typically observes the characteristics of an individual unit – a child, a class, a school or a community. The purpose of such observation is to probe deeply and to analyse intensely the multifarious phenomena that constitute the life cycle of the unit.

Case studies are very popular with students, probably because they find it easier to focus their research on one organization, or part of an organization. When applying a case study approach, students incline towards using interviews as their main, or sole, means of data collection, although more enterprising students use a mixture of data collection techniques, such as questionnaires, individual interviews and group interviews, aiming not only for a rich output, but higher marks.

A *survey* is a representative selection from the population of a particular type, for instance, a survey of 30 universities from the population of universities in the UK or a survey of 200 retail companies in Europe. Surveys can be time-consuming and so rather than interview the sampled population, students often favour questionnaires. For a sound grounding on survey research methods, read Fowler, F. (2001). *Survey Research Methods*, Thousand Oaks, CA: Sage.

Ethnography has its roots in anthropology, the study of people in their natural environment, in effect, the study of *cultures*. For example, the study of Amazon tribes would qualify as ethnographic research. The ethnographic researcher has not only to record patiently what he observes but he is also expected to provide some sort of interpretation of what he sees. His is a difficult job, not just in terms of the patience that is required, but also with respect to the difficult conditions that these researchers often have to work under. The traditional ethnographic researcher has to be admired. These days, however, ethnography has taken a wider meaning, referring to the study of any culture, old or modern. A modern example of ethnography would be the study of gang culture. Ethnographic research is not something that the novice student ought to attempt without clear guidance from an experienced tutor. If you are interested in pursuing ethnographic research, then you may find the following book of value: Davies, C. A. (1999). *Reflexive Ethnography: A Guide to Researching Selves and Others*, London: Routledge.

Experimental research tends to be the domain of the scientist, where he attempts to test an hypothesis (i.e. a theory) through some type of experiment. He will first try to define the problem that he is looking at; next, he will formulate his hypothesis; and finally, he will implement his experiment to test whether or not his hypothesis was correct. The experimental researcher is normally well versed in using statistical tools and techniques.

Historical research, as the name suggests, is research that focuses primarily on events that occurred in the distant past (e.g. the conditions under which soldiers lived during the First World War), but it can also deal with events in the recent past (e.g. the growth of the Internet). Historical research is a bit like ethnographic research in the sense that the researcher requires skills in observation and interpretation, except in the case of historical research the subjects under research tend to appear in documents, videos, etc., rather than in real life. You could say that historical research is akin to a detective mystery, but where all the suspects are (normally) dead! When the historical researcher investigates events in the recent past, the issue arises of whether he is engaging in historical research or contemporary research.

Action research is where the researcher starts with a particular problem that he wants to solve, or understand better, usually within the environment where he is working (Cunningham 1995). A teacher could carry out action research to improve his teaching. Perhaps his pupils are having difficulty understanding his subject. He would define his problem, plan a means of solving the problem (e.g. more interesting, topical discussions, use of groupwork, etc.), implement his proposed solution, and evaluate the results. The key to understanding action research is to realize from the outset that the researcher is *involved* in the research not just as a (research) observer but as a participant, i.e. he is part of his own research and his participation can influence his findings. Writing about your own participation in a research project can be problematic: there is the question of objectivity and the temptation to show yourself in a good light in your findings. To gain credibility in the research community, action research, although problem-based, nevertheless follows accepted research procedures: elucidation of research objectives, review of relevant literature, applied research, discussion of results, conclusion. Some students attempt what they think is action research, but omit the research aspect, and are left with what is in effect a work-based project rather than a well-rounded piece of credible research. For further assistance in understanding action research, read Reason, P. and Bradbury, H. (2000). *Handbook of Action Research: Participative Inquiry and Practice*, Thousand Oaks, CA: Sage.

Grounded theory (Glaser and Strauss 1967) is quite a difficult theory to apply in practice, and only a very confident student ought to attempt grounded theory. It is demanding in the sense that it does not follow the normal procedures for implementing a research project: that is, start with a clearly defined research focus, find out through a Literature Review what others have to say about your research problem, implement your own practical research, discuss the findings, come to a conclusion, etc. Instead, grounded theory is a bit higgledy-piggledy, in that you do not start with a clearly defined set of research objectives but follow where your research takes you, building up theory as you go along. You start with a rough idea of the area that you are interested in researching; next, you carry out some empirical research; then you refer to literature that you think is relevant to the work that you carried out; you then, depending what you have read, implement further practical work; and so on, jumping back and forth between your empirical work and your review of relevant literature, until you develop a sustainable theory grounded in your practical research, but influenced by reference to appropriate literature. In other words, the relationship between the Literature Review and your practical research is not sequential but symbiotic, where one feeds into the other. It is very exploratory in nature, and so means that you need to be aware of when to call a halt to your research, otherwise it will be never-ending. It is very much like the relationship between an artist and his painting: what the artist thinks, will influence what he paints; what he paints, will influence what he thinks; but at some point he needs to put down his brush or he could ruin what was a work of art. For more information on Grounded Theory, read:

- Dey, I. (1999). *Grounding Grounded Theory: Guidelines for Qualitative Inquiry*, San Diego: Academic Press.
- Glaser, B. and Strauss, A. (1967). *The Discovery of Grounded Theory*, Chicago: Aldine.

Incidentally, some staff, and so students, refer to the aforementioned research strategies – case study, survey, etc. – as examples of a research *method* ('The research method that I will be adopting is a case study . . .'), equating a research strategy with a research method. This is fine, but it can be confusing. Your overall research strategy is only one of the *methods* that you will be using to carry out your practical research: the other methods, which you also have to discuss in your dissertation, include your *method* of data collection and also the *method* by which you expect to analyse your collected data. That is why this chapter in your dissertation is usually called the Research Methods chapter, to reflect the fact that you will be writing about a number of methods related to implementing your empirical research (research strategy, data collection techniques, framework for data analysis, etc.). Otherwise, logically, if you equate a research method only to a research strategy, and you call your chapter 'Research Methods', then all you ought to be writing about is your case study, or survey, or whatever, which is clearly wrong because you also need to discuss how you intend to collect and analyse your data. So, instead of writing 'The research *method* that will be adopted is a case study . . .', you ought to be writing either 'The research *strategy* that will be adopted is a case study . . .' or 'One research method that will be adopted, related to research strategy, is a case study . . .', but not '*The* research method that . . .'.

Quantitative vs qualitative research

Some researchers mistakenly group research strategies under two opposing headings: quantitative vs qualitative. Students often replicate this mistake. At a simple level, the former type – *quantitative* – refers to research that is concerned with quantities and measurements, such as the number of people who smoke in a given period on 5th Avenue in New York, or the success rate of dissertation students in the London School of Economics, or the proportion of a population that use a particular type of transport to get to work in Bombay. The number crunching can be more complicated than just gaining simple quantitative information: it can involve calculating, for pension and personal insurance purposes, the probability of dying before retirement for those in a given profession. Hence much of the scientific research that occurs, because it deals with quantifiable data, tends to be grouped under the heading quantitative research. *Qualitative* research, on the other hand, is linked to in-depth exploratory studies (exploring, for example, *why* students pick a particular module to study), where the opportunity for 'quality' responses exist. Denzin and Lincoln (1994: 2) hold that qualitative research involves studying 'things in their natural settings, attempting to make sense of, or interpret, phenomena in terms of the meanings people bring to them'.

In general, quantitative research answers the *how* questions, whereas the *why* questions are left to qualitative research. Of course, the reality is that it is rare that professional researchers, and dissertation students for that matter, stick to only collecting and analysing either quantitative or qualitative data. They usually mix and match (Myers 1997). A student could be interested in quantitative issues such as how many postgraduate students picked a particular module for the taught part of their course, the number that passed that module, as well as qualitative matters such as why students selected the module in the first place and what they liked/disliked about the module. This mix of quantitative/qualitative questions is common in everyday life: someone might ask you if you attended so-and-so's party at the weekend (begging a quantitative y/n response) but also enquire what you thought of the party (encouraging a qualitative answer).

A common mistake by students

A common mistake by students is to equate *research strategies* with quantitative or qualitative research. Too many students think that it is the research strategy that determines whether their research is quantitative, or qualitative, in nature. For instance, it is common for students to relate surveys to quantitative research and case studies to qualitative research. Although it is generally true that a case study, for example, *suggests* a qualitative study and that a survey, for example, *suggests* a quantitative piece of research, it is not necessarily the case. It is not the research strategy – case study, survey, experimental, action research, etc. – that determines whether or not your empirical study is quantitative or qualitative in nature: that is dependent on a combination of your research strategy, your individual research objectives and your data collection technique(s).

Suppose that you decide to do a case study of one university in Paris (e.g. the Sorbonne). A case study is normally associated with an in-depth exploratory study, so a case study of one university in Paris must be a qualitative study, yes? Well, not necessarily. If your case study was intended to determine issues surrounding pass rates, such as the number of students passing each module, the progression rates for different courses and years, including direct entrants, and that you want to collect your data through the use of closed questionnaires, then the nature of this research would be quantitative in nature because the research objectives relate mainly to *how* questions (*how* many students passed each module, etc.) and because questionnaires limit the opportunity for in-depth exploratory responses, tending to yield answers that are easily quantifiable (six people said this, four said that, etc.). On the other hand, you could implement a survey of universities in France, but instead of focusing on how many students failed modules, etc., you could focus on *why* students are failing, and collect your data through interviews. The 'why' nature of the research and the use of interviews – where the opportunity to explore matters in depth exists – provide evidence that the research would now be primarily qualitative in nature. For more information on qualitative research, read:

- Denzin, N. K. and Lincoln, Y. S. (2000). *Handbook of Qualitative Research*, 2nd edn, Thousand Oaks, CA: Sage.
- Silverman, D. (1997). *Interpreting Qualitative Data: Methods for Analysing Talk, Text and Interaction*, London: Sage.
- Silverman, D. (2000). *Doing Qualitative Research: A Practical Handbook*, London: Sage.

So do not write in your dissertation that you are doing quantitative, or qualitative, research because of the research strategy that you have chosen. A research strategy cannot be, in itself, qualitative or quantitative – it is the combination of your research strategy, your research objectives and your data collection techniques that help determine the quantitative or qualitative nature of your research. When you are explaining why you have picked a quantitative (or qualitative) approach do so by reference to not only your research strategy, but also to your research objectives and your means of data collection. Do not exclude the possibility that your research is both quantitative and qualitative in nature. If so, indicate which parts are mainly quantitative and which parts relate to the qualitative aspects.

Sampling techniques

Regardless of whether your research is quantitative or qualitative in nature, it is highly unlikely that you will be in a position to collect data from your whole target population (e.g. all customers who frequent Marks & Spencer), in which case you will need to collect data from a sample of your population (e.g. a sample of those who frequent Marks & Spencer). There are a number of sampling techniques that you can use, including: random sampling, simple random sampling, stratified sampling, cluster sampling, systematic sampling, quota sampling, and convenience sampling.

Sampling techniques

- *Random sampling* is where you select, entirely at random, a sample of a population. For example, if you want to know how people intend to vote in a local election, in a particular town, rather than ask everyone in that town (because it may be too costly and perhaps impossible to accomplish in a set period), you might decide to stop a selection of people at random in the street and ask them. Be aware, though, that samples are often open to the accusation of bias – the street you stood in, the time of day you carried out your survey, the number of people you asked, etc., will never please everyone! Whenever politicians do not like the results of a survey, they are inclined to criticize the sampling methods employed. Implementing a random sample helps you reduce bias.

- *Simple random sampling* is a variation of random sampling. In random sampling it does not need to be the case that each member of your population has the same chance of being selected (e.g. if you pick a Saturday afternoon to sample your population, then football fans, many of whom may be watching their favourite football team at the time of your sampling activity, have less of a chance of being sampled), whereas with simple random sampling every member ought to have an equal chance of being selected. Of course, if you have a large population where it is impossible to identify every member (so as to allow everyone an equal chance of being selected), then your sample may be subject to significant bias.

- *Stratified sampling* is where you break down your target population into identifiable groups (strata) and then take samples from each of your groups. For example, students attending a lecture could be classified under the strata 'male' and 'female' or 'school leaver' and 'mature entrant', and samples taken from each stratum.
- *Cluster sampling* is where you break down your target population into clusters (or groups or strata) but, unlike stratified sampling (where you immediately select samples from each of your groups), you then randomly select a sample of your clusters. From within each of your chosen clusters, you will then select random samples. It is actually quite simple to understand, as the following example shows. Suppose that you want to investigate the health of chickens in Scotland. It would be too time-consuming and expensive to check on the health of every chicken, so you decide to use the different regions of Scotland as your clusters (Strathclyde, Highland, Grampian, South Lanarkshire, etc.) and you then randomly select a subset of these regions, thus reducing the clusters that you need to target. From these clusters you randomly select the chicken plots that you will visit for inspection. You have to be careful that your clusters are of comparable size, so it may be appropriate to merge some of your clusters at the very start of your research before you randomly select the clusters that you will then explore in detail.
- *Systematic sampling* occurs when you take a sample of your target population at equal or regular intervals. For example, you select every fifth name on a list or every tenth customer record from a customer computer database.
- *Quota sampling* does not involve random sampling and is therefore vulnerable to the criticism that there is no way of telling if the results are representative of a larger population. Sampling that does not involve random sampling is sometimes referred to as non-probability sampling. In quota sampling, you decide beforehand the type and number of members (i.e. your selection quota) that you intend sampling. When you are stopped in the street and asked about your choice of breakfast cereal or how you will vote in the next election, then it is likely that you are the victim of quota sampling (you have been picked because you are one of the '5 old females' or '10 young males' or '15 professionals' that are on their list for selection).
- *Convenience sampling* is another non-probability approach to sampling, i.e. it is non-random. It is implemented because, as the name suggests, it is convenient to the researcher. You might decide to interview your fellow students for your dissertation because it is convenient for you to do so; similarly, you might interview staff in an organization where you have worked and have ready access. That is not to say that your research findings will not prove valuable, although they must be treated with caution (if your

sample has not been selected randomly then it is difficult to claim that it is representative). Convenience sampling tends to be used as a form of exploratory research, giving ideas and insight that may lead to other, more detailed and representative research. If you are interested in exploratory research, and not claiming that your findings will be representative of a larger population, then convenience research is perfectly acceptable.

'DEWEY DEFEATS TRUMAN' announced the *Chicago Daily Tribune* in 1948. Quota sampling was used by Gallup to predict the outcome of the Presidential election in the 1948 USA elections. Using quota sampling – which we know is unlikely to produce results that are representative – Gallup predicted that Truman would lose the election to Dewey. The next day the big newspapers led with the headline story that Dewey had won the election. In fact, as history shows, the opposite happened and it was Truman who had won the election. Gallup quickly dropped the use of quota sampling to predict election results and ever since that embarrassing episode has used clustered sampling of interviews nationwide. After his victory Truman was asked to comment on the earlier headlines – 'DEWEY DEFEATS TRUMAN' – to which he replied, 'This is for the books'. He was right, because it has appeared in this book!

Another example of a disputed survey occurred when *The Herald* newspaper (2007: 1) led with the headline 'Labour leads in new poll but 50% still to decide'. The headline refers to the Labour Party in Scotland apparently in poll position to win the up-and-coming elections for control of the Scottish Parliament at the expense of the Scottish National Party (SNP). This survey contradicted all previous surveys of voter intentions, which hitherto had shown the SNP with a sizeable lead. *The Herald* (2007: 6) provided details of the sampling methods adopted:

It surveyed a random sample of 1000 adults across Scotland by telephone between March 22 and March 27. The survey was quota controlled by geography, age, gender, and socio-economic grade, and results then re-weighted to ensure balanced representation was obtained. The margin for error is plus or minus 3%.

Yet the survey could be criticized on a number of fronts. First, 50% of respondents identified themselves as undecided on how they would vote in the forthcoming election, therefore that fact alone would seriously damage the credibility of the survey (or rather any claim to 'balanced representation' based on the survey). Macleod (2007: 6), reporting for *The Times* newspaper, comments that 'the poll's validity was damaged by the fact that as many as 50 per cent of the respondents were "undecided" and that it was conducted by an organisation with no discernible track record on political polling'.

Also, quota sampling appears to have been used to collect voter intentions ('*The Survey was quality controlled . . .*'). In quota sampling, the selection process is dependent on human judgement and so subject to bias. The attractiveness of quota sampling to organisations lies in the relatively inexpensive costs and case of implementation, but such practical advantages may not be enough to compensate for the methodological weakness inherent in quota sampling: lack of confidence in the results.

Sample size is an issue in quantitative research, particularly when you want to claim that your findings are representative of a larger population. Generally speaking, the larger your sample size, then the more representative your results. Students who interview two people, asking each only three questions, are unlikely to convince their tutor that the results are representative of a larger population. The Internet site http://www.surveysystem.com has produced a calculator to help you determine your sample size (Figure 5.1) with different *degrees of confidence*.

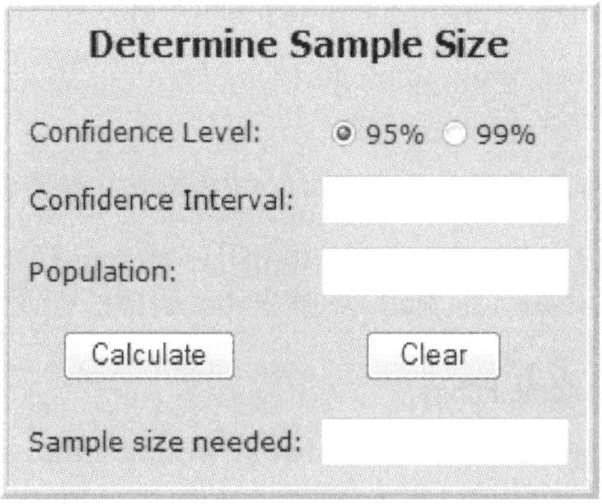

Figure 5.1 Calculating your sample size

To use the calculator, you need to understand the terms *confidence level* and *confidence interval*. To quote the site (http://www.surveysystem.com/sscalc.htm#terminology):

> The confidence interval is the plus-or-minus figure usually reported in newspaper or television opinion poll results. For example, if you use a confidence interval of 4, and 47% of your sample picks an answer you can be 'sure' that if you had asked the question of the entire population [then] between 43% (47–4) and 51% (47+4) would have picked that answer.

> The confidence level tells you how sure you can be [about your results]. It

is expressed as a percentage and represents how often the true percentage of the population who would pick an answer lies within the confidence interval. The 95% confidence level means that you can be 95% sure; the 99% confidence level means you can be 99% certain.

If you are not comfortable using statistical techniques, then stick to qualitative research, where you typically use case studies, open questionnaires and/or semi-structured interviews. You will still need to justify your sample selection, though. For further reading on quantitative research, refer to:

- Buglear, J. (2001). *Stats Means Business*, Oxford: Butterworth Heinemann.
- Buglear, J. (2004). *Quantitative Methods for Business: The A to Z of QM*, Oxford: Elsevier.
- Field, A. (2000). *Discovering Statistics Using SPSS for Windows: Advanced Techniques for Beginners*, London: Sage.
- Henry, G. (1990). *Practical Sampling*, Newbury Park, CA: Sage.
- Sapsford, R. and Judd, V. (1996). *Data Collection and Analysis*, London: Sage.
- Sapsford, R. (1999). *Survey Research*, London: Sage.

For a useful overview of research approaches, both qualitative and quantitative, refer to:

- Dawson, C. (2006). *A Practical Guide to Research Methods*, Oxford: How to Books Ltd.
- Saunders, M., Lewis, P. and Thornhill, A. (2007). *Research Methods for Business Students*, 4th edn, Harlow: FT Prentice Hall.

Positivism and phenomenology

Researchers can sometimes get carried away with terminology and instead of using the terms *quantitative* and *qualitative* to describe the nature of their research, they substitute the term *positivism* for quantitative research and the term(s) *interpretavism/phenomenology* for qualitative research. Tutors teaching research methods to students sometimes reiterate this fusion of terminology. Unfortunately, there are occasions when students, without grasping the meaning of these new terms, mimic their tutors with disastrous consequences. They see their tutors using such terminology, and so they themselves feel obliged to incorporate the same terminology into their dissertations. If you do not understand what these terms mean then why use them? You are only highlighting your ignorance, and will lose marks as a result. It is depressing for a tutor to see students using terms which they clearly do not understand, yet insist on using because they feel that is what their tutors want to see. No! If you are not sure about research terminology, ask your tutor. That is what he gets paid for – to help you. It is better to show your ignorance during the process of writing your dissertation than at the end, after you have submitted: in the former you only lose virtual marks, whereas in the latter you lose real marks.

Nevertheless, some explanation will be provided here of the terms *positivism* and *interpretavism/phenomenology*, just in case you feel the need to use them in your dissertation. A researcher with a *positivist* view of the world is someone who holds that reality is objective and independent of the observer and so can be measured and predicted (Orlikowski and Baroudi 1991; Remenyi *et al.* 1998). Measuring the temperature at which different types of metals melt could fall into the category of positivist research (since the melting metal is not influenced by human observation). What the positivist researcher is really saying is that his type of research – positivist research – is not influenced by the unpredictable behaviour of human beings and that, as a result, his findings are more reliable (e.g. such-and-such a metal melts at such-and-such a temperature, full stop). Positivist research is common in the world of science (mathematics, physics, chemistry, etc.) and less prevalent in the arts-based research world (e.g. sociology, history, history of art, etc.), where the latter normally involves, and is influenced by, human participation and observation. The emphasis on quantifiable data is the reason that positivist research is equated with quantitative research, but the two concepts, although similar, are not exactly the same (e.g. providing students with questionnaires to complete, with a view to obtaining quantifiable data, is an example of quantitative research, but is not an example of *positivist* research, because the questionnaire responses are dependent on human participation, and therefore human influence).

Interpretative researchers, on the other hand, hold to a very different view of the world than positivist researchers. Interpretative researchers believe that there are many, equally valid, interpretations of reality, and that, further, these interpretations are dependent on when they are made and the context in which they are made, i.e. they are *time* and *context* dependent. A student who accepts the 'ontological assumption associated with interpretative/constructivism that multiple realities exist that are time and context dependent . . . will choose to carry out [their] study using qualitative methods so that they can gain an understanding of the constructs held by people in that context' (Mertens 1998: 161). If your research concentrated on, say, interviewing your fellow students on their views of their dissertation tutors, then you would be engaging in interpretative research: students would present a variety of views, some praising their supervisors, others offering criticism, with a range of views expressed on why students like/dislike their supervisor (a student who previously applauded his supervisor might change his mind if he failed his dissertation and vice versa for a student who disliked her supervisor but changed her mind when she gained a high mark!). One colleague carried out research recently where he interviewed students as they progressed from first year to third year, capturing their views on how they were coping with group-based coursework. He was adopting an interpretative philosophy to his research study in that he was interested in his students' interpretations of their group-work experiences, which he also recognized might alter as they advanced through their studies (i.e. time and context dependent). For interpretative researchers, human participation and observation, and the context and time these occur, are fundamental to their research. The emphasis on human interpretations of events leads interpretative research to be identified, correctly, with qualitative research.

Phenomenological research is just a fancy word for interpretative research, i.e. the focus on individual perceptions of events. Phenomenology has strong philosophical foundations, where the phenomenological philosopher, just like his later phenomenological research cousin, is interested in how the world appears to others, i.e. in subjective experiences. Some researchers divide phenomenological research into two categories: phenomenological research that deals with *describing* events and phenomenological research that attempts to *explain* as well as *describe* events. Mostly it is the latter interpretation – description and explanation – that is accepted as phenomenological research: what is the value of just describing what has happened when you could go further and try and explain why something happened? Your interpretation of your qualitative data might be wrong, but at least it will have value in trying to engender further debate, or lead to further lines of enquiry.

One could argue that the positivist researcher's view of his research – that it is untainted by human influence and so more reliable – is erroneous and just wishful thinking. In the first place, positivist researchers are often wrong. Scientists once thought that the world was flat. That the Sun rotated around the Earth. Airplanes continue to crash. Missiles go astray. Economic forecasting, based on quantitative modelling, is often wrong; and so on. There is also the argument that even in the world of positivist research, human influence cannot be avoided. Once measurements have been taken, and results produced, the results themselves require human interpretation. Scientists often disagree about how to interpret the same research data (e.g. global warming); and they have been known to interpret research data that best suits their own career interests, or the interests of their political or financial masters. For instance Dinwoodie (2007: 6) reports that the Director of the Information Services Division (ISD), a body that produces statistical data on health issues in Scotland, laments that:

> *The independent, neutral and honest interpretation of statistics is often lost in the middle between opposing interpretation poles . . . On the one hand the media and political opposition concentrate on negative themes and interpretation. The Scottish Executive* [the ruling political body] *and ministers naturally press for any positives to be highlighted . . . We find it difficult to steer a neutral course when publishing statistics, especially so because most of the statistical collections . . . have the Executive* [the ruling political body] *as the main sponsor.*

That is not to say that interpretative research is any more reliable, or somehow 'better' than positivist research. Both types are useful, and have their place; and both types are fallible, because humans are fallible.

Justifying your research strategy

After identifying the research strategy that best meets your own research objectives, you now have to do two things: first, explain that research strategy, to show your tutor that you understand your chosen research strategy and, second, justify why that approach best meets your research needs.

A common mistake by students

A common mistake by students is to select a research strategy (survey, case study, historical research, etc.) and then to try and see how it fits in with their research objectives. That is a back-to-front way of doing things. What you ought to do is consider your main research questions/objectives and reflect on which research strategy best meets your needs. In short, a *survey* is used when you are seeking representative views; *experimental* strategy is required when you are interested in causal relationships; *historical* research for events that occurred in the past; a *case study* when you seek an in-depth, investigative study; and so on.

Of course, there are practical considerations that might influence your choice of research strategy, given the reality that students tend not to have much time to implement their empirical research (your dissertation usually has to be completed in a short time-frame). So, although you might decide that a survey of 50 employers, using interviews, might provide the basis for an excellent empirical study, you have to take on board practical issues: do you have the time for such a survey (using interviews)? Will you get access to all your research subjects? Do you have the time to analyse all your collected data? In brief, are you being unrealistic and over-ambitious? Practical considerations can form part of the justification for your chosen research strategy and data collection techniques.

Let us look at the e-Learning sample research objectives identified earlier in this book as an example of how to select and justify a particular research strategy:

---

1   *Identify* the forces driving e-Learning and the barriers to the successful delivery of e-Learning programmes.
2   *Evaluate critically* models and frameworks relevant to supporting academic staff in coping with e-Learning.
3   *Explore* staff stakeholder views and practices related to e-Learning preparation, including drivers and barriers to e-Learning.
4   *Formulate* recommendations on staff preparation issues.

Objectives 1 and 2 above could initially be covered in the Literature Review. Objective 3 ('Explore staff stakeholder views and practices . . .') is a practical objective, requiring the implementation of empirical research. Which research strategy should we adopt to meet this objective and how can we justify our selection? Central to this objective is the keyword 'explore', which implies an in-depth, exploratory study of staff stakeholder views and practices. Suppose that you have decided that a case study best allows you to implement objective 3. Within a sub-section of your research methods chapter entitled research strategy, make it clear: (a) which research strategy you have decided to adopt; (b) your understanding of what that strategy is; and (c) your justification for choosing that strategy. Saunders *et al.* (2000: 92) stress the importance of justifying the relevance of your chosen research strategy to your work: 'what matters is not the label that is attached to a particular strategy, but whether it is appropriate for your particular research . . .' Below is a sample answer tackling these very points for the above empirical research, where examples of what is to be addressed appear in square parentheses – [a], [b], and [c] – to let you see how the sample answer in Appendix E is constructed:

[a] The research strategy that will be used to implement the empirical research is a case study. What is a case study approach and why is it suitable for this research? [b] Cohen and Manion (1995: 106) describe a case study thus:

> '. . . the case study researcher typically observes the characteristics of an individual unit – a child, a class, a school or a community. The purpose of such observation is to probe deeply and to analyse intensively the multifarious phenomena that constitute the life cycle of the unit.'

According to this definition, a case study is therefore concerned with close observation of how a particular population group behave in a particular context. [c] A case study approach facilitates this researcher's drive to probe deeply into a university's response to e-Learning, by devoting time and energy concentrating on specific aspects of e-Learning in one higher education institution. [b] However, there is some disagreement about what constitutes a case study. Yin (2003: 13), for example, defines a case study in a different way:

> 'A case study is an empirical inquiry that
> * Investigates a contemporary phenomenon within its real-life context, especially when
> * The boundaries between phenomenon and context are not clearly evident'.

Continuing . . .

Yin, with the above definition, is trying to distinguish a case study from other research strategies. An *experiment,* he argues, intentionally separates

phenomenon from context; *historical* research, although integrating phenomenon and context, normally deals with non-contemporary events;
surveys can investigate phenomena and context together, but lack the in-
depth investigation of a case study approach. That a case study is an in-
depth study of a phenomenon is not evident from Yin's definition (Cohen
and Manion's definition makes the depth of study clear – *probe deeply and
analyse intensely*), although his book *Case Study Research* makes it obvious
that he knows that case study research is a detailed and time-consuming
undertaking. [c] This research is concerned with an in-depth study of
the phenomenon e-Learning in a contemporary context – a university
environment – where the boundaries between e-Learning and a university
environment are not obvious. For example, the review of literature showed
clearly that there is confusion over what is meant by the term e-Learning;
further, it is difficult to compartmentalize e-Learning in a teaching
and learning institution; also, the boundaries, if there are any, between
e-Learning and learning, a university's primary focus, whether it be
through teaching or research, are not *clearly evident*.

Adding . . .

[b] **and** [c] Although this research meets Yin's second condition – *the
boundaries between phenomenon and context are not clearly evident* – it seems
likely that Yin's second condition has more to do with emphasizing the
interpretative/constructivist view of the world than insisting that complexity of environment is a necessary condition that needs to be satisfied
to justify the use of a case study as a research strategy (in any case, the
university environment is a complex environment and one that
encompasses different stakeholder perspectives and interest groups). Thus,
either definition of a case study, whether it be Cohen and Manion's simple, but helpful, description of a case study, or Yin's conditional definition,
meets this researcher's aim of delving deeply into a contemporary phenomenon, e-Learning, within the context of a university environment.

Finishing with . . .

[c] Given the nature of this research – in-depth study of a contemporary
phenomenon (e-Learning), in a complex environment (a university),
where a variety of stakeholder perspectives are sought (with a specific
focus on academic staff preparing for e-Learning, but where other staff will
form part of the study to place the study in the context of a complex
environment), and where the underlying research philosophy is based on
an interpretive understanding of the world – a strategy that meets the needs
of this research is a case study. . . . the case study approach provides the
focus that is required, emphasizes depth of study, is based on the assumption that reality can only be understood through social constructions and

interactions, and that the context in which the phenomena under study is situated is complex. These facets of case study strategy fit perfectly with the aim of objective 3 of this research: to implement an in-depth exploratory study of staff stakeholder views and practices related to e-Learning preparation, including drivers and barriers, focusing on a specific unit of analysis (a team of academic staff preparing for e-Learning for a particular programme), but obtaining other stakeholder views in recognition that a university is a complex environment and academic staff views need to be placed in context.

Notice that in attempting to justify the choice of a case study for the above research, the student has reflected on what a case study is in order to map its benefits onto what he is trying to achieve in his research objective 3, thereby justifying his research strategy. As stated previously, a sensible approach is to state quite categorically the research strategy that you will choose, define that strategy – to show your dissertation marker that you understand the strategy you have chosen – and then, as above, justify your selected strategy. Try and refer to literature when laying bare your reasoning: this demonstrates that you are well read and allows you another opportunity to exhibit your skills in critical evaluation.

Essentially, what you have to remember is that you need to **define your chosen strategy and justify why it meets your research needs**. As long as you do that, then your marker will see that you understand the strategy that you have picked and, importantly, why you have picked it (once again, it is the *what* and *why* questions that you focus on in your chapter on research methods). Of course, the length of your answer will depend on the type of dissertation that you are doing and the number of words that you have to play with.

Appendix E – Sample Research Methods – contains an example of a research methods chapter, exaggerated in length in order to try and explain, in depth, issues germane to writing a chapter on research methods. For now, look at the sample Introduction and sample Research Strategy sub-sections. Notice the techniques adopted in writing these two sub-sections. The sample Introduction reminds the reader of the initial research objectives and identifies the core objective that relates to the gathering of empirical research, as well as reminding the reader that the Literature Review findings point to the need for empirical research. The sample Research Strategy also underlines the main research objective/question to be addressed through empirical research, clarifies whether it is qualitative research and/or quantitative research that is sought, dismisses research strategies that are inappropriate, identifies the preferred research strategy, and justifies it. Finally, the sample chapter acknowledges criticisms of a case study because sometimes it is good to face criticisms of your chosen research strategy head-on – remember, no research strategy is perfect.

It is unlikely that your Research Strategy sub-section will be as large as the sample research strategy in Appendix E, unless you are doing a PhD. The sample sub-section is deliberately enlarged to underline key points of discussion. Nonetheless, you will still be expected, as a minimum, to say what your strategy is and why it is appropriate to your research.

The question of reliability (and validity)

Is your empirical research reliable? Is it valid? And what is the difference between the two? If your postgraduate dissertation is subject to a viva – an oral examination – then the question of validity and reliability is likely to be raised by your examiners. Which means that you will need to be prepared to defend against the charge that your research is invalid and unreliable. Even if you are not subject to an oral examination, your marker may expect you to face the issues of validity and reliability in your research dissertation. Play safe – include a paragraph or two on why your research is valid research and why it can be relied upon.

What counts as *valid* empirical research? Valid research is research that is acceptable to the research community. How, then, do we know what is acceptable to the research community? What is acceptable to the research community – academics and practitioners engaged in research – is research that: is based on tried and tested research strategies and data collection techniques (to be discussed on p. 101); uses data analysis techniques (to be discussed on p. 113) that are deemed *appropriate to your research*; all of which are implemented properly. So, if you use a survey as your research strategy, and it is appropriate to your research (i.e. you have successfully argued the case), then you are heading towards the goal of achieving valid research. Similarly, if you collect your data using data collection techniques (e.g. questionnaires, see Appendix F) that are relevant to what you want to achieve, then you are building up the case that your research is valid. And if you analyse the data that you have collected in a way that is apposite to your research, then you are helping to achieve research that is valid. In other words, *valid research* is all about implementing your empirical work – from selection of an overall research strategy to the collection and analysis of your data – in a way that uses research approaches and techniques suited to each of these activities.

Here are a few hypothetical examples of research that would be open to the accusation of being invalid. You seek to ascertain from the general public their views on the war in Iraq, which you wish to claim are representative of the general population. You adopt a case study of those staff working in an Army Recruitment Office. This research would be invalid because the target population – Army Recruitment Officers – could not be said to represent the general population; and besides, a survey would be more appropriate. You are keen to implement an in-depth discussion with old people about how they are being cared for in their old age and you decide to base your results on a survey questionnaire. This research would be invalid because a questionnaire, however detailed, would be inappropriate to your aim of achieving an 'in-depth discussion': interviews would be more appropriate, or a combination of questionnaires and interviews. *Valid* research is about the appropriateness of the choices you make in terms of your research strategy and data collection/ analysis techniques.

What counts as *reliable* empirical research? Central to reliable research is the concept of *trust*: can your results be trusted? Your work could be valid but unreliable, that is to say you could adopt a research strategy that is appropriate to your research (e.g. a case study), use data collection techniques that you consider relevant (e.g. interviews, sample documents), and apply a suitable means of analysing your collected data, yet your work may be untrustworthy. How could that be? If you interview your research subjects but keep no record of your interviews, then your research may be viewed as unreliable. Or if you are vague about who you interviewed and when the interviews took place, then your research may not pass the reliability test. The best way to achieve research that can be relied upon is to make available to your examiner, either in the body of your dissertation or in your Appendices, details of where you did your empirical research (i.e. research site), who you researched (i.e. sample selection information), together with evidence of what you did with the sample population (e.g. experiments, interview questions, etc.) and what you found (e.g. experiment results, transcript of interviews, etc.). Yin (2003: 38) states that the way to deal with reliability is to 'make as many steps as operational as possible and to conduct the research as if someone were looking over your shoulder'. That is sound advice.

The issue of bias may also impact on the reliability of your research. For instance, if you are claiming that your results are representative of a larger population but your sampling was non-random, then your results (as in the earlier 'DEWEY DEFEATS TRUMAN' example) are not reliable. Similarly, interviewing as a means of data collection is a tricky business because sometimes the respondent is trying to please the interviewer and so gives answers that will please the interviewer (or show the respondent in a good light). Gavron (1996: 159) recognized the problem of eradicating bias altogether, particularly in relation to interviews: 'It is difficult to see how this [bias] can be avoided completely, but awareness of the problem plus constant self-control can help'. Even the simple act of observation is not bias-free: in trying to make sense of what we are looking at we are influenced by own prejudices, experiences, and personal baggage. Phillips and Pugh (2007: 50) agree: 'There is no such thing as unbiased observation.'

So, *valid* research relates to how you gather and analyse your empirical data, i.e. the strategies and techniques that you use (e.g. surveys, interviews, etc.), whereas *reliable* research focuses on the need for a record of evidence that you did indeed do the research (in a fair and objective way). If a tutor, or external examiner, asks you about the validity of your research, then you need to answer in terms of the appropriateness of the research strategy that you picked, the relevance of the data collection techniques that you used, and the (fitting) way that you analysed your data. If you are questioned on the reliability of your research, then you should answer with reference to your record of evidence (e.g. detailed information provided on your site and sample selection, sample questionnaires, interview transcripts, etc.) and the steps that you took to achieve fairness and objectivity (e.g. random selection of subjects). You can also argue that your research is reliable because you used valid strategies and techniques appropriate to your research objectives AND you have a detailed record of your research plan (e.g. people interviewed, questions asked, etc.) and its implementation (e.g. completed questionnaires, transcripts, etc.) AND you took steps to minimize bias in your work (e.g. random selection of research subjects). In other words, although valid research is not proof that your research is reliable, it can be used to strengthen the case for trusted research when combined with the other tests for reliability.

A further argument for reliability relates to the experience of the researcher. Companies that have a long record of trusted research publications, such as Ernst & Young or PriceWaterhouseCoopers, have a good chance of their research output being accepted as reliable work because of their experience in the field. Similarly, many of your tutors will have a record of publishing that, in turn, will add weight to the reliability of future research that they intend pursuing. Although it is unlikely that you, a student, will have similar research output as your tutor or large companies, you can argue that any classes that you attended on research methodologies, together with close supervision, will have aided you in producing research work that can be deemed reliable. If you have indeed produced a research paper which, for example, was presented at a conference, then you can certainly argue that your work, in summary form, was accepted by your peers and, hopefully, received enthusiastically!

Data collection

Preparation, preparation, preparation

Once the research strategy has been selected, a method of collecting the research data is required. Data collection methods include a variety of techniques: sampling (discussed earlier), secondary data, observation, interviews, and questionnaires. Researchers may use more than one technique to collect data. Using more than one technique allows you to *triangulate* results. Triangulation occurs when you use different sources of data to get a range of perspectives (particularly useful in qualitative research) and so achieve a more rounded picture, or 'thick description' of what you are looking at (Geertz 1973). If you were to ask a fellow student how he got on in his exam he might reply 'I did fine'; but if you then decided to check his results on the examination board you might discover that he barely passed; and, further, if you were able to see his examination script and read the examiner's comments you might get a better insight into what he did well at and where he lost marks. Triangulation can be time-consuming but it has its rewards.

Preparation is absolutely crucial to successful data collection: making arrangements to obtain your supervisor's views on your proposed research methods; putting together, and implementing, a pilot study if you have time; negotiating access to your data subjects; development of your actual questions (interview questions, questionnaires); and giving yourself enough time to collect your empirical data and write up your results. Unfortunately, when students are asked to collect and analyse their own data, they often leave themselves little time to do justice to these tasks, and it can show in the final output: rushed, confused, superficial, and vague.

If you intend interviewing your research subjects, then plan your questions beforehand. You can impose a rigid structure to your interview by sticking strictly to your pre-arranged questions. Or you can introduce a degree of flexibility to the interview process by using a semi-structured questionnaire. That is, you can go into the interview with a limited number of pre-arranged questions but with a willingness to let the interview ebb and flow, following associated leads and new issues as they arise.

Qualitative interviewing, using semi-structured questions, makes use of open-ended questions to encourage meaningful responses (Patton 1990). Open questions are so-called because the respondent is not confined to a limited number of responses. Examples of open questions are:

> What do you think of the benefits, if any, of e-Learning?
> Why did you register for this course?
> What are your views on capital punishment?
> What problems have you encountered with train travel?
> Tell me about your marriage?
> How would you define *happiness*?

The flip side of using open questions is that they can prove difficult for respondents to answer. Respondents might be tempted to give you an 'answer' that either shows themselves in a good light or which they think will please you; or they might blurt out the first thing that crops into their head! How many times have you been asked an open question and given a quick response, one which you later regret as inadequate and not reflecting what you genuinely believe or wanted to convey?

Closed questions are an alternative to open questions. They are used when you want a specific answer to a limited range of responses, such as:

Please indicate your sex:
Male __Female __

Which of the following reflects your views on capital punishment?

1. Support capital punishment __
2. Against capital punishment __
3. Indifferent __

You can combine open and closed questions in the same interview or within the same questionnaire, or even within the same question by including the option of 'Other (please specify)' as shown below:

What problems have you encountered with train travel?

A.   Overcrowding __
B.   Delays __
C.   Expensive __
D.   Discomfort __
E.   Other (please specify)

_____

_____

_____

If your research is primarily quantitative in nature and you are using questionnaires to collect your data, then make sure that your questions are precise and suitable for later software analysis. SPSS is a standard data analysis package that students can use to aid their quantitative research. Although the acronym SPSS stands for Statistical Package for the Social Sciences, its use is not confined to research in the social sciences. Statistical packages such as SPSS depend on you creating data sets or files, which in turn are extracted from your completed questionnaires; therefore your questionnaires need to be thought through with the resulting data analysis process in mind. You could work backwards and imagine the type of data file that you will be entering into your chosen statistical software package, as shown in Table 5.2 (where M = male, F = female, 0 = degree, 1 = diploma, 2 = school qualification, 3 = other).

Table 5.2 Example of coded data file

Age	Sex	Qualification
19	M	0
23	F	2
30	M	2
18	M	3
20	F	1
Etc.		

From there, you can then work out the sort of questions you need to ask to enable you to create that data file:

Please enter your age: ____
Sex: Male ____ Female ____

Qualification(s):
    Degree   ____
    Diploma   ____
    School   ____
    Other (please specify): _____

Do not start your empirical research unprepared, hoping somehow that things will come together. Give yourself enough time to write your chapter on research methods. Seek your supervisor's advice on how you intend to collect and analyse your data (e.g. does she think that your data collection techniques are appropriate?). Work out your questionnaires/interview questions in full. Ask yourself if the responses to your questions, whatever they may be, will help you meet your specific research objectives (i.e. are your questions relevant?). Plan your physical collection process (e.g. interviews with data subjects) and give yourself plenty of time to analyse your results. For more information on questionnaire design and interviewing, read Oppenheim, A. N. (1992). *Questionnaire Design, Interviews and Attitude Measurements*, London: Pinter.

What and why?

> #### *A common mistake by students*
>
> A common mistake committed by students, when writing about the data collection techniques they propose using for their empirical research, is to be vague about what *they* did, and why, opting instead to concentrate their efforts on providing the reader with a dull list of data collection techniques that are available to researchers in general.

This is very boring to the reader, and it is not going to get you many, if any, marks. In this section of your dissertation you will need to identify:

1 Where you will get your data from (people coming out of a shopping centre, fans in a football stadium, employees from a number of companies, or wherever).
2 Your sample size (number of experiments/companies/people).
3 Your sampling technique (random, stratified, quota, convenience, etc.).
4 How you will extract your data (interviews, observation, questionnaires, tests, etc.).

In addition, when you write all this down in your dissertation make sure that you justify each of your choices for the aforementioned points 1, 2, 3 and 4. Also, as evidence of point 4 – how you will collect your data – you should place your intended questionnaire/interview questions in your appendices section at the back of your dissertation. After you have collected your data, insert in your appendices an example of a completed questionnaire/interview session, taking care to remove identifying information that your research subjects may wish to remain hidden (such as employee names or company details). The key to your data collection sub-section is to provide enough detail so that the reader can, if he wishes to, repeat your research. In that way the information that you provide about your empirical work will be unambiguous and transparent, and so avoiding potential examiner comments such as 'not sure how many companies this student sampled' or 'this student fails to make it clear why he has adopted the use of questionnaires as his means of data collection' or 'this student has not included his questionnaire so the actual questions asked remain a mystery!'

Let us take the e-Learning case study as an example of how to record information about your intended empirical work. In Appendix E, 'Sample Research Methods', there are two fully worked-out sub-sections which are relevant: *Data Collection: Site and Sample Selection*; and *Data Collection Techniques*. You can peruse the detail of these sub-sections at your leisure, but for now we will focus attention on specific points. Remember, the sample chapter on research methods is longer than one would expect to see in a Master's dissertation, and that is because certain parts have been exaggerated in length to emphasize key issues for you, the reader.

The empirical research for the e-Learning example is based on a case study of one university from which a number of staff are to be sampled, to meet objective 3 of the research study ('Explore staff stakeholder views and practices related to e-Learning preparation, including drivers and barriers to e-Learning'). Hence the heading *Data Collection: Site and Sample Selection*. If your empirical work is different, then you should have a different heading. If you intend visiting a number of companies, i.e. more than one site, then change your heading accordingly, e.g. *Data Collection: Sites and Sample Selection*.

What forms the content of a sub-section entitled *Data Collection: Site and Sample Selection* and how do you go about recording this information? First, *you state where you are getting your data from*: the physical location(s)/departments *and sample size* (number of research subjects). Also, take the opportunity to remind the reader about your research strategy and do not forget to justify your site selection. If you are investigating the behaviour of crabs on a number of beaches, then say which beaches you will be using – i.e. your research sites – and why you have chosen those particular beaches. If you intend sending out questionnaires to a number of companies about their e-security measures, then say which companies (or types of companies, if anonymity is a requirement laid down by your research subjects) and why you have chosen those particular companies (you may have selected them at random). If you are going to interview students from a particular undergraduate programme, from a particular year-group, then state the basic details (university/course/year) and why that particular site/course/year-group.

To begin with, you need to state quite categorically the 'site(s)' and the number of research subjects (people/crabs/etc.) that will form the source of your data. Taking the e-Learning example as an illustration one would need to identify (a) the university (as it is a single case study); (b) the main department; and (c) the programme, and the number of staff that go to make up the source of the data. Once again, points (a), (b) and (c) appear in square parentheses in bold below to make it easier for you to identify the constituent parts of the sample answer:

[a] The site will be Inverclyde University (IU). This case study is not intended to be an exhaustive study of all the e-Learning initiatives operating in the university. Such a study would, in order to produce meaningful results, be enormously time-consuming and perhaps never-ending (e.g. as one moved the study from one School or Faculty to another School or Faculty, or indeed between departments, new blended e-Learning programmes may suddenly appear and others may just as quickly disappear). [b] Instead, one division within the Inverclyde Business School (IBS) will form the focus of academic staff interviews. [c] Specifically, those staff involved in preparing lecture and seminar material on the VLE software platform Blackboard for a suite of post-graduate programmes in E-Business, Knowledge Management and Management of Information Systems will receive structured interviews. This will allow a focused, achievable approach to the study, giving academic staff the opportunity to express detailed views on e-Learning preparation. Eight teaching staff who have been involved in preparing material for their modules for Blackboard usage on the China programme will be interviewed.

Next, you need to justify your choice of data sources. In the e-Learning example, this could be justified by, first of all, drawing attention to the hitherto lack of in-depth studies in this area:

The opportunity to implement a case study within a university to explore staff stakeholder views and practices related to e-Learning training, including drivers and barriers to e-Learning, is an exciting one. Empirical research in e-Learning tends to take place via the mechanism of e-mailed questionnaires (examples include: Britain and Liber 1999; Rockwell *et al.* 2000; Gerrard 2002; Massey 2002), resulting in a preponderance of quantitative data (such as '61% of all respondents rated the overall quality of e-Learning as fair or poor') rather than probing, qualitative data. In addition, such surveys tend to be sent to one individual or centre for response, hence lacking in different stakeholder views. This empirical research will attempt to delve deeply into an institution's approach to e-Learning by implementing a case study and by concentrating on collecting qualitative data from pertinent stakeholders. It is hoped that the results of this study will provide the reader with a three-dimensional picture of e-Learning and, through its *relatability*, add to the tapestry of knowledge that is forming around the field of e-Learning.

Then you can establish why you are focusing on Division X within your selected institution:

Given that a major focus of this research is to gain a deeper understanding of how staff, in practice, prepare for e-Learning, in whatever form, and that these staff have prepared aspects of the e-Learning part of this blended approach, then selecting X [name of Division] as part of the case study presents an excellent opportunity to address issues surrounding staff views and experiences of e-Learning preparation. Selecting X is not a pretence that X is representative of other Divisions, or Departments, within Inverclyde University and that what happens in X in this context happens, or will happen, elsewhere. Instead, it is to the concept of *relatability* – discussed earlier – that is expected to be of interest to other Departments in other universities. E-Learning is of great interest to universities and the experiences and perspectives of one department will add incrementally to the knowledge base of e-Learning research.

There are two other reasons for choosing X's postgraduate programme as the main focus for this case study. The UK Council for Postgraduate Education (1999), in a report – *The International Postgraduate: Challenges to British Higher Education* – raised the issue of the potential for using new technologies for teaching and learning with international postgraduate students but revealed that evidence of staff e-Learning experiences with international postgraduate students were from 'anecdotal' sources (section 7: 2). Selecting X's postgraduate programme provides an excellent opportunity to obtain empirical data on how X's staff prepare for e-Learning and how they prepare for the challenge of dealing with students (and staff) from a different culture. Secondly, The Commission of the European Communities (2002: 5) lamented that the 'most successful players [in e-Learning initiatives] to date, however, remain the well-established and prestigious institutions'.

If there are other research subjects from whom you wish to extract data, then remember to include them, saying why you are incorporating them in your sample:

If Division X is viewed as central to this case study, then, in order to achieve a three-dimensional perspective of e-Learning at IU, other stakeholders need to form part of this research. To concentrate solely on staff from Division X would produce, at best, a two-dimensional perspective: experiences and views of academic staff and their Head of Department. To gain a fuller perspective, the research needs to be widened to include staff outwith Division X. Those who have a part in training academic staff to cope with e-Learning ought to form part of the study. Similarly, *elite* staff – staff with influence, and who are well-informed in the organization (Marshall and Rossman 1989) – need to be included. . . .

To capture a School/Faculty view of e-Learning issues, the Dean of the Inverclyde Business School (IBS) will be included in the case study; similarly, the Principal and Vice-Chancellor is included to give a strategic perspective on e-Learning. The Pro Vice-Chancellor of Learning and Information Services will be part of this study, for his over-arching role in achieving strategic objectives related to the use of ICT. And because Division X is located in IBS, the C&IT Fellow located in IBS (someone with direct responsibility for encouraging and supporting e-Learning initiatives in the IBS) will also be interviewed. This thick view of e-Learning will be enhanced further by including members of those who have a role in best teaching practices within IU: the Head of the Academic Practice Unit (APU), together with a member of the Teaching and Learning Team (LTAS). In effect, empirical data will be obtained from academic staff involved *in the field* of e-Learning preparation, from staff in the e-Learning Innovation Support Unit, as well as staff with a specific role in offering guidance and strategy on teaching practice; and, for a wider management perspective, data will be captured from the Head of X, the Dean of IBS and the Principal and Vice-Chancellor.

Finally, in relation to your data sources, it is good practice to summarize, for easy reference, the information in the form of a diagram, as shown in Figure E2 (taken from the sample chapter on Research Methods in Appendix E).

Next, you can explain your sampling method (state what it is and justify your approach):

Convenience sampling was used to select both the university and the postgraduate program. It is convenient because the researcher works at the university. This means that the subjects under study have not been chosen at random and that therefore there can be no claim to achieving representative views related to the broader university community. Instead, this research has as its focus the aim of achieving an in-depth and qualitative insight into e-Learning preparation issues. The review of relevant literature established that e-Learning is an area of increasing interest in the wider university community and so the results of this study will be of

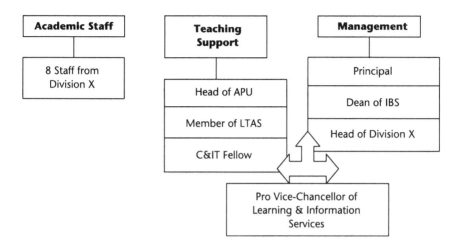

Figure E2 Inverclyde University (IU) Research Units

interest to those grappling with similar staff preparation issues. Convenience sampling is also used because of time issues and easy access to research subjects.

In truth, you can disclose your sampling method just about anywhere in your data collection sub-section – it does not need to be *immediately* after you have revealed your sample size. It can be before it or after it, or even within your earlier sub-section on research strategy.

Now you will need to start explaining *how* you will collect data from your sources, i.e. clarify and justify your data collection techniques. Do not get bogged down in the common mistake of just listing the general benefits of the techniques that you intend using: try and discuss the relevance/benefits of *your* chosen techniques to *your* research. In other words, articulate the type, or types, of data collection techniques that you will be adopting, indicating who will be subject to what data collection technique, and assert your rationale for using those techniques. For instance, if you want to email questionnaires to your research subjects, then state this and justify why you are using email questionnaires as opposed to, say, interviews. If you are interested in interviewing employees from a particular company, then say so, explaining how you will conduct your interviews (i.e. structured or semi-structured interviews?), who will be subject to these interviews, and how interviewing will help you collect the data that you need to complete your empirical research.

Incidentally, a structured interview – where you have a pre-prepared set list of questions that you would like answered – allows you to keep a tight grip over the interview process and maintain a focused interview; while semi-structured interviews – where you have an outline structure with key pointer questions, hoping to generate a fluid, dynamic interview – gives you, the interviewer, an opportunity to confront core issues and at the same time allow the interview process to take unexpected twists and turns. Of course, there is nothing to stop you having a completely structured set of interview questions, to establish a focus, but where you are quite prepared to let the interviewee expand on issues as he sees fit (this can be done through the use of open questions, such as 'What are your views of x?'). You may wish to use a mix of data collection techniques, in order to achieve a more rounded view of what you are researching. The advantage of interviewing is that you can explore interviewee responses and get at the root of issues. In effect, interviewing is 'a conversation between interviewer and respondent with the purpose of eliciting certain information from the respondent' (Moser and Kalton 1971: 271).

The following extracts from the e-Learning example in Appendix E – where interviews and secondary data, such as in-house reports, form the main data collection techniques – illustrate the previous points, *viz.*: [a] clarify your main data collection technique(s); [b] justify it/them; and [c] indicate who is subject to which technique and type of questions:

[a] Qualitative data will be obtained primarily through the vehicle of interviews. [b] This will open the opportunity to discuss, with the various stakeholders, e-Learning issues in depth. [a] However, in order to establish a framework around the interviews, and to focus on specific issues with different interviewees, the interviews will be structured with questions prepared beforehand, but the interviewer will be open to new issues and follow different, associated leads depending on the responses and willingness of the interviewee. Qualitative interviewing, using structured questions, makes use of open-ended questions – such as, for example, 'What do you consider to be the benefits, if any, of e-Learning?' – to encourage meaningful responses (Patton 1990).

[c] Interviewing different staff (e.g. Principal, academic staff, member of LTAS, etc.) will allow for cross-comparisons of responses, encouraging different perspectives of similar e-Learning issues to emerge (e.g. rationale for involvement, perceived barriers, staff support required, etc.). For example, the Vice-Chancellor and Dean of IBS will be questioned mainly on strategic issues related to e-Learning, whereas the Head of X, although receiving questions on strategic issues, will be questioned mainly on implementation issues linked to strategic objectives, including support for staff training. The interviews will be recorded, where possible, for two reasons: to ensure that the analysis of data is based upon an accurate record (e.g. transcript) and to allow the interviewer to concentrate on the interview.

Continuing with details of staff to be interviewed . . .

The following staff will be interviewed:

1 Principal and Vice-Chancellor of Inverclyde University (IU)
2 Pro Vice-Chancellor of Learning and Information Services
3 Member of e-LISU
4 Head of Academic Practice Unit (APU)
5 The Dean of the Inverclyde Business School (IBS)
6 The Head of the Division X
7 Member of Learning and Teaching Strategy (LTAS) Team
8 C&IT Fellow
9 8 Academic Staff from Division X: module teaching team involved in development of teaching and learning material, using Blackboard, for the delivery of an MSc E-Business to students in China.

Including the benefits of choosing the above stakeholders:

[b] By selecting a variety of e-learning stakeholders, from those involved in strategic decision-making (1, 2, 4 and 5), those charged with providing training to academic staff (2 and 3), those involved in providing IT Support (2 and 5) and learning and teaching advice (3, 4, 7 and 8), and by selecting a Division that has recent experience of implementing e-learning strategy (6 and 9), it is expected that an enriched understanding of e-learning will emerge, one that will better inform the e-learning process and assist in the development of, for instance, the ingredients for improved guidance to support those faced with implementing e-Learning: academic staff.

If you are making use of secondary data (such as company records), then state explicitly what secondary data you will be using, and why:

Secondary data, in the form of university documents and academic staff teaching and learning material, will also be collected to form part of the analysis. The secondary data will come from a variety of documented sources:

• University Strategic Plan
• IBS Plan for 2002/03–2005/06
• Division X's Strategic Plan
• Learning, Teaching and Assessment Strategy (LTAS) 2000–2004
• APU E-Learning Strategy

The secondary data, coupled with the interview data, will assist in providing a rich picture of e-Learning in the university by facilitating a comparison of the stated University/Business School/Divisional objectives against staff perceptions, at various levels within the institution.

Finally, you should inform the reader in which Appendix you will be placing your questions and raw data, for example:

Appendix A contains the collection of structured questions to be used for the academic staff; Appendix B contains the actual interview transcripts of interviews with academic staff; and Appendix C contains the questions and transcripts of interviews with elite staff.

A convenient and cost-effective way to collect qualitative data, often favoured by students, is to use *focus groups* (Marshall and Rossman 2006). Instead of interviewing subjects on a one-to-one basis, in a formal, uninviting environment (e.g. an office), focus groups provide an opportunity to gather together a predetermined number of interview subjects, usually in a relaxed setting, to discuss their attitudes towards whatever topics you want discussed. The emphasis on capturing people's views means that focus group-based research is phenomenological in nature and linked to qualitative research. However, getting data from a focus group is not straightforward. You need to plan your discussion topics in advance, decide how to collect your data, pay attention to the flow of discussion (allowing others to contribute), recognize when to call a halt to particular discussions; as well as making every effort to minimize bias. On this last point, it is very easy to manipulate inadvertently what you want people to say, by the questions that you ask and in your responses – oral and facial – to comments given by members of the focus group. This can happen to such an extent that your input may contort what you think you are witnessing, or as Heisenberg (1958: 288) put it: 'What we observe is not nature itself, but nature exposed to our method of questioning'. Perhaps complete objectivity is a fallacy, something that can never be achieved, as posited by Zukav (1979: 328):

> *'Reality' is what we take to be true. What we take to be true is what we believe. What we believe is based upon our perceptions. What we perceive depends upon what we look for. What we look for depends upon what we think. What we think depends upon what we perceive. What we perceive determines what we believe. What we believe determines what we take to be true. What we take to be true is our reality.*

Zukav's perspective on objectivity, although perhaps over-cynical, underlines the need for you not to covet deliberate bias and to make every effort to minimize accidental bias.

When you engage in focus groups you are in effect participating in a form of action research. You are not a full participant because you are not answering the questions you pose. At the same time, it cannot be claimed that you are a neutral observer, because you are asking questions, directing the flow of discussion, interrupting debate, inviting others to contribute, revealing unwitting approval/disapproval (a slight frown here, a quiet smile there, laughing at a joke, shaking your head at an argumentative participant, and so on). Indeed, your mere presence impacts on the group dynamics and the questions that you ask influences the nature and tone of group member responses. It is probably more accurate to describe your role as a *participant observer*. That said, there is a dynamism to be found in focus groups that make them suited to exploratory, in-depth qualitative studies (e.g. case studies).

You do have some flexibility on how you structure this part of your chapter on research methods. You are free to have one sub-section in your chapter to cover both your site/sample selection information and your data collection techniques (e.g. *Data Collection Information*), i.e. there is no rule that you need to separate *where* and *how* you collect your data into different sub-sections (as done in Appendix E). As long as you give the information in a detailed and clear manner, that is what is important. It is worth repeating that the length of the sample answers are not indicative of how much you need to write: that all depends on the type of dissertation you are writing and the number of words at your disposal. That said, the research issues that need to be addressed and the principle of how you can record your answers remain the same.

Framework for data analysis

After you have disclosed how you propose to collect your research data, you should then go on to explain how you intend analysing what you have collected.

> **A common mistake by students**
>
> A common mistake by students is to collect the data with no prior plan of how to go about making sense of their raw data. The inevitable consequence is that they become quickly bogged down and confused about what to do next, and this sense of befuddlement becomes evident in their final submission.

When you get your empirical data you need to *describe* what you have collected and then *analyse* the data (although you can describe and analyse simultaneously), producing what is called your 'empirical research findings'. Your overall research findings, in effect, are the combination of your literature review work and your empirical findings. Collectively, this is sometimes referred to as *synthesizing* your research work, i.e. the bringing together of your main research output from both your Literature Review and your empirical research. However, you first need to elucidate how you envisage going about the task of describing and analysing your empirical data. This can be done by outlining a *framework for data analysis*.

Before you can produce such a framework, though, you need to know the difference between *data description* and *data analysis*. Suppose that you issued a questionnaire and that it was completed by 100 respondents. You start to describe the results for question 1, which asked 'Do you like the [UK] Prime

Minister (Y/N)?' You count how many people responded 'Y' and how many people responded 'N'. A description of what you found could be as follows: '82% of respondents stated that they do not like the Prime Minister.' (At a simpler level, describing your raw data can entail prerequisite tasks such as transcribing taped interviews or writing down notes about an organization you recently visited.) Interpreting what this means is not so simple, and is unlikely to occur after looking at the results of just one question. Instead, analysis tends to be a cumulative process, dependent on the results from a number of question responses combined with cross-referencing of related Literature Review findings. For instance, if other parts of the same questionnaire highlighted that most people objected to the 2003 invasion of Iraq, then you might start to analyse the Prime Minister's unpopularity in terms of the war in Iraq, i.e. by combining questionnaire results you can begin to place meaningful interpretation on aspects of your collected data. Data description is a necessary step before data analysis, with the former simpler and relatively easy to do, involving a straightforward statement of what you found, while the latter takes you into the realm of interpretation, usually requiring cross-referencing of data descriptions, together with references to your Literature Review findings.

If you are attempting to analyse quantitative data, you could exploit the power of statistical data analysis software. For instance, you could use simple cross-tabulation together with elementary graphical models to convey basic statistical information (allowing you to describe your empirical data) as well as utilize more advanced features such as statistical correlation and regression, hypothesis testing and time-series analysis (giving you evidence to support detailed analysis). Table 5.3 provides a list of some of the statistical tools and techniques that you can use to describe and then analyse your quantitative data. Descriptive statistics are used to help you present your quantitative data in a manageable form.

In the context of a student dissertation, a framework for data analysis is usually straightforward. Once again, let us return to the e-Learning case study for illustration purposes (*Framework for Data Analysis*, in Appendix E) to see how easy it is to develop, and explain, a framework for data analysis (in this

Table 5.3 Examples of statistical techniques for quantitative research

Descriptive statistics	Advanced statistics
Summary Statistics (mean, median, mode, range, central tendency, standard deviation, variance); **Tabulation** (simple tabulation and cross-tabulation); **Graphics** (bar chart, pie chart, line chart, multi-series line chart).	Student's *t*-test; Chi-square test; Analysis of variance (ANOVA); Regression analysis; Correlation; Fisher's least significant difference test; Time-series analysis.

case related to qualitative research). The case study raw data comes mainly from two sources: interviews from academic staff who are preparing e-Learning material for a postgraduate programme, and *elite* staff interviews, i.e. those staff who are in a position of power to influence the direction of e-Learning at Inverclyde University. How can we go about analysing these two sets of data? One way to analyse qualitative interview data is to first of all break down the interview data into easily identified *themed* subsets, and then compare and contrast staff responses to each themed group of questions. For example, if a number of questions in the interview related to 'drivers for e-Learning', then the data for that particular theme can be described and analysed as a separate unit. Similarly, if another group of questions centres on 'barriers to e-Learning', then you can compare and contrast staff responses relative to the theme 'barriers to e-Learning', and so on. However, at some point you need to cross-reference how staff have responded to different questions in order to build up a fuller picture of what your data is telling you.

How you prepare to collect your data has an impact on how easy it will be to analyse it once collected – so, if you wish to analyse data via themes within your subject area then incorporate these themes in your initial questionnaires/ interviews, etc. using appropriate headings (e.g. Computer Security Breaches Suffered, Impact of Security Breaches, Countermeasures Adopted, Views on Government Advice, Recommendations to Other Companies, etc.). Appendix F contains a sample questionnaire which illustrates how to group your research questions into themes: there are six themes in this example and each theme is clearly headed. For instance, the first theme – e-Learning drivers – consists of questions linked to that theme:

A. THEME: University Drivers for e-Learning

Question 1A
The university's Strategic Planning Document makes reference to e-Learning targets and objectives.
Do you know what these are?

Question 2A
The Inverclyde Business School's (IBS) plan for 2002/3 to 2005/6 also makes reference to e-Learning targets and objectives.
Do you know what these are?

Question 3A
Why do you think university management wish academic staff to become involved in e-Learning?

Question 4A
What advantages do you think e-Learning will have for students?

Question 5A
What advantages do you think e-Learning will have for academic staff?

The general structure of the sample questionnaire, with the themes evident from the section headings, is designed to make the task of data analysis easier:

A. THEME: University Drivers for e-Learning

(Questions)

B. THEME: Barriers

(Questions)

C. THEME: Preparation

(Questions)

D. THEME: IT Infrastructure

(Questions)

E. THEME: Academic Staff Motivation

(Questions)

F. THEME: Reflections and Future Directions

(Questions)

It makes sense when you are preparing your data collection techniques to reflect on your questionnaire/interview design in terms of their impact on your later data analysis. Grouping related questions together under an appropriate heading, as above, will make life easier for you when you eventually get around to undertaking your data analysis.

Returning to the e-Learning example, a useful start would be to explain to whoever is reading (and marking) your dissertation that the analysis of the interview data, obtained from the academic staff and the elite staff, will revolve around the idea of themes. As such, these themes have to be made apparent to the reader:

To help focus the interviews in terms of reflecting the main objectives of this research and ease the analysis of the qualitative data, the interviews will be structured according to themes. These themes reflect the overall aim and objectives in this research and also echo main areas arising from the review of literature: *University Drivers for e-Learning, Barriers, Preparation, IT Infrastructure, Academic Staff Motivation* and, to conclude,

Reflections and Future Directions. It is important not to view these themes as separate topics: they are inter-related. All of the topics could have been placed under the heading 'Preparing for e-Learning'. For example, questions on academic staff motivation relate specifically to what motivates/demotivates staff to become involved in e-Learning; similarly, IT Infrastructure concerns the IT support suitable for an e-Learning environment. The themes are there to help the interviewer and interviewees focus, and as an aid to the analysis of the transcripts.

If you want, you could also indicate the spread, or type, of questions to your stakeholders:

Further, as an indication to the quest for depth as well as focus to this research, academic staff will be asked 4 questions on Drivers, 5 questions on Barriers, 2 questions on IT Infrastructure, 5 questions on Motivation, 3 questions on Reflections and Future Directions, and over 30 questions (including sub-questions) on Preparation. Table E1 reveals the breakdown of questions (including sub-questions) under each theme, for academic staff and elite staff. An additional theme – e-Learning Strategy – is included for elite staff, to reflect their role in the strategic shaping and delivery of e-Learning.

Using a diagram, or table, is an effective way to communicate summary information, adding a professional touch (e.g. Table E1, from Appendix E):

Table E1 Case study: breakdown of themes and questions

Theme	Academic staff questions	Elite staff questions
X. e-Learning Strategy	–	10
A. Drivers	5	4
B. Barriers	5	6
C. Preparation	33	12
D. IT Infrastructure	2	6
E. Academic Staff Motivation	6	3
F. Reflections and Future Directions	3	4

Although the e-Learning example explains that interview questions will be analysed in terms of themes – drivers, barriers, etc. – there is still the big picture to consider. By that, one means your general approach to data analysis. For the e-Learning example this involves collecting interview data, describing it (i.e. interview transcriptions + simple written statements of who said what), followed by interpretation of the descriptions (= analysis). Wolcott (1994) refers to this approach as a process of *description, analysis* and *interpretation*, while Miles and Hubermann (1984) and Creswell (1997) emphasize that such an approach is non-linear, involving repetition and reflection.

Once again, where possible, produce a diagrammatic summary of your approach to data analysis (in this case, taken from the sample chapter on research methods, Appendix E), with a little preamble to introduce it:

> Figure E3 illustrates graphically the approach that will be adopted to analyse data from the Case Study, based around the iterative process of *description, analysis* and *interpretation* (Wolcott 1994) of the collected data, particularly with regard to extracting and understanding emerging themes. However, analysis of qualitative data is not a linear activity and requires an iterative approach to capturing and understanding themes and patterns (Miles and Huberman 1984; Creswell 1997).

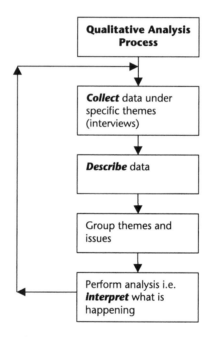

Figure E3 Qualitative data analysis process for Inverclyde University case study

You might also wish to raise any issues about how you collected your data (from transcribing, to data protection issues, use of notes, dependence on memory, etc.), as shown in the e-Learning example:

> The question of how to record the interviews is one that has been given much consideration in this case study. Taking notes as respondents talk is one simple alternative. However, the disadvantage of having to write as respondents are talking, and so failing to give respondents your full attention and, in turn, perhaps omitting crucial comments and nuances,

together with the problem of having to interpret summary comments some time after the event, in the end made this mode of recording unsuitable. Instead, all interviews will be recorded on tape and transcribed. Such an activity will prove time-consuming, but the resulting data will aid in the researchers aim of gathering enriching, qualitative data. Over-riding advantages include the freedom to concentrate on the interview process and, crucially, the capture of everything said by the respondents. As each interview will be structured under the themes mentioned earlier (Drivers, Barriers, etc.), the transcriptions for each interview will not form one mass of oral text, but rather be categorized under predetermined topics and sub-topics, in turn aiding the analysis phase. One last point on transcribing: all the interviews will be transcribed. As Strauss and Corbin (1990: 31) recommend: 'better more than less'. The researcher has decided to err on the side of caution and have all interviews transcribed.

Data analysis rarely consists of only description and analysis of themed groups of sub-questions in isolation (i.e. looking at Theme A, then Theme B, then Theme C, and so on). For the richer dimension it is often necessary to cross-reference respondent data, linking different sub-groups of data (or, in this case, 'themes'), adding cumulative meaning through an iterative process, and, particularly in the context of a student dissertation, comparing and contrasting your raw data description and analysis with your Literature Review findings. Therefore, if you have some raw data under a theme entitled e-Learning Barriers, then you could interpret your raw data findings not only in relation to what your respondents tell you within that specific theme, but also what they told you in other related themes that might give you a better understanding of their views, and against what the literature said about the barriers to e-Learning. In other words, you are comparing and contrasting your raw data at a number of levels. In your chapter on research methods you can let your supervisor know how you will analyse your collected data:

> An important part of this research is to analyze the Case Study data, comparing and contrasting different stakeholder perspectives (as above), and to reflect on the Case Study results with respect to the findings in the Literature Review. Figure E3 is updated (Figure E4) to show this overarching reflective process.

Even if you think your diagram is self-explanatory, take your reader through your diagram. This helps remove any misunderstanding and shows your tutor that you have a clear understanding of your data analysis framework. A summary of Figure E4 could be as follows (notice that the summary finishes with a quotation, taking the opportunity to add weight to the approach to data analysis):

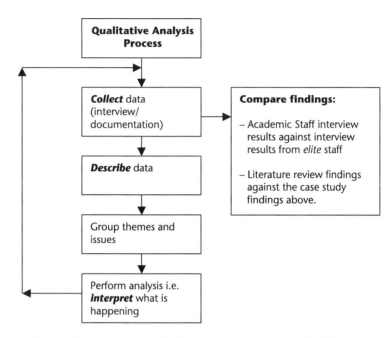

Figure E4 Qualitative data analysis process for Inverclyde University case study [updated]

In terms of analysis, there will be a two-pronged approach: first, the academic staff case study findings will be described and analysed; second, the elite staff case study findings will be described and analysed, not only comparing elite staff findings against each other, but also comparing elite staff findings against academic staff findings. However, it is in the second phase that, as well as comparing elite staff findings against academic staff findings, relevant literature review findings will also be compared and contrasted against the case study findings (this is to avoid repetition of comment with reference to the findings in the literature review). The essence of this qualitative analysis paradigm reflects accepted practice in dealing with qualitative data, and is perhaps more succinctly described by Bogdan and Biklen (1982: 145) as 'working with data, organizing it, breaking it into manageable units, synthesizing it, searching for patterns, discovering what is important and what is to be learned, and deciding what you will tell others'.

Too often students populate their dissertations, from beginning to end, with unexplained diagrams. Worse, students can be seen embedding diagrams in their dissertation yet fail to refer to their diagrams in the body of their text, in which case the diagrams are not even acknowledged by the students themselves and so serve no purpose, and therefore gain no marks, and might even lose some!

There are many approaches to data analysis. This sub-section has merely described one approach, based on the concept of *themes*, using the e-Learning case study example to illustrate key points. The important factors that you should take on board are:

1 You ought to inform the reader how you intend analysing your data.
2 How you implement your data collection techniques can impact on your data analysis (so think carefully about how you design your interviews, questionnaires, experiments, etc.).
3 Your data analysis framework will involve data description followed by data interpretation.
4 Cross-referencing of data results, coupled with references to related Literature review findings, will help produce a more meaningful analysis of your empirical data.
5 Remember to illustrate your data analysis approach through the use of diagrams/figures/tables. And do not forget to explain your diagrams/figures/tables!

Limitations and potential problems

It is unusual for researchers, at any level, not to recognize limitations in their own work. In a paper published in *Women in Management Review* by Ogden *et al.* (2006: 43), for example, the authors acknowledged the limitation of using a case study as their research strategy but justified it with an appeal to capturing a rich picture of individual human experiences:

> *Due to the combination of the depth and sensitivity of the research topic, a case study approach is adopted (Yin 1994). Although the lack of probability sampling inherent in the case approach means the results cannot be generalised, the results provide a rich and detailed picture of the experiences and perceptions of individuals working within the industry. Analysis of this data provides a valuable insight into contemporary inhibitors and enablers of females' career development in financial services.*

Similarly, the student dissertation that is problem-free or not limited in some way does not exist, so do not try and fool your examiner and pretend otherwise. On the other hand, your examiner is not interested in every single problem that you have encountered while doing your dissertation, from perceived bad supervision to your initial inability to find relevant literature. If you include a section on 'Limitations and potential problems' (or whatever you want to call it) within your chapter on Research Methods, then it is limitations and problems related to your empirical research work that your examiner expects to read about, not problems in general. By facing possible criticisms of how you conducted your empirical research, you are displaying a certain level of research maturity. Of course, do not go overboard and undermine your good work!

As stated above, in such a section – *Limitations and Potential Problems* – you ought to focus on issues connected to your empirical research and not your dissertation as a whole. Such issues tend to concentrate on your chosen research strategy, data collection techniques, including site and sample size and selection where appropriate, and analysis of collected data.

Questions that you can reflect on

- What are the known criticisms of my chosen research strategy? (If you read the literature on your chosen research strategy, then you are bound to unearth criticisms – every research strategy has its critics as well as its supporters, some more vociferous than others!)
- Is my approach to collecting my data limited in any way? (E.g. why am I using questionnaires when interviews might give me more meaningful results? Perhaps you are unable to get access to your research subjects or they are so geographically dispersed that it is impractical to visit them.)
- Is my sample population big enough? (E.g. a criticism may be that your experiment/questionnaires/interviews etc. are limited in number, but the lack of time available to you, as a student, may form part of your justification.)
- Is my research open to the accusation that it is invalid? (I.e. have I argued successfully that the way I approached my research is appropriate to achieving my research objectives/questions?)
- Am I vulnerable to the claim that my empirical work is unreliable? (I.e. have I provided enough detail to show that I did the research and that my findings are trustworthy, e.g. provided site and sample selection information, questionnaire samples, made efforts to reduce bias, etc.?)
- Can I generalize as a result of my empirical work? (Does it matter if I can't?)
- What efforts have I made to ensure that my empirical research is, as far as possible, fair and free from bias? (E.g. if you know the research subjects – for instance, they may be fellow students whom you wish to interview – what mechanisms have you set in place so that your views of them and, equally, their views of you, do not influence your findings?)

It is important to recognize potential problems and to show how you have addressed them. Avoid producing just a *list* of issues. Identify perceived limitations of your work/potential issues and *explain* what you have done to negate those risks. It is the top students who do well in this section because they are confident in putting up a stout defence of their work, even with identified shortcomings.

To help clarify the question of limitations/potential problems linked to your research methods, a defence of potential issues in the empirical research for the sample e-Learning dissertation will now be developed. To begin with, below is recognition that a case study – the chosen research strategy for the practical research – is limited because generalizations cannot be made from case studies. However, a defence of the case study is also given, with the author appealing to *relatability* as his goal rather than *generalizability*.

There are limitations to this research, as well as issues related to implementing a case study in an environment where one is employed. The results of this study cannot be generalized to the wider research community. Indeed, the results of this research cannot even be generalized to represent the university under study: although key elite staff will be interviewed, and strategic documentation will be referred to, the study of a different programme team in the institution, preparing for e-Learning, may lead to different results. The question of the validity of case study research, in the sense that generalizations cannot normally be made, has already been discussed and addressed. This researcher is using a tried and tested research strategy, appealing to the concept of *relatability* rather than *generalizability*, although it was also argued that generalization, although not immediate, can take place over a period of time – incremental generalizability – as more empirical research case studies are implemented. This researcher is sacrificing immediate generalizability for depth of study.

Next, the issue of the reliability of the research work is discussed:

Nonetheless, there is also the question of the *reliability* of using such a strategy, particularly when interviews are used as the main means of data collection. In the first place, there is the matter of studying one instance of one phenomenon, the results of which are not open to immediate generalization. Next, there is the question of depending on a data collection technique – interviews – that relies on personal opinion, and so open to bias and inaccuracy. Even more problematic, how can the researcher maintain *objectivity* when he interviews colleagues in an environment wherein he works!

In terms of the reliability of case study research, Yin (2003: 38) states that the way to deal with reliability in a case study is to 'make as many steps as operational as possible and to conduct the research as if someone were looking over your shoulder'. This research work met this test of reliability by providing details of the appropriateness of the case study strategy to this research, as well as the data collection techniques to be used, the site selected, the type of staff to be interviewed, their roles, the specific themes that will be addressed, the actual interview questions, and the method of data analysis. In addition, full transcripts are provided. Reliability is sought through a highly structured, transparent and detailed approach to this study, using a research strategy and data collection techniques that have validity in the research community.

And then dealing with the question of bias.

The issue of depending on interviews as the main source of data, when interviewees can exhibit bias or poor memory recall, was dealt with by ensuring that the researcher was not depending on his results from only one or two respondents, but on a number of sources. To begin with, a team of academics preparing for a new suite of programmes will be interviewed. A number of views are collected on the same issues, from staff working on the same programmes, ensuring that the researcher is not dependent on one or two respondents for key data. Second, staff from outwith this programme will be interviewed, further removing the dependence on opinion that may be factually wrong or skewed and to place academic staff views in a wider context, lessening the opportunity for bias or misinformation. Third, the interview questions are extensive and detailed, where some of the same issues are tackled in different themes (e.g. barriers to e-Learning), which presents an opportunity for staff to consider some topics in different contexts and acts as a check on the consistency of staff views. Fourth, documentation will be used as a means of understanding the university's e-Learning objectives and implementation issues, and also used to compare against interview answers. It must also be accepted that people are not robots and that to err is human, both in terms of expressing occasional bias and making honest errors of recollection; but that for the most part respondents will answer interview questions in a professional, competent manner. Nonetheless, by adopting the aforementioned procedures, it is expected that any bias or misinformation will be minimized.

If your research subjects are people known to you, for example, work colleagues or friends, then you need to be prepared to meet the claim that your work is vulnerable to bias. The findings from the sample e-Learning research case study are based, for the most part, on interviews of work colleagues (fellow academics). This is openly recognized in the discussion below, but, in addition, the researcher outlines how he intends to achieve objectivity and, therefore, trust in his findings:

Interviewing one's colleagues raises the issue of objectivity. Implementing a case study within one's place of employment has the comforting advantage of access to subjects. However, such a scenario brings with it problems that, if not managed properly, may hinder the research and endanger relationships between the researcher and the participants in the research project. There may be the concern expressed that 'how can a colleague, albeit one engaging in research, not be influenced by his prior knowledge of his fellow colleagues' views and bring such knowledge to bear when interpreting transcripts of interviews?' This indeed was a concern expressed by a colleague, and relates to the objectivity of the researcher. To minimize such an influence, the researcher adopted the following strategy: until he had secured all staff interviews and completed the transcripts, the researcher would refrain from attending any e-Learning seminars within Division X (to avoid directly or indirectly presenting his views of e-Learning or acquiring the views of his research subjects); after the transcription of interviews, staff names would be replaced by codes (Lecturer A, Lecturer B, Senior Member of Staff A, and so on); and a deliberate and significant time-gap created between the transcriptions and transcription analysis to further minimize the possibility of bias when interpreting staff views. Furthermore, as far as is practical, staff transcriptions will be edited to remove identifying comments. This may help allay any concerns that staff may have concerning their transcriptions, with the added benefit that they may speak more freely.

Still on the theme of reliability, the researcher now attempts to reduce fears that, while carrying out his interviews, his colleagues may have difficulty in perceiving him as a researcher rather than just a colleague:

> Another issue, connected to objectivity, is that it may prove more difficult for colleagues to view the researcher other than a colleague than it may be for the researcher to view current colleagues as research subjects. This is a danger that the researcher is aware of and will attempt to minimize by clarifying the researcher's role and by informing participants of the purpose of the research, the uses of the collected data and the manner in which participants could assist in the research. The fact that the researcher is recognized within Division X as a researcher with publications in the field may go some way to gaining the respect and trust of colleagues.

As you can see, what you have to do is confront openly any perceived limitation of your research methods (selected research strategy, site and sample selection, data collection issues, etc.) and associated problems, such as achieving objectivity in your findings. The aforementioned issues do not exhaust all the possible problems that you might encounter in your empirical work. For example, if you are new to implementing empirical research, like most students who embark on a major dissertation, then you might claim justifiably that your lack of experience in this area, and shortage of practical skills (e.g. in carrying out interviews, questionnaire design, data analysis, etc.) present a possible limitation in implementing your empirical research. If this is your first attempt at a dissertation, then it will be a learning experience, one where you will make mistakes (and hopefully learn from them). Nevertheless, you should not submit yourself as incompetent! Explain how your attendance at classes on research methods, sage advice from your supervisor, your own learned reading and, where appropriate, pilot testing have all contributed towards mitigating this apparent limitation.

Another potential barrier that might hinder the smooth implementation of your empirical work is the possibility that you may encounter difficulty in getting access to your research subjects when you want them – the answer may lie in the timing of your practical research and maintaining regular contact with those whom you want to 'research'. Too many students fail to appreciate how time flies. Naively, they leave their empirical research to the last minute and neglect to consider the possibility that their research subjects might be too busy to see them. As one student wrote in her dissertation:

> While carrying out the required research the author had to take into account the amount of time she had in which to collect the necessary data for analysis before the date of [submission for] the dissertation . . . However, while arranging interviews the interviewees often found it difficult to make time to take part in the interview as they were occupied with their own duties or unavailable for interviewing. This posed a problem for the author as she already had time constraints of her own to manage in order to complete the dissertation in time.

Another student made the same point:

> The time allocated for completion of this project was restricted to one academic year. One might think that this is a considerable length of time, however, given other priorities and commitments, the time left to conduct research was limited . . . as a consequence there was no time to research every aspect of the subject, therefore strategic decisions had to be made as to what was relevant . . . Moreover, there was no time to properly evaluate [sic] the work as it was being done, meaning that some relevant issues may have been overlooked.

Student complaints about lack of time are quite common, particularly as submission deadlines approach, and are usually evidence of a lack of planning and foresight on the part of the student. Year after year, tutors witness numerous dissertation students, at various levels, leaving their dissertation work to the stage where the best that the student can hope for is a basic pass. Plan your work from the start; as far as possible adhere to your anticipated milestones; do a bit of work on your dissertation every week; and keep in touch with your supervisor.

With respect to your intended empirical work, try and maintain contact with your research subjects, from the moment that they have agreed to participate in your research up until the moment you make use of them, or they will forget all about you! It is not uncommon for students to approach their supervisor with a hang-dog expression, complaining that the people who had agreed to be interviewed three months ago are no longer available or have changed their mind. Do not leave your empirical work to chance: be organized. And leave enough time to accommodate mishaps.

Summary of key points

- Your research methods chapter is where you describe the methods that you will use to implement your research and, importantly, explain the reasons behind your choices. An appropriate structure would cover: research strategy, data collection techniques, approach to data analysis, and acknowledged limitations of your work.
- The *research strategy* refers to your over-arching approach to your empirical research, and there are a number of tried and tested strategies to choose from, examples of which include: case study, survey, ethnographic, experimental, historical, action research, and grounded theory. You must *identify* your research strategy, *describe it* and *explain* why it is appropriate to your research.
- The question of whether your research is *quantitative* or *qualitative* in nature, or a mixture of both, depends not on your choice of research strategy alone but on the combination of your research strategy + research objectives + data collection techniques.
- *Sampling* is the process of selecting a portion of a target population. Sampling techniques available to you include: random sampling, simple random sampling, stratified sampling, cluster sampling, systematic sampling, quota sampling, and convenience sampling.
- *Positivist research* is research that is objective and independent of the observer and which can be measured and predicted. *Interpretative/phenomenological research*, on the other hand, accepts that there are many interpretations of phenomena and that these interpretations are time – and context – dependent.
- Your research work should be *valid* and *reliable. Valid* research is about the appropriateness of the choices you make in terms of your research strategy and data collection/analysis techniques pertaining to your research objectives. *Reliable* research refers to the trustworthiness of your research findings, which you achieve through transparency on how you implemented your research.
- In your sub-section on data collection techniques, you need to state from where you will get your data (a football stadium, employees from a number

of companies, or wherever), your sample size (number of experiments/ companies/people), your sampling technique (random, stratified, quota, convenience, etc.), and how you will extract your data (interviews, observation, questionnaires, tests, etc.). Justify your choices.

- A *framework for data analysis* is an outline of how you expect to analyse your collected data.
- Identify perceived limitations of your work and/or potential issues and explain what you have done to reduce those risks.

6

Writing up your findings

The general approach • The process of description, analysis and synthesis: an example

The general approach

The task of writing up your results is a necessary, if somewhat time-consuming and laborious, process. If you have worked out a way to analyse your results beforehand, then your job will be so much easier.

> **A common mistake by students**
>
> A common mistake by students is to write their chapter on research methods devoid of any reference to data analysis, with the result that when they eventually have the data in front of them they are not sure what to do with it!

Create a simple structure for your *findings* chapter. Have an uncomplicated title, such as 'Case Study Results' if you carried out a case study, or 'Survey Findings' if you implemented a survey, or the more generic 'Empirical Research Findings', or even 'Findings and Discussion'. The latter title captures the idea that you will describe and discuss your results. Better still, you could call your chapter 'Survey Findings: Description, Analysis and Synthesis', thus identifying the type of empirical research that you did – in this case, a survey – as well as informing the reader that you will partake in three main types of intellectual activity: a simple description of your results; discussion about what you found; and, finally, an integrative analysis of your empirical data against your Literature Review findings (i.e. the synthesis bit). Although your chapter title may give the impression that the content is purely about your empirical findings, this is not the case – yes, you are expected to report on the data that you collected but you are also expected to compare and contrast your empirical findings against what you discovered in your Literature Review, otherwise what was the point of initiating a Literature Review?

Give a brief introduction to your chapter – you should by now be well versed in writing an introduction to each of your chapters. Start by [a] reminding the reader of what you *set out to do*, followed by [b] a brief description of how *you intend approaching* the write-up of your empirical results. You should also [c] place your empirical research *in context*. For example, if your data were derived from a case study of an organization, then give some background information about that organization, as in the sample e-Learning case study:

> [a] **This chapter reveals** the results of the case study described in Chapter 3 Research Methods . . . The research concentrates on two groups of stakeholders: academic staff within Division X, located in the Inverclyde Business School (IBS) at Inverclyde University (IU) and recently involved in preparing teaching and learning material on an e-Learning environment and senior staff in Division X, IBS and ICU who have an influence on the implementation of e-Learning in the university, i.e. *elite* staff . . .
> [b] **The case study is approached in a highly structured way.** First, a description is provided of academic staff results, theme by theme . . . The gathering of empirical data for this research is based on a case study, to allow an analysis of real problems in **a set context.** Prior to a description and analysis of the case study results, a profile of related aspects of ICU will now be made **to set the study in context [c]** . . . It is in the context of these developments, self-perceptions, and aspirations in which the context of this study is implemented. It should be appreciated that universities are complex organizations and that the above is not an attempt to *explain* ICU nor describe fully its operation or culture, but merely to place the study in context . . . [d] The transcripts of the interviews for academic staff can be found in Appendix B; the transcripts from the senior staff interviews are in Appendix C.

Also, let the reader know [d] *in which Appendix* they will find evidence of your interviews, experiments, questionnaire responses, as in the example above: 'The transcripts of the interviews for academic staff can be found in Appendix B; the transcripts from the senior staff interviews are in Appendix C.'

The heart of the chapter on your empirical findings will revolve around the tasks of *description* (of your empirical data), *discussion/analysis* (of what you have described) and *synthesis* (of your discussed empirical results against your literature findings). Bogdan and Biklen (1982: 145) describe this process as 'working with data, organizing it, breaking it into manageable units, synthesizing it, searching for patterns, discovering what is important and what is to be learned, and deciding what you will tell others'. You cannot evaluate the worth of your research findings unless you have had an attempt at going through the intellectual exercise of description → analysis → synthesis.

If you recall Bloom's (1956) taxonomy of learning, you are being tested that you have the cognitive skills illustrated in his learning triangle (basic knowledge → comprehension → application → analysis → synthesis → evaluation); and the higher up his learning triangle you go, the more marks you get! Your ultimate goal is to show that you can *evaluate* what you are looking at with reference to your Literature Review + Empirical Findings. You need to describe your empirical data before you can discuss/analyse it; you need to have discussed/analysed your descriptions before you can synthesize your empirical results with your Literature Review findings. Only then can you evaluate the worth of your findings and decide if you have met your specific research objectives and, in turn, your overall research aim. The actual evaluation of your overall research work should appear in your Conclusion Chapter, not this one. Figure 6.1 captures the cyclical nature of writing up your empirical findings, culminating at some stage (usually in your concluding chapter) in a self-evaluation of your overall findings:

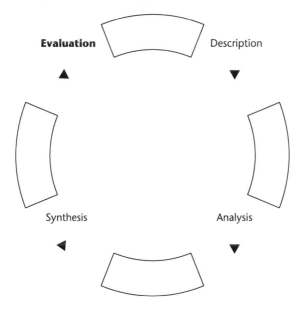

Figure 6.1 Process of description, analysis and synthesis leading to evaluation

Once you have carried out your description, analysis and synthesis (and leaving the overall evaluation to your final chapter, the Conclusion), it is good practice to provide a summary of your findings. Even here, if you are running short of words you can make the alternative decision to summarize your findings in your Conclusion chapter. This makes sense because if you summarize your findings in this chapter you will also find yourself having to repeat this summary, in whatever form, when you discuss your conclusions and recommendations in your final chapter. If you have plenty of words to spare, then there is no harm in doing both; if you are running close to your word count, then think strategically and put the summary of your findings in your Conclusion.

The process of description, analysis and synthesis: an example

To demonstrate data *description*, *analysis* and *synthesis* in practice, we will revisit the e-Learning case study, where two sets of university staff – academic staff and senior staff – were interviewed on aspects of e-Learning. The early stages of reporting on responses to questionnaires or interviews tend to yield basic information, with little to get your teeth into, as illustrated in the example interview question and answer:

Question 1A
The first question – Question 1A – was: '*The University's Strategic Planning Document makes reference to e-Learning targets and objectives. Do you know what these are?*'

Response
Seven of the eight members of the programme team replied 'No' and one member of staff answered 'Eh, to be honest with you, I don't. I know that there is some vague push for e-Learning but I'm not clear on the specifics.' Thus, no members of staff knew what the university's strategic objectives and associated targets were in relation to e-Learning.

It is only when you get deeper into your reporting that you can then begin to show cognitive skills beyond mere description. Suppose both sets of staff were asked the question: 'What, in your view, is the rationale behind the university's drive for e-Learning environments?' You record the responses from the academic staff as follows: Nonetheless, the early part of your empirical findings chapter will necessarily involve much basic description of your results, which you build up with cross-referencing of empirical data, as shown in the following example.

Question 3A
What, in your view, is the rationale behind the university's drive for e-Learning?

Response

Three members of staff viewed it as a cost-saving exercise. Two members of staff believed the university's interest in e-Learning was driven by their competitors and perhaps cosmetic. Two members of staff gave the combined reasons of efficient use of resources coupled with university image. One member of staff held a positive view, believing that the university management did not intend that e-Learning be seen as 'a replacement for traditional modes of delivery, but to complement traditional modes of delivery' and that there existed the potential for professional development initiatives for those 'who can't attend traditional face to face modes'.

Summarizing academic staff views as follows:

Of the eight respondents, only one viewed management intentions in a wholly positive light, with the majority suspicious that management were introducing e-Learning to make cost-savings or to 'look good' or a combination of both. Only one member of staff made any explicit reference to university management intentions as an attempt to 'enhance the student experience as well'.

Next, we could describe the responses from the senior staff to the same question. At this stage we might still only be engaged in simple description – the analysis and synthesis will come later. Note that the question number – labelled Question 3A for academic staff but Question 2X for senior staff – might be different because the number of questions, and type, might differ from one group to another. So, starting with:

Question 2X

What, in your view, is the rationale behind the university's drive for e-Learning environments?

Response

One respondent responded curtly: 'I don't know. But I know what the Business School's is.' Another did not answer the question directly other than to say that the university has 'a good rationale in terms of its vision for the future of where the University is to go and how e-Learning can support that', but added that 'what it hasn't considered is how it will embed e-Learning in the systems throughout the university'. One member of staff thought that 'there wasn't a big overall university picture' and that there were many perspectives on the subject. Emphasizing that he was presenting his own personal perspective, he conjectured that the rationale behind the university's drive for e-Learning was linked to student freedom of choice in terms of 'how, when, where, what to learn', in effect, issues related to flexibility of access and delivery.

Continuing with . . .

The above four senior staff then went on to suggest a university rationale for e-Learning. One member conjectured that he would like to think that it had reasons to do with 'effectiveness of learning', but suspected that the rationale was more to do with efficiency, specifically releasing staff from teaching duties to pursue research income and consultancy activities. A second member agreed that the rationale might be linked to efficiency – 'I can give you a rationale' – in making the university more cost-effective by enhancing quality and reducing costs at the same time. However, he made it clear that he did not agree with this rationale and that, contrary to this rationale, the quality/cost trade-off remains the same: 'I think all the evidence so far is that the quality–cost trade-off stays the same, em, in other words if you use e-Learning, if you invest in e-Learning you push quality up but you also push costs up . . . I don't believe it actually'.

The two other staff members cited the same two reasons behind the university's push for e-Learning: to compete with other universities engaging in e-Learning ('that competitive element, a need to go for a wider global market'; 'maintaining some degree of presence relative to other universities') and to implement the university's objective of wider access ('wider access in terms of outreach to more remote communities'; 'widen our inclusiveness and accessibility').

Building up your descriptions and cross-referencing of the data . . .

One member of staff explained the IBS's e-Learning strategy:

> '. . . we want to roll out Blackboard in a sequential way, year on year, eh, as the delivery mechanism, em, that we are now up to level 3 modules . . . So, level 3 modules will be rolled out next year . . . So that's part 1 of the strategy, to roll out with the, em, the framework. And secondly to broaden that, em, across all modules through a period of time. And thirdly, our strategy is to deepen our engagement with the VLE and with, with web-based learning, em, through, em, eh, further staff developments . . .'

In essence, the IBS plan is to, in the first instance, convert year 1 undergraduate modules onto the VLE software platform Blackboard; do the same with year 2 modules of the School framework, then years 3 (along with Master's programme modules) and 4. Currently, modules in years 1 and 2 of the undergraduate framework have been placed on Blackboard and year 3 and Master's (at the time of interview) was planned for Semester A of the academic year 2003–2004.

Another member of staff explained that Division X had no e-Learning strategy as such, but that the Division was implementing the university's Learning and Teaching Assessment Strategy (LTAS), 'and the LTAS plan has very clearly this kind of dimension of e-Learning within it, and that's quite implicit as well, you know this kind of moving responsibility to the student for learning etc.' He did add that although there was not an e-Learning strategy in Division X, the Divisional Plan had 'a number of objectives which relate specifically to e-Learning' and that he was in the process of creating an e-Learning Task Force. As well as the afore-mentioned activities, Division X was implementing the IBS's e-Learning strategy.

Although the descriptions above are quite prosaic, with no analysis, quotations have been included to colour and support the descriptive process. When you are describing raw data, particularly people's views on a topic, then it is also worthwhile to put together a summary of what you have described, particularly if there are salient points that you wish to highlight:

> No member of staff stated that they knew the rationale behind the university's drive for e-Learning. One respondent said categorically that he did not know, another respondent offered a view on the rationale without saying what she thought it was, and five others made it clear that they had a personal view on what it might be. Two staff suggested that the rationale may be about efficient use of resources (with one member suspecting this to be the unstated university rationale, and the other disagreeing with the logic of that rationale); two staff thought that it might concern the twin elements of competitiveness and student access; with one member of staff suggesting that the rationale was connected to student freedom of choice. Even where the staff offered a suggested rationale, their suggestions were varied.

There are various tools and techniques that you can use to describe and analyse your empirical findings, ranging from simple descriptive graphs, such as bar charts and tables, to more complicated statistical analysis. It all depends on the type of data that you have and what you want to do with that data. If your research is essentially qualitative in nature, then using themes (as in the case study example) coupled with basic descriptive tools will suffice; if your research is mainly quantitative in nature, then you will exploit quantitative instruments for measurement and analysis.

Once you have assembled a certain level of description, you can then enrich your work by offering intelligent comment, i.e. analysis. You can now take the opportunity to show off your analytical skills by expressing an opinion on the views given by both sets of staff. In this case the analysis occurs through the vehicle of cross-referencing which, for the purpose of highlighting, appears in **bold**:

> Academic staff were asked a similar question. Three academic staff members believed it to be a cost-saving exercise; two that the drive for

e-Learning was driven by their competitors (and perhaps cosmetic); two that it was linked to efficient use of resources and university image; and one that it was to enhance the student learning experience. **The replies from the elite staff and the academic staff suggest that neither the senior staff nor the teaching staff had a consistent idea amongst their own group of the university's rationale for e-Learning. However, some staff produced suggestions that coincided into two similar groupings (competitiveness, cost-cutting/efficiency); but elite staff members also introduced the idea of accessibility (not mentioned by academic staff) and academic staff offered a less charitable gloss on the university's reasons for advancing e-Learning. Also of interest is that whereas five of the eight academic staff viewed cost-cutting/efficiency as a reason for the university wishing to engage e-Learning, only two elite staff believed the rationale was linked to cost-cutting/efficiency.**

In effect, when you are *analysing* your empirical data, you are offering comment which you support with reference to your described data.

Finally, findings from the Literature Review on the forces driving e-Learning can then be recalled with a view to synthesizing theory with practice, adding another layer of understanding and depth:

The literature review highlighted a number of forces driving e-Learning, with the main drivers reflecting a desire to improve *quality*, *flexibility* and *effectiveness* of educational delivery (with the latter referring to value for money), all within the context of the Government's target of achieving substantial increases in the student population (Dearing 1997; Jung 2000; Farrell 2001; Epic 2002; Department of Education and Skills 2003). Only one member of staff interviewed (an academic) referred to enhanced quality as a driver, with the other staff, elite and academic, highlighting either flexibility of delivery (e.g. on and off campus) or cost-cutting/efficient use of resources as primary motivators for Inverclyde University adopting e-Learning. The primary focus for introducing new technologies in an educational environment ought to be to enhance the student learning experience, i.e. improve the quality of educational delivery. Indeed, SHEFC (2003) warn against introducing e-Learning as a way to cut costs, reflecting that it can cost six times as much to develop an e-Learning programme than a traditional programme. Similarly, a report for the CIPD (Sloman and Rolph 2003) echoed SHEFC's views by stating that if institutions believe that e-learning will automatically save them costs then they will be disappointed.

It is interesting to note that in the interviews above, it was mainly the academic staff that saw the rationale behind e-Learning as a cost-cutting/ efficiency exercise, not the elite staff. Perhaps this reflects the earlier point that an e-Learning strategy is important, not only to convey an institution's direction in e-Learning, but also to explain the rationale behind its usage, and so removing misconceptions.

As you can see, at each stage of description/analysis/synthesis, you are build-ing up a thick account of your results. It is a tedious process but one that is necessary, if you want to do justice to your research.

Everything you do in your dissertation leads to your concluding chapter – Conclusions and Recommendations – wherein you collate your work in summary form, underline your main conclusions and, based on these, make pertinent recommendations. This means that your concluding chapter is a crucial one because it is there where you capture the essence of your research output, achieving what supervisors call 'cyclical closure'. So do not dismiss your final chapter lightly: it is an integral part of your dissertation.

Summary of key points

- Create an appropriate chapter heading: 'Case Study Results' or 'Survey Findings' or 'Empirical Research Findings' or 'Findings and Discussion' or 'Case Study Findings: Description, Analysis and Synthesis' or 'Survey Findings: Description, Analysis and Synthesis', etc.
- Write a brief introduction to your 'Findings and Discussion' chapter: (a) reminding the reader of the data that you set out to collect; (b) identifying how you will write up your findings (this should be based on the *framework for data analysis* you outlined in your research methods chapter); (c) placing your practical research in context; and (d) naming the appendix/appendices wherein you have placed your questionnaire(s)/responses, etc.
- Your empirical findings should be *described*, *analysed* and *synthesized*.
- *Description* is a simple process, entailing the basic reporting and chronicling of empirical results (who said what, etc.).
- *Analysis* is intelligent interpretation of the aforementioned descriptions.
- *Synthesis* occurs when you compare and contrast your empirical findings against your Literature Review findings.

7

Concluding your dissertation

What's in a Conclusion? • Research objectives: summary of findings and conclusions • Recommendations • Contribution to knowledge • Self-reflection

What's in a Conclusion?

By this stage you are probably mentally exhausted and sick of the sight of your dissertation. Besides, you may have exams to concentrate on or holidays to arrange or employment opportunities to explore. Reject the temptation, however appealing, to scribble down a quick ending to allow you to submit your work and finally see the back of it. It is at this stage where you need to make a final push and finish with a flourish. If your concluding chapter is epitomized by unstructured and ill-disciplined rambling, then you will leave your dissertation marker with the clear impression that you lacked the necessary skills to compose an acceptable Conclusion and/or you lost interest in your own work. A Conclusion is the final big piece of the dissertation jigsaw and your supervisor/marker is expecting it to contain certain things.

So, what is in a Conclusion? Quite a lot, actually! Here is what is expected, as a minimum, in your Conclusion:

• Research Objectives: Summary of Findings and resulting Conclusions
• Recommendations.

If you omit either of these elements, then you are missing out on potential marks. If, in the Conclusion, a student has not summarized his work or informed the reader what he has concluded as a result of his research or outlined his way forward, then he may lose substantial marks. So include these things and avoid throwing away marks. Doing so shows discipline and a structured mind, i.e. a research-based approach to rounding off your dissertation.

One other point: for most postgraduate dissertations you are not expected to contribute *new knowledge*, so you can normally omit this requirement. The exception is the PhD. For PhD students (a route you may wish to take after your Master's), an acceptable structure for a Conclusion could be:

- Research Objectives: Summary of Findings and Conclusions
- Recommendations
- Contribution to knowledge.

Additionally, regardless of the type and level of dissertation, inserting a sub-section on self-reflection adds a little something different to a dissertation. As with most chapters in your dissertation, you should also begin with a short introduction. A solid structure for a dissertation could look like:

- Introduction
- Research Objectives: Summary of Findings and Conclusions
- Recommendations
- [Contribution to knowledge]
- Self-reflection.

Although the sub-section in square brackets – *Contribution to knowledge* – is directed at those students studying for a PhD, it may be that, even as a Master's student, you have indeed produced new knowledge, in which case by all means include a sub-section on 'Contribution to knowledge', but be warned, this is a rare event for non-PhD student work.

It is acceptable to combine some of the above sub-sections (e.g. 'Recommendations and Implementation', 'Self-Reflection and Contribution to Knowledge'), particularly if you are running close to your dissertation word limit. Very often it is just a matter of personal choice.

If you did not cover the limitations of your work in your Research Methods chapter then you can include it here, giving you an acceptable Conclusion chapter, the structure of which is shown in Figure 7.1.

Advice is now offered on how to write up each of these sub-sections. The sub-section 'Limitations' was covered in the research methods chapter, so will not be covered here in any great depth.

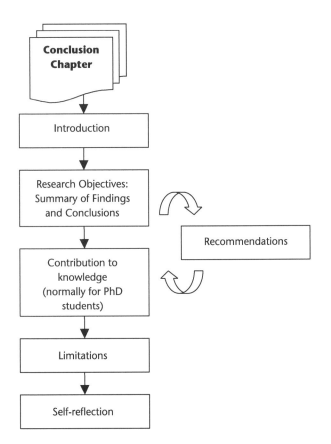

Figure 7.1 Structure for Conclusion chapter

Research objectives: summary of findings and conclusions

Prior to summarizing your findings, it is good practice to present a brief introduction at the start of your Conclusion, before your first sub-section 'Research
Objectives: Summary of Findings and Conclusions', reminding the reader of
your initial research objectives, and setting out what you intend to cover in
your Conclusion chapter. If your reader has an idea of the topics that you will
be covering in your Conclusion, then she will be more at ease. Keep things
simple, using matter-of-fact language. To begin with, remind the reader of
your overall research aim, together with the individual objectives that you set
out to meet in order to achieve your overall research aim: 'The overall aim of

this research was to advance an understanding of . . . The specific research objectives were . . .'. Then list your objectives. For example:

The overall aim of this research was to advance an understanding of e-Learning in the university environment, particularly in relation to academic staff preparation issues. The specific research objectives were, within the context of higher education, to:

1   *Identify* the forces driving e-Learning and the barriers to the successful delivery of e-Learning programmes.
2   *Evaluate critically* models and frameworks relevant to supporting academic staff in coping with e-Learning.
3   *Explore* staff stakeholder views and practices related to e-Learning preparation, including drivers and barriers to e-Learning.
4   *Formulate* recommendations on staff preparation issues.

Next, state the sub-sections that your Conclusion will cover. You are not expected to *discuss* the actual content of these sub-sections at this stage. Just let the reader know what they are, for example:

This section will revisit the research objectives above, summarize the findings of this research work and offer conclusions based on the findings. The previous chapter – Case Study Results – was large and requires to be summarized, hence the summary in this chapter. Recommendations for future research will be discussed, in terms of how to progress this research study. Importantly, the contribution of this research to the development of e-Learning will be clarified. Additionally, a section reflecting on the research process that has been undertaken is included. By adopting this structure it is intended that the research work will be concluded so as to reflect on whether or not the objectives stated at the start of this research have been met, including consideration of the value of this study. Guidance will be offered on how this research work can be progressed.

The sub-section 'Research Objectives: Summary of Findings and Conclusions' is a simple matter. All that is required is that you answer two straightforward questions:

1 As a result of your Literature Review *and* empirical research (if you did both), what did you find out in relation to your individual research objectives?
2 What conclusions have you come to?

You do not need to go through all the swirling and interlinking analysis that you went through in the write-up of your data collection. No – at this stage of your dissertation you can put aside your debating skills. Information rather than persuasion is the goal of your concluding chapter. *Informing* – rather than *persuading* – the reader of your summary findings, your conclusions, your research limitations, and your recommendations.

In the sub-section 'Research Objectives: Summary of Findings and Conclusions' you are, in effect, writing a summary of the work you carried out to fulfil each of your research objectives; and at the end of each of these summaries you are coming to some sort of conclusion about your work. Think of 'conclusions' as key points you wish to make about the findings for each of your research objectives. So, when you write about what you found out for, say, your first research objective, you then make a *key point* that you think captures what your findings are telling you in relation to that research objective. You then approach your other research objectives in the same way: summarize your findings for each objective, ending each time with a key point. Your structure for the sub-section 'Research Objectives: Summary of Findings and Conclusions' could take the following shape:

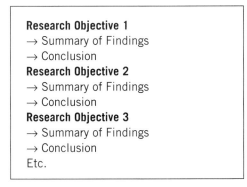

Research Objective 1
→ Summary of Findings
→ Conclusion
Research Objective 2
→ Summary of Findings
→ Conclusion
Research Objective 3
→ Summary of Findings
→ Conclusion
Etc.

For example, if you were the researcher involved in the e-Learning example, did you 'identify the forces driving e-Learning and barriers to the successful delivery of e-Learning programmes' (objective 1) and, if so, what did you find out from your Literature Review and your empirical work? What 'models and framework relevant to supporting academic staff in coping with e-Learning' (objective 2) did you examine and what were your findings? Similarly, what were the 'staff stakeholder views and practices related to e-Learning' (objective 3)? If you have a research objective that is phrased in terms of making recommendations as a result of your work, as in objective 4 of the e-Learning example ('formulate recommendations on staff preparation issues'), then this objective would be addressed when you get to the Recommendations sub-section within your Conclusion chapter.

As described above, a convenient way to tackle your summary is to create separate headings in your 'Research Objectives: Summary of Findings and Conclusions' chapter that cover each of your individual research objectives, and under each heading summarize what you found out related to that research objective, ending with relevant conclusions. Such a structure, related to the e-Learning example, might look like:

5. CONCLUSION

(brief intro)

5.1 Research Objectives: Summary of Findings and Conclusions

    5.1.1 Research Objective 1: e-Learning Drivers and Barriers

        → Summary

        → Conclusion

    5.1.2 Research Objective 2: Models and Frameworks

        → Summary

        → Conclusion

    5.1.3 Research Objective 3: Staff Stakeholder Views and Practices

        → Summary

        → Conclusion

Fleshing out Research Objective 1 above, to illustrate the structure in practice:

Research Objective 1: e-Learning Drivers and Barriers
The literature identified the main reasons why universities have become involved in e-Learning: external pressures from government to accommodate greater student numbers; wider access; flexible delivery; competition; access to global markets; use resources prudently; and because of the assumed inherent benefits to staff and students (enhancing the educational environment). Yet, in practice, the picture is not so clear. In practice, as evidenced in this case study, those in charge of shaping e-Learning in an institution (elite staff) may not have a firm collective view of why they are introducing e-Learning (other than to be viewed as 'modern' by potential students and be different from their competitors); and that academic staff, as in this case study, may hold an erroneous view of why their institution is pushing e-Learning (cost-cutting exercise, a view the elite staff were at pains to dismiss).

Continuing with . . .

Similarly, whereas elite staff held that the main benefit of e-Learning to academic staff was the opportunity for them to become reflective practitioners, academic staff either did not see any benefits for them or were concerned or cautious. Both sets of staff identified similar benefits of e-Learning to students (revolving around flexible access), but academic staff were not convinced that these benefits would materialize. In terms of drivers for, and benefits of, e-Learning, it is clear that a major discrepancy can occur between theory and practice, and between different stakeholders, with elite stakeholders having a positive view of the impact of e-Learning, and those who have to implement e-Learning, academic staff, having a cynical view of elite stakeholder intentions.

Adding . . .

The main conclusion, and lesson, that can be drawn from this research on these issues – *forces driving e-Learning* – is not any dispute of what these forces are (for they can differ between countries, and indeed between institutions, and there exists much literature to educate those interested), but rather, **that [Conclusion 1] a lack of communication is at the heart of much of the confused picture for the reason behind why an institution wishes to integrate e-Learning into their environment and the perceived benefits to the different stakeholders.** In this case study, elite staff were unsure of why their university was interested in e-Learning and, furthermore, academic staff misunderstood elite staff intentions. Such misunderstandings may be complicated further by imperatives to integrate e-Learning into teaching environments without the rationale being discussed with, or explained to, academic staff, as in this case study.

Followed by your findings on the barriers to e-Learning . . .

What conclusions can this research come to regarding barriers to the successful delivery of e-learning progammes? There are many potential barriers that can impede e-Learning in a university environment (ranging from fear of high costly failure, inadequate IT infrastructure, opposition to distance learning through globalization, job insecurity, intellectual property rights, perceived poor progression rates, and so on) but a main barrier identified in the literature was a lack of pedagogical training for academic staff. In this case study the main barriers to academic staff becoming involved in e-Learning were inadequate training on e-learning *and* lack of time. Although the academic staff under study contributed to a blended e-Learning environment, they did so because they were paid and also because they were instructed to do so. Internal barriers were discouraging, such as the compulsory manner in which e-Learning was implemented and suspicion over management intentions, as well as lack of confidence in IT support and lack of confidence in their students to cope with e-Learning; but, nevertheless, academic staff remained interested. Academic staff 'buy-in' is crucial to success in e-Learning, something recognized by elite staff. Most of the academic staff were getting involved in e-Learning where they are told to get involved, and so, to that extent, barriers identified by the literature review and academic staff were not preventing the delivery of e-Learning within the institution. However, it then becomes an issue of what type of e-Learning is being delivered, particularly when academic staff complain of a lack of time to get involved in any meaningful way and admit to not understanding what e-Learning involves, or how to use it to best advantage. This may help partly explain why the literature laments that e-Learning is very much fragmented and piecemeal, pursued by isolated 'e-nthusiasts', and not mainstream academia.

which you can then summarize as follows:

The lesson of this case study appears to be, with respect to barriers and motivation, that e-Learning ought not to be viewed as a natural part of being a professional teacher to be done in the tutor's own time; on the contrary, e-Learning is not a simple piece of technology, like word-processing, but a new way of teaching and learning, and so staff require guidance as well as time to learn about e-Learning. **The conclusion that can be drawn from this research on barriers to e-Learning [Conclusion 2] is that two main barriers hindering academic staff in meaningful and voluntary involvement in e-Learning programmes are a lack of time to learn about e-Learning (and prepare associated teaching material) and a lack of pedagogical training on e-Learning.**

You then repeat the above process for each of your research objectives: summarize your Literature Review findings and your empirical research, ending, in each case, with a conclusion (or conclusions, as in the above example). You can, if you wish, provide an additional (overarching) summary statement, a final paragraph in your sub-section 'Research Findings: Summary of Findings and Conclusions' that looks at your work in the round. Or you may introduce an unexpected conclusion, something that you did not set out to study but which became apparent through your research:

There is one other, unexpected, conclusion that this research work has uncovered, and that is that **although there is no agreed definition of e-Learning among e-Learning gurus, nonetheless the absence of one at a local, institutional level is a hindrance to meaningful discussion of e-Learning itself.** The Literature Review showed that e-Learning definitions varied widely, that there was no consistent definition and that some prominent figures in e-Learning concluded that any attempt to provide an absolute definition was an impossible task ('herding cats', 'comparing apples to oranges', etc.). This may be true but during the case study staff were repeatedly peppering their responses with phrases such as 'well, depends on what you mean by e-Learning'. A small sample of such phrases made by both groups of staff – elite staff and academic staff – are listed below, to illustrate this very point:

- *I think it depends what you mean by e-Learning here, because I'm not quite clear what people mean when [they] say e-Learning;*

- *Genuinely, I don't quite know what e-Learning means any more;*
- *does depend on the dimension of what is a blended approach . . .;*
- *if by e-Learning you mean . . .;*
- *there is e-Learning and e-Learning . . .;*
- *I'm not sure what that means precisely;*
- *Again, it depends on what our definition of e-Learning is;*
- *I am not quite sure how we would define that.*

This suggests that a lack of a definition of e-Learning may present an initial barrier to progressing discussions about e-Learning, and that definitions are not abstract, academic activities unrelated to practical concerns. It may not be important on the actual definition of e-Learning that an institution decides upon, but that one is required is evidenced from above.

Or you may take the occasion to remind the reader that your research, although solid, has some limitations and that your work has to be placed in this context:

The conclusions have to be viewed in terms of a caveat. The conclusions are based on an extensive review of related literature and a case study, which means that the conclusions are linked to these two sources only. One is not generalizing that what was concluded in this research automatically applies to all other institutions in higher education. Instead this research is appealing to the concept of *relatability*: that what was researched in this study will be of interest to other researchers and institutions interested in e-Learning and that it will add, incrementally, to the patchwork of research in e-Learning.

Ending with. . . .

Another limitation, is that student perspectives on e-Learning have not been explored. Such empirical data would have added further richness to the study, but this would have compromised the focus of the research and perhaps made the burden of work unmanageable (the decision to include so many elite staff, although of enormous benefit to the study, did increase dramatically the workload).

Or you may decide to sign off with a statement on how much you enjoyed your research work, ending with a pithy quotation:

This research was hugely enjoyable and worthwhile. One, though, cannot be complacent, and should appreciate that research is a slow, deliberate process and that the outcomes from research studies may not impact on other researchers and institutions for significant periods. As Professor

Richard Sennett (1998: 96) observed: 'It takes institutions a long time to digest the technologies they ingest.'

After you have summarized your research findings, and made concluding observations, you are normally required to indicate what happens next in terms of addressing perceived issues or taking your research forward.

Recommendations

Normally your tutor will want to know what recommendations you are making as a result of your research work. It would be very odd indeed if you finished your dissertation and you offered the reader no advice on what you think should happen next, so much so that you might lose a significant number of marks if you omit this sub-section in your concluding chapter. Having said that, some institutions do not require their dissertation students to make recommendations in relation to their research findings, so check with your institution's regulations on whether or not you are required to do so.

A common mistake by students

A common mistake by students is to hide their recommendations by embedding them in a sentence or two within an obscure paragraph. If the marker has to look hard to find them then you are at risk of, once again, losing marks. Either have a full sub-section in your Conclusion headed 'Recommendations' or group together an obvious collection of paragraphs dealing with the implications of your completed research. Remember, though, if one of your research objectives referred explicitly to making recommendations, as in objective 4 of the e-Learning example case study ('Formulate recommendations on staff preparation issues'), then it is best that you devote a properly headed sub-section to your recommendations.

There are two types of recommendations that you can make: recommendations specific to the evidence presented in your study; and suggestions for future research. If your dissertation was on how governments make the decision to go to war with other countries and that your work concluded – based on a case study of the UK and the 2003 invasion of Iraq – that there was scant regard both to democratic process and the need for concrete evidence of the case for war, then you might recommend that, in the future, procedures are in place to ensure Parliament has a crucial role to play before war is declared and that part of that process necessarily involves the independent collection and analysis of any data related to such a decision. In terms of future research, you might propose that other researchers examine why some countries, under the same pressures, decide not to go to war.

One way to deal with your recommendations is to link them to your previous conclusions (which in turn were linked to each of your specific research objectives). For example, if one wished to make recommendations based on the e-Learning case study, then one would look to see what conclusions were made for each of the research objectives, and then write recommendations specific to those individual research objective conclusions. If you adopt this approach, make sure that you remind the reader what your conclusions were so that they do not have to keep flipping back over your dissertation to find them. Looking at the conclusion for objective 1 of the e-Learning example case study, related recommendations could develop as follows:

> Conclusion 1 stated that **a lack of communication is at the heart of much of the confused picture for the reason behind why an institution wishes to integrate e-Learning into their environment and the perceived benefits to the different stakeholders.** From Conclusion 1, the first recommendation to be made is that elite staff should be aware of: why they are introducing e-Learning, the external factors that are influencing their university's decision to engage e-Learning, the benefits to staff and students; and, importantly, they need to ensure that the e-Learning strategy is clear, justified (in terms of rationale) and communicated to those charged with integrating e-Learning in to the teaching and learning environment, i.e. academic staff.

Also, try and explain the benefits of your recommendation(s), i.e. do not just present the reader with an unexplained recommendation, unless you feel that what you are recommending is blatantly obvious and requires no explanation. Explaining the above recommendation:

> This recommendation would have a number of benefits. Firstly, elite staff themselves would understand collectively why e-Learning is important to the university and what the benefits are to the institution as a whole, as well as to staff and students, and so they would be in a much better position to win staff 'buy-in'. Communicating the rationale – whatever it turns out to be – to academic staff would remove any misunderstandings of university intentions and may help avoid cynical guesswork. Further, a university's e-Learning strategy should be clearly headed and be easy to find (whether it be on a website, or contained in university strategic planning documents) and not buried under obscure objectives such as, for example, 'Campus Development'. In effect, e-Learning strategy, rationale and benefits should be visible and communicated to management and teaching staff.

You are entitled to group recommendations together, as follows:

> From conclusion 2, it is recommended that to encourage staff to become involved in e-Learning, a reward in the form of time to prepare for e-Learning, both in terms of studying e-Learning and preparing e-Learning material, is made available. And, importantly, from Conclusions 2 and 3 – related to pedagogical training – there follows the recommendation that academic staff receive meaningful pedagogical training, in a structured way, that is aimed specifically at preparing academic staff for integrating e-Learning into their teaching, covering the topics: benefits of e-Learning, practical advice on the changing role of staff and students, including supporting infrastructures, a well as guidance on what works and what does not.

Where possible, try and show your recommendations diagrammatically. And do not neglect to explain your diagram (a common failing by students). For example:

> The recommendations are diagrammatically represented in Figure 7.2. This diagram conveys the essence of the conclusions and recommendations, underlining that each of the recommendations flow to provide a sensible

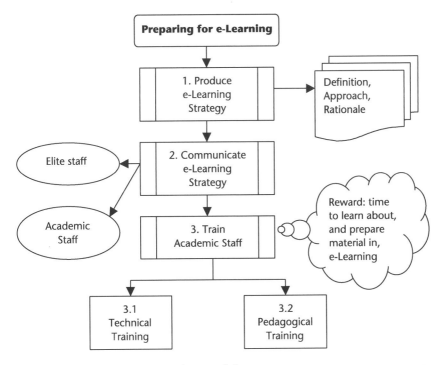

Figure 7.2 e-Learning preparation model

framework which universities can adopt to prepare their academic staff for e-Learning. First, a university should develop its e-Learning strategy. This strategy should be readily accessible to staff, supported by a local definition of the term e-Learning, details of the approach to be adopted (e.g. voluntary, blended, etc.), including a rationale of why the university wishes to become involved in e-Learning. Next, this strategy should be communicated to all elite staff with a part to play in shaping the direction of e-Learning. Then, the strategy should be communicated to academic staff. Following that, academic staff should receive training on e-Learning. This research showed that two types of training were necessary to prepare academic staff for e-Learning: technical training (to cope with the software platform to be used, as well as to cover necessary computer skills); and training on e-Learning pedagogy. There was a great deal of evidence to show that technical training predominated and that pedagogical training to help staff prepare for e-Learning was largely omitted. Staff should also be given time to engage in e-Learning activities.

The above recommendations are examples of the first type of recommendations, ones that originate from your specific research findings. Remember that you can also make more general recommendations, based on possible avenues for future research. To help you handle this type of recommendation, ask yourself the question: 'If I had to recommend to someone else – another student – who was interested in picking up where I left of, how would I advise him on how to progress my work?' You are really asking yourself to reflect on the second type of recommendation: recommendation(s) for future research. You do not need to go into convoluted detail for this type of recommendation, just a sentence or two might suffice (e.g. 'Although thorough research has been conducted for this project, there are other related areas of study that could benefit this work in cybercrime [if that was your dissertation area]. For example, further research could focus on areas that were touched on only briefly in this dissertation, such as legislative or technological developments in the context of cybercrime, . . .')

Finally, you might want to offer advice on how to implement your specific recommendations (a common issue at a viva):

Another recommendation concerns the implementation of the model discussed. The culture of an organization can impact on staff development and on how a model can be received. For example, this study illustrated that some teaching staff were resistant to change, others were amenable, whereas others, still, were cynical but interested in e-Learning. Similarly, senior staff exhibited different types of traits towards staff development: for example, some held the view that it was part of the tutor's job to engage in e-Learning and that a tutor should not be rewarded for doing so, while others believed that staff should be rewarded. These traits, or *leanings*, were reflected throughout a number of themes, from views on e-Learning strategy, to the benefits of e-Learning, through to motivational issues, perhaps demonstrating different cultural stances by the various stakeholders. Also, at the risk of generalizing, this study showed that the Inverclyde Business School policy was to impose e-Learning on subordinate departments while, according to elite staff, other parts of the university had a more liberal attitude. To offer an improved chance of the model being adopted successfully, it would be fruitful to revisit the university under study and, applying a framework of organizational behaviour, try and determine the detail of the various cultures in operation at Inverclyde University. A formal understanding of the culture (or cultures) of an institution by the deliberate mapping of cultural traits against a credible behavioural framework would allow the proposed model to be implemented in a way that was appropriate to different cultures within a university.

To reflect the importance of making recommendations in a Master's dissertation, students often call their final chapter 'Conclusions and Recommendations', rather than simply 'Conclusions'. Regardless of the title of your concluding chapter, central to a praiseworthy sub-section on recommendations are a number of elements, *vis.*:

• You base your recommendations on your research conclusions.
• You explain, where you think it is necessary, your recommendations.
• You present them diagrammatically, where convenient.
• You offer advice on how to implement your recommendations.

Figure 7.3 may help you to remember these salient points.

A common mistake by students

A common mistake by students is to produce recommendations 'out of the blue', i.e. recommendations that have no or little obvious link to their research conclusions. If you follow the aforementioned advice, you should avoid that mistake.

Contribution to knowledge

It is unusual for MSc./M.Litt./MPhil. postgraduate students to be challenged on how their work has *contributed to new knowledge*. Usually such a requirement is reserved for a special type of postgraduate dissertation: the PhD. If you are

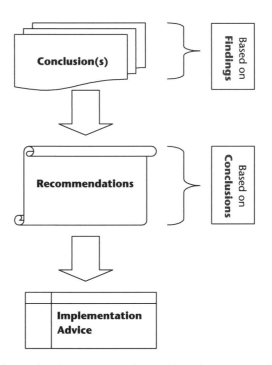

Figure 7.3 Relationship between conclusion(s) and recommendations

studying for a PhD, then you will need to confront the question of how your research has enhanced existing knowledge. If you are studying for a Master's but wish to progress your work to PhD level, or if you believe that your Master's work is exceptional, then you should understand how to answer the question: 'So, what's different about your work?' One way to tackle this question is to have a sub-section in the concluding chapter devoted to how your work has contributed to the field of x, y or z. 'Contribution to knowledge' is as good a title as any. But how do you deal with this issue?

Let us look at what a 'contribution to knowledge' means. Implicit is the idea that you are required to make an *original* contribution to knowledge, that there is something unique about aspects of your work, either what you studied, or how you researched something, or the specific problems that you addressed, or the angle from which you approached a subject area, or the light that you have shed in a rarely researched subject, and so on. Doing the same research, in the same way, and coming to the same conclusions as others is unlikely to be viewed as making an (original) contribution to knowledge.

However, it is almost impossible to produce *completely* unique research. In some way, however distant, original work owes much to what has gone before. Even Albert Einstein's work on relativity was built on the shoulders of giants. Do not panic that you might be expected to invent a new branch of physics or emerge with the meaning of life. Here lies the clue to managing your approach to writing about your contribution to knowledge: articulate how your research compares and contrasts with research done by others in your field, eliciting what is *different* about your work.

Be bold. Do not try and avoid the issue of your contribution. Meet the matter head on: 'How has this research work contributed to knowledge? In terms of . . .'. There are two areas where you can look for an original contribution to knowledge: in your Literature Review and in your empirical research. For example, if in your Literature Review you explored a facet of an important subject area that had hitherto been neglected or treated superficially, or erroneously, and your detailed study of secondary sources revealed new insights, then you can claim to have made an original contribution to knowledge. In which case, say so:

> The review of literature made it clear that e-Learning usage is fragmentary in the world of education and that there is an acute lack of in-depth research of e-Learning practices. This study has redressed that anomaly in a number of valuable ways. First, the review of literature provides a critical investigation of e-Learning theory pertinent to institutions, dovetailing into a critique of guidelines and frameworks as they relate to preparing academic staff for e-Learning. Knowledge derived from this review of literature can educate and further inform debate on the drivers and barriers to becoming involved in e-Learning (too often, literature uncritically lists drivers and barriers, failing to give a more rounded, research-based picture). Second, . . .

Your main contribution to knowledge, however, probably lies in your empirical work. It is less common, although not unheard of, for the Literature Review to be the principal source of your original contribution. If your experiment/survey/case study/action research/etc. is unique, then you could be making an original contribution to knowledge. Even if you do the same type of study as someone else, you still might be making an original contribution to knowledge. For example, suppose that a previous researcher implemented a survey looking at student debt. Suppose further, that his study was done in the USA. You use the same, or very similar, survey questions, but your target population is UK students. Your work compares and contrasts the two sets of results, producing new knowledge. At a simple level, even if you think up, for example, a case study from scratch, designing your own questions and selecting a specific target population, then it is statistically unlikely that someone else has carried out the *exact* same study as you. So, if your empirical work is unique then say why that is the case, as in the example:

> The empirical research work is unique: no other researcher has carried out a study of such depth within Inverclyde University, interviewing elite staff on strategic e-Learning issues and academic staff on e-Learning preparation, including issues surrounding drivers and barriers to e-Learning. The

lack of empirical data to support research theory was recognized as a particular failing in much of the current e-Learning literature. In that respect this research offers an insight into the views of two important university stakeholder groups on e-Learning that other institutions can relate to and learn from, allowing practice to be fed back into theory. The richness of material provided is, without doubt, fascinating. The themes addressed, in terms of their collectivity, are unique in one case study in e-Learning: e-Learning strategy, drivers, barriers, preparation, IT infrastructure, academic staff motivation, and future directions. The findings help in understanding issues related to these themes, and provide other researchers with a unique spotlight on two different types of stakeholders within an institution.

One other source of evidence to support your 'contribution to knowledge', other than your Literature Review and your actual practical work, can be found in your recommendations. It is likely that your recommendations contain proposals that are different in some respects from what has been produced before. If, for example, you have developed some sort of model or paradigm which you believe, if implemented, can resolve a problem that you identified earlier, then your model/paradigm itself becomes part of your original contribution to knowledge. Imagine that in the e-Learning case study example, two models were produced in the Recommendations sub-section: a Pedagogical Training Framework as well as an e-Learning Preparation Model. These models could be argued as making an important contribution to knowledge:

> The specific e-Learning models produced at the end of this research – the *e-Learning Preparation Model* and the *Pedagogical Training Framework* – encapsulate what needs to be done to encourage academic staff to engage meaningfully with e-Learning initiatives, ranging from the need to develop an e-Learning strategy that is clear, defines e-Learning, and justifies the rationale for introducing e-Learning and the approach adopted, to the communication of this strategy to elite staff and academic staff, and the crucial importance of pedagogical training on specific areas. In effect, a collective framework has been created that is specifically devoted to e-Learning preparation and based on in-depth research. This has been a highly successful piece of research with many points of learning for both theory into practice and practice into theory, resulting in a significant contribution to knowledge.

An obvious way to show your contribution to knowledge is to identify what other researchers have done and how your work builds on theirs; but importantly in what respects your work differs:

> How has this research made a contribution to knowledge? To date, the work produced by other researchers has concentrated on . . . This research,

on the other hand, differs in the following respects . . . The importance of this work, compared to what has been produced hitherto, lies in . . .

It would also be worthwhile, prior to your viva (if you are subject to one) to attend a conference – or if you cannot afford that, then try and get hold of the conference proceedings – and obtain up-to-date evidence that continues to offer support on the need for your research. For example:

At the recent Ed-Media 2004 Conference (attended by this researcher), Zellweger (2004: 161) complained that anecdotal advice can be found on how to use e-Learning in universities but that 'so far there is a lack of systematized scientific knowledge'. The lack of methodical research into e-Learning in Higher Education continues to this day to be an area of concern, but this research study, by adopting a highly disciplined and structured research-based approach to acquiring knowledge on e-Learning, has made an important and unique contribution, as discussed above, to an understanding of e-Learning in Higher Education. As more researchers adopt a research-based approach to e-Learning, then less will we hear the sentiments expressed by concerned researchers such as Zellweger.

Finally, if you have published aspects of your research in journals or conference proceedings then that in itself can support the claim that you are making a contribution to knowledge:

Furthermore, research publications produced as a result of this research have contributed to the field of e-Learning in that the opportunity to publish and discuss e-Learning issues with one's peers has not only engendered fruitful debate but also allowed other researchers to have access to research deemed by conference committees as making a contribution to the e-Learning academic community. These publications are listed below:

1. Burns, J. (2004). 'Students are not the only ones who need Guidance on e-Learning', in *Proceedings of the AACE Ed-Media 2004 Conference*, Lugano, Switzerland, June.
2. Burns, J. (2003). 'Toward a Conceptual Framework for the Development of Online Learning Systems', in *Proceedings of the AACE Ed-Media 2003 Conference*, Honolulu, Hawaii, June.
3. Burns, J. (2003). 'Identifying and capturing knowledge for website usage: a platform for progress', in *International Journal of Electronic Business*, 1(3): 225–236.
4. Burns, J. (2002). 'The Drive for Virtual Environments in Higher Education: University Initiatives and the Need for Student Support Infrastructures', in *Proceedings of the BEST Conference*, Edinburgh, Scotland.

5. Burns, J. (2002). 'Quality Guidelines and Virtual Learning Environments: Supporting Academic Staff in Meeting New Challenges', in *Proceedings of the 14th International Conference on Assessing Quality in Higher Education*, Vienna, Austria, July.

As you can see, the question of how to cope with writing about your contribution to knowledge is not as problematic as it first appears. Basically, look to see what aspects of your Literature Review are unique, or different, from what others have done; look at how your empirical work contributes to knowledge; and look to your recommendations in terms of making a contribution. In short, look at what other research has been done in your field and how your contribution differs, and if you have publications to boast of then your work has already achieved peer recognition!

Self-reflection

How do you reflect upon an activity that has become an integral part of your life? Throughout the life-cycle of your dissertation, from submitting your proposal to writing your concluding chapter, a wide range of conflicting emotions have been experienced: the excitement of starting a large research project; angst at trying to get a handle on your subject area; delight at reading the work of other, more experienced, researchers; confusion over the plethora of material; frustration at following blind leads; satisfaction in structuring one's own thoughts and arguments; the pain of having to remove work that is, on hindsight, not relevant; and relief in completing the concluding chapter. Panic, pride, tedium, exhilaration . . . there are many nouns that could be used in equal measure to convey the feelings that you will have experienced in undertaking your dissertation. Of more practical benefit may be the need to reflect on lessons learned.

Placing a sub-section in your concluding chapter, entitled 'Self-Reflection', lets the examiner see that although you did the dissertation because it was an academic requirement, it was also a learning process for you. Try and recall how you overcame difficulties at the various stages of your project. If you have kept a diary, then that will make this sub-section easier to complete. When you are mulling back over the stages of your dissertation you should focus on two questions: 'What advice would you give to other students' and 'If you had to do it [your dissertation] again what would you do differently, if anything?'

Be honest (but fair to yourself and others), or there is no point in the exercise. For instance, if your work started badly then say so, explaining why:

This research work started badly. The (first) research topic was e-Learning and Knowledge Management, with a vague idea of some sort of connection between the two, and an ill-defined view that managing knowledge in e-Learning was problematic. A full chapter was then written, comparing how Knowledge Management researchers define knowledge against how philosophers down the ages (such as Descartes and Locke) defined knowledge. There was a sense of satisfaction at completing the chapter and the work was published and presented at an international conference. However, the overall area of study lacked adequate focus and was approached with little enthusiasm. As a result, this work was abandoned belatedly and a new research topic started from scratch.

And do not forget to offer advice to future students:

> The first piece of advice would be to select a topic that genuinely interests you. This researcher's academic interests have deep roots in education: completion of an Open University degree in order to become a mathematics teacher; and a Post Graduate Certificate in Education (PGCE) – with Merit in Teaching – to become a secondary school teacher.
>
> E-Learning is an area that will have a huge impact on teaching. Bringing together a vocation in teaching with research on e-Learning was an exciting prospect. Accordingly, the research focus was changed to accommodate a genuine interest in teaching, rather than what seemed clever and innovative.

The above scenario highlights a common student scenario: an initial failure to find a research topic. Another big problem area for students tends to be the chapter on research methods. For many students it is such a difficult part of the dissertation to comprehend, yet it is so pivotal to their empirical work. Sometimes the problem lies in the concepts used in the teaching of research methods, where terms such as 'phenomenology', 'positivism', 'ontological', etc., are so abstract that they confuse students; or perhaps there is a problem deciding whether or not the approach you are taking to collect and analyse your data is indeed the right one for your research, as discussed below:

> The Research Methods chapter was, initially, unbalanced in that it was biased towards providing details on how the research would be implemented rather than any philosophical underpinning to justify the research approach. There needs to be a balance, but in the initial Research Methods chapter, this was missing. Sometimes the researcher can be too close to his work and so fail to notice obvious failings. That is why your supervisor is there. Listen to him. In fact, the deeper one became immersed in this research, the more difficult it became to step back. A trick someone suggested, which worked, was to have a few days break, return to the work, but select a page at random and try to determine how one could justify what was written, and work backwards to see if indeed that is how you approached the discussion related to the selected text. Not all the research

work relates to justification of arguments, but nevertheless such an exercise does prove interesting, if only to improve the flow of what is written.

It is good to warn students that research is not a smooth, seamless activity, that things can and do go wrong:

> The case study required careful planning, not only in working out the thematic structure of the interviews (based on issues from the literature review) and the questions to ask within those themes, but also in terms of how to analyse the data. Despite such planning, one has to be prepared for hiccups. For example, during the transcription process it was discovered that part of a respondent's replies to a number of interview questions were missing from the tapes! During the interview the tape had stopped and this had gone unnoticed. One has to admit the mistake and simply re-do that part of the interview.

Similarly, a dissertation does not always follow an uninterrupted linear path, where the Introduction is completed to order, followed by the Review of Literature, then the Research Methods, etc. The reality is that the stages of the dissertation tend to be undertaken in an iterative fashion, even within the one sub-section, as detailed in the following narrative:

> When writing about barriers to e-Learning, one would discover an interesting article that was relevant to the section on e-Learning definitions, and so serious consideration would be given to revisiting that earlier section, even if the research work was at an advanced stage or one had believed that an earlier section was complete. This was time-consuming, and in some cases led to much re-thinking, but it was beneficial and gave a freshness to the work, making it as up-to-date as possible. E-Learning is a vast subject area, growing by the day, but one had to discipline oneself to ignore work that was simply replicating what was already written – not an easy task.

You can also remind the reader of the limitations, as you see it, of your work. For example:

> Although this research has achieved its overall aim of acquiring a deeper understanding of e-Learning in Higher Education and related objectives – drivers, barriers, pedagogical issues – one also has to acknowledge limitations in this research work. In the first instance, the case study is not representative of all institutions in Higher Education. Indeed, it is not even representative of what happens at Inverclyde University, despite the university-wide roles of many of the elite staff. This is a deficiency in that this work cannot be generalized to be applicable to any Higher Education institution. Yet, if one takes into account that the purpose of the research

was to appeal to *relatability*, then there is no intention to mislead or misrepresent the results. It is expected that as more researchers study the issues confronted in this work, and implement more in-depth case studies, that an understanding of the issues addressed in this work will increase incrementally, adding to the rich tapestry of e-Learning research.

Another limitation is that student perspectives are not investigated fully. Such empirical data would have added another layer to the study, but this would have compromised the focus of the research and perhaps made the burden of work unmanageable (the decision to include so many elite staff, although of enormous benefit to the study, did increase the workload dramatically).

A third limitation is that the empirical study was a snapshot of e-Learning at Inverclyde University. A study of e-Learning at Inverclyde University, taken over different timescales, would have provided a more rounded and representative picture, as well as showing a cycle of activity, decision-making, and responses, but such a study was outwith the scope of this dissertation. Nevertheless, such an approach would have been interesting, but in a different way from how this study was implemented.

You do not need to concentrate all the time on the problems you encountered, or perceived limitations of your work. You can also let others know what worked well:

The analytical structure that was decided beforehand – deal with academic staff first, compare their answers against each other, deal with elite staff next, not only compare their answers against each other, but against academic staff replies and compare and contrast both sets against the findings from the review of literature – forced the researcher to concentrate on processes rather than people, which helped to minimize potential bias when it came to interviewing people whom the interviewer knew.

One piece of useful advice is this: do not undersell your research findings. Too often, students are reluctant to boast about their work and it is common for tutors to read concluding chapters that are reticent in expressing what has been achieved. The results are understated, offering tentative concluding remarks. Students, even though they produce good work, are still disinclined to express their contribution in positive terms. Sometimes they think it is ridiculous, or embarrassing, or even ill-mannered, to praise oneself, and so they underplay their achievements. You are not expected to engage in an unseemly paroxysm of self-eulogy, but you can, and ought to, assert and defend your good work with confidence.

Research is a discipline, but one that should be done with genuine conviction in an area that is of interest to you. Writing a dissertation is a demanding intellectual odyssey, but it should also be an enjoyable experience. If there is one concluding piece of advice that one can give to those contemplating a similar research journey, it is that there is no royal road to research. It takes hard work, and a disciplined mind, but the finished product is something to reflect on with pride. Or, in the words of Nick, a rebellious character in Shakespeare's *King Henry VI*, Part 2 (Proudfoot *et al.* 2001: 520), who, when defending his craft, quotes with pride a common saying: 'Labour in thy vocation'. George, his rebellious comrade, echoes that sentiment when he responds: 'Thou has hit it; for there's no better sign of a brave mind than a hard hand.'

Summary of key points

- A comprehensive concluding chapter could comprise of the following sub-sections: Introduction; Research Objectives: Summary of Findings and Conclusions; Recommendations; Contribution to Knowledge (normally only expected of PhD students); Limitations; and Self-reflection.
- In the *Introduction*, refresh the reader's memory about your research objectives and give a quick run-down on the content of your concluding chapter.
- In the *Research Objectives: Summary of Findings and Conclusions*, answer the following questions: 'As a result of your Literature Review and empirical research (if you did both), what did you find out in relation to your individual research objectives?' and 'What conclusions have you come to?' For each research objective, inform the reader of your findings and offer a view on what your research is telling you.
- Your conclusions are derived from your research findings and your recommendations are based on your conclusions. In your *Recommendations* sub-section, you deal with two types of recommendations: recommendations linked to your conclusions and suggestions for future research. Explain your recommendations and, if you find it convenient, summarize them in the shape of a diagram. Finally, offer advice on how to implement your recommendations.
- Normally it is not a requirement that Master's students make a contribution to knowledge. However, if it is, then insert a sub-section in your concluding chapter entitled *Contribution to Knowledge* and consider your contribution in two ways: as a result of your Literature Review findings and your empirical work. Emphasize your contribution by comparing and contrasting your work/findings against the work of other researchers.
- In the *Limitations*, qualify your research work with reference to perceived limitations, e.g. inability to generalize your findings (if that is the case), lack of time to do more (in-depth) research, restrictions on access to research subjects, etc. It is not absolutely necessary to create a Limitations

sub-section, as long as you refer to the limitations of your work somewhere in the Conclusion. You can, cleverly, turn some of the limitations of your research into recommendations ('This research revealed valuable insights into staff views of e-Learning. It is recommended, for a wider perspective, that students also be interviewed . . .').

- In the *Self-reflection*, reflect on two questions: 'What advice would you give to other students' and 'If you had to do it [your dissertation] again what would you do differently, if anything?'

8

Finally: Writing the abstract

What is an abstract? • How to write an abstract • Abstract template

What is an abstract?

Postgraduate students are normally required to include an *abstract* in their dissertation. An abstract is essentially a *synopsis* of your work. If an abstract is mandatory, it may not necessarily be assessed formally. This section will assume that you need to write an abstract for your dissertation and that it is assessable, but find out from your university's regulations whether one is needed and the weighting, if any, of marks accorded to the abstract.

An abstract is the first piece of work that readers encounter in your dissertation. It is a summary of your work and normally appears after your Title Page and Acknowledgements. It should capture the essence of your research in a lucid and succinct way. Some institutions differentiate between a *descriptive* abstract and an *informative* abstract: the former concentrates on the structure of the dissertation and not its content (and so is of limited value), whereas the latter provides a condensed summary of the actual work carried out by the researcher. It is the informative abstract that is the norm in postgraduate dissertations and, consequently, the one covered in this chapter.

Unfortunately the (informative) abstract is often treated as an afterthought by students. Ignorance of what an abstract is, and how to write one, further undermine student attempts to put together a competent abstract. Yet it is so easy to score marks in this area, despite the claim by Saunders *et al.* (2000: 418) that 'writing a good abstract is difficult'.

Like everything else in your dissertation, there is a technique to writing an abstract. A good abstract will normally contain the following elements:

- a statement of the problem/issue that you are investigating, including an indication of the need for your research;
- your research methods;
- your results/findings;
- your main conclusion(s) and recommendation(s).

Importantly, try and keep your abstract to one paragraph and to one page. Some institutions will also require your abstract to be *italicized*. Each of the above aspects that collectively form an abstract will now be discussed in detail. You should take into account the preferences of your examining institution as well as the preferences of your supervisor who may well be marking your dissertation.

How to write an abstract

If your abstract is to be assessed formally, it might only be worth about 10 marks at most, but it is very easy to obtain a high score; it is also just as easy to lose silly marks. Students who gain few marks for their abstract do so because they have no idea what an abstract is or how to write one. You can learn by examining the following abstracts against the criteria set down below of what an abstract ought to contain:

- a statement of the problem/issue that you are investigating, including an indication of the need for your research;
- your research methods;
- your results/findings;
- your main conclusion(s)/recommendation(s).

Example 1 (an abstract on cybercrime)

Abstract
The purpose of this dissertation is to explore the adverse effect of Internet crime on the modern business community.

Cybercrime is a recent computer security issue that has evolved quickly without adequate opportunity for the issues surrounding it to become widely acknowledged and subsequently acted upon. Although there has been an abundance of tools to try and protect organizations from cyber breaches, existing research shows that e-security breaches are commonplace. Furthermore, cyber-related legislation has been slow to keep pace with computer security breaches, even to the extent of creating additional barriers for those attempting to combat crime.

Out of 10, this would get a mark of 1 or 2, for a number of reasons. The student identifies his research area only in vague terms: something to do with 'cybercrime'. There is no indication of *what* area in cybercrime his dissertation tackles (the actual dissertation was a study of current preventative measures with a view to understanding why cybercrimes appear to be on the increase), although he does suggest the motivation behind his studies: the continued proliferation of cyberattacks on organizations. So, in terms of the first task that a student ought to do in an abstract – identify his research area and motivation behind his research – this student has failed to be specific about his research area. Worse, this student threw away marks by failing to address the other aspects that ought to be covered in a good abstract: how he approached his research (e.g. research strategy and data collection techniques), his findings and conclusions, and his way forward. In effect, his abstract is quite empty and devoid of meaningful information.

An improved abstract is as follows (for the purpose of emphasis, the key abstract elements are in bold, and in square parentheses – they would not appear so in the finished version):

Abstract
[**Motivation**] *Cybercrime – crime on the Internet – is of growing concern in the business community. Despite UK Government initiatives (such as BS7799) and growing sales in software solutions (e.g. anti-virus software), cyber attacks are on the increase.* [**Research Focus**] *This dissertation focuses on ways to assess the effectiveness of current preventative measures to cybercrime and to understand why organizations continue to be vulnerable to cybercrime.* [**Research Methods**] *This dissertation met these twin research aims through an extensive study of relevant literature and the implementation of practical research. The latter was carried out through a Case Study with Company XXX using semi-structured interviews with key I.T. security personnel.* [**Findings**] *This research produced a number of key findings: recent surveys confirm a significant increase in the incidences of cybercrime and their impact on the business community but also the types of cybercrime (viruses, hacking, spam, identity theft, fraud, privacy issues, web vandalism, etc.); organizations lacked the security expertise to deal with cybercrime and so depended too much on readily available technical ways to combat cybercrime (and failing); organizations were not aware of Government recommendations on how to address internet-based security issues; and Governments and law enforcement agencies tended to localize cybercrime, allocating scant resources to contributing to a global solution.* [**Conclusions**] *The main conclusions drawn from this research were that current approaches to fighting cybercrime are deficient because they fail to embrace an holistic approach, instead opting for a narrow local software-based focus, and that a lack of*

communication between major stakeholders at local, national and international level has hindered security development. [**Recommendation**] *This research argues for a multi-pronged model to reduce incidences of cybercrime. One that takes into account Risk-Assessment models, local management of company policies, implementation issues (including proper resourcing and review policies), the need for global support infrastructures, and a means of fostering communication networks.*

Notice that each of the features expected of a good abstract – research focus, motivation behind the research, research methods, findings and conclusions/recommendations – are to be found in the rewritten version. Note also that you can start with the motivation before identifying your specific research focus.

A common mistake by students

A common mistake by students is to think up their abstract from scratch, without taking into account what they have written in their completed dissertation. This is harebrained, because you can get the information about your research area – motivation, research approach, findings and conclusions/ recommendations – by referring to the relevant chapters in your dissertation and summarizing the appropriate segments, then sticking them in your abstract. For instance, when summarizing your *research area* for the abstract, go to your dissertation Introduction, locate your specific research objectives, summarize them into one or two sentences and insert this summary into your abstract. Do the same for the other parts that go to make up your abstract. Students often lose stupid marks in their abstract by either ignoring what they have actually written in their dissertation or, worse, contradicting their own work!

Example 2 (an abstract on software piracy)

Abstract

The aim of this project is to examine the impact of software piracy facing the modern business. With the Internet becoming an ever-present phenomenon, in homes and the business community, the problem of software piracy – in all its various guises – appears inexorable. As a result, many organizations continue to toil in the on-going battle to prevent this phenomenon escalating.

The question has to be posed: is software piracy a problem that is solvable or do organizations have to concede that it is here to stay? This project tackles these difficult questions. However, it is possible to deal with piracy in a strategic and cost-effective way.

Once again, as in Example 1, this is a poor abstract, deserving of only 2 or 3 marks out of a possible 10. Why? To begin with, although the student makes her research area clear ('The aim of this project . . .') and suggests the importance of her work ('With the Internet becoming an ever-present phenomenon . . .'), she fails to state her research methods. It is also unclear if the sentence beginning 'As a result . . .' is personal opinion or based on her research findings. Similarly, is the last sentence ('However, it is possible . . .') a conclusion to her research or is it a personal comment plucked out of thin air? And what is she recommending as a result of her research? This vagueness has cost her marks.

What follows is an improved version, incorporating the main abstract elements (research focus, motivation behind the research, how the research was implemented, findings and conclusion/way forward):

Abstract

[**Research Focus**] *The aim of this dissertation is to investigate the extent and nature of software piracy, concentrating on three types of software piracy facing organizations today: applications software piracy, music piracy and movie piracy.* [**Motivation**] *The use of modern technology, in particular the Internet, to facilitate new avenues for software piracy makes the need for this research timely.* [**Research Methods**] *This research project was based on a review of relevant literature and questionnaires sent to one organization in Scotland.* [**Findings**] *The findings underline that there is an increase in software piracy and that different types of piracy have different markets (e.g. applications software piracy directed at the business community whereas music piracy is aimed at the young) and, correspondingly, different, although overlapping, solutions.* [**Conclusion**] *The main conclusion to be drawn from this work is that software piracy is both a criminal problem and a cultural issue,* [**Recommendation**] *at the heart of which lies a solution based on ethical awareness training.*

Keywords: software piracy, music piracy, movie piracy, ethics, training.

Notice that the abstract includes a line for 'keywords'. This is good practice: it helps the reader even more to get a handle on what your research is about and is a professional touch that ought to meet with approval from your tutor. Try to use no more than five keywords or terms, otherwise it just gets confusing for the reader.

Example 3 (an abstract on plagiarism)

What follows is an example of a very good abstract (on Plagiarism), even though the 'motivation' part drags on somewhat:

Abstract

[**Motivation**] *In this digital age where plagiarism is a growing phenomenon* *in universities, it is imperative that senior management, tutors and staff understand collectively how to deal with the problem. The term plagiarism itself is often vague, leading to misunderstandings about what is acceptable and unacceptable practice. Similarly, at the chalk-face level, tutors may lack the skills necessary to detect plagiarism. At a wider, institutional level, procedures may lack coherence and consistency, leading to potential claims by students of unfair treatment.* [**Research Focus**] *This dissertation develops a workable definition of plagiarism, explores how students plagiarize, offers guidance on how to detect plagiarism, and presents a formal model on how to deal with cases of suspected plagiarism.* [**Research Methods**] *The research methods consisted of a wide review of relevant literature on plagiarism, coupled with the collection and analysis of empirical data. The latter is based on a survey of staff from 10 universities in the UK, using questionnaires.* [**Findings/Conclusions**] *The findings from this research show that the term 'plagiarism' is often misunderstood; that the Internet is a core vehicle for plagiarism; and that central to combating plagiarism is the need for a coherent, consistent university-wide approach.* [**Recommendations**] *This dissertation proffers such an approach, through the use of a Staff Awareness and Training module.*

Keywords: plagiarism, e-plagiarism, cheating, plagiarism software, essay banks.

What is good about this abstract? It is contains all the ingredients of a complete abstract: it provides a statement of the 'problem/issue' – in this case, plagiarism – including 'an indication of the need for' the research (growing problem, lack of staff understanding on how to deal with it); it identifies the chosen research methods (literature review + survey of staff from 10 universities); it outlines the findings (confusion over the term plagiarism, use of the Internet to facilitate plagiarism, etc.); and it points to a way forward (adoption of a Staff Awareness and Training module).

Finally, keywords are included to add a nice, professional touch. Note that you can merge your findings and conclusions together if you find it convenient to do so.

The next section provides an *abstract template* to help you write an abstract.

Abstract template

As an aide-mémoire, an *abstract template* has been created which highlights the main elements that you ought to include in your own abstract (i.e. research problem, need for your research, how you did your research, your findings, and your recommendation(s)). You can refer to this template when you are doing your own abstract. In that way, you should avoid missing out key abstract elements and so, in turn, create a favourable impression with your dissertation tutor/marker.

Abstract

The focus of this research is in the area of . . . *Such a study is important in order to* . . . The *research approach adopted* in this dissertation includes . . . *The findings from this research* provide evidence that . . . *The main conclusions drawn* from this study are . . . *This dissertation recommends that* . . .

Keywords: a, b, c, d, e

For tidiness, try and keep your abstract to one paragraph and no more than one page (a third of an A4 page normally suffices). Your institution's dissertation guidelines might even indicate the maximum number of words for your abstract. If your abstract starts to stretch over several paragraphs, there is the real danger that you are drawn into writing a disjointed, incoherent mini-essay, rather than concentrating on what you are supposed to be doing: writing an abstract. Keeping your abstract to one paragraph, as indicated in the abstract template, should assist you in the task of producing a tidy, coherent and focused abstract.

If you find the business of writing an abstract initially difficult, then you are not alone: even your tutors can sometimes struggle with writing an abstract. For example, many tutors submit their research, in the form of a research paper, to up-and-coming conferences, with the aim of disseminating their recent research work to the wider research community. As part of their paper submission, they must include an abstract, summarizing their work. However, for their paper to get accepted, it is first judged by 'reviewers', fellow academics trusted by the conference committee to review submitted papers. One of the criteria that conference paper submissions are judged on is the quality of the abstract. When reviewers come to rate the full paper, they also tend to mark the quality of the abstract as well. On occasion, paper submissions are returned with comments such as 'abstract is lacking in detail' or 'no indication of type of study employed' or 'abstract requires to elucidate main findings'. Paper reviewers apply the above abstract template, if not consciously, then intuitively, when judging the quality of an abstract. For example, here is one such abstract (with the subject topic altered to avoid identification) that was reviewed recently, together with the reviewer's comments:

Abstract
This paper will delineate the efforts that have been done in applying technology as a scalable, adaptable, harmonized resource among

geographically distributed employers, employees and customers, in the context of the business community. By implementing this technology in the world of commerce, using web service and agent technology, we are able to reuse functionalities in a flexible and high performance manner. This way, many service and content providers can contribute in developing a very large-scale integrated technology-based business community, giving rise to more acceptable, and accepted, computer systems.

Key Words: Grid, Resource Sharing, Technology, Web service, Agent.

Reviewer's Comments (related to abstract):
The abstract is too short (approx 80 words). Need to state *methodological approach* adopted and clarify your *findings* (see conference website for guidance on writing an abstract).

As you can see, writing an abstract can be problematic, even for academics. When you write your dissertation abstract, make sure that your abstract can answer the following questions:

- Have I identified the focus of my research?
- Have I indicated my motivation/rationale behind this study?
- Have I stated how I did my research?
- Have I summarized my findings/results?
- Are my main conclusions and recommendations included?

If you follow the abstract template, i.e. have addressed the above questions, then you should have an abstract that avoids the common pitfalls and is a credit to your dissertation.

Summary of key points

- The (descriptive) abstract, sometimes referred to as a *synopsis*, is a summary of your work.
- In the abstract you should: identify the focus of your research; point out the rationale for your research; reveal your research methods; state your main findings/conclusions; and, where applicable, specify your way forward/ recommendations.
- Write your abstract in a single *italicized* paragraph.
- At the end of the abstract, in a separate line, include up to five keywords that you feel best captures the nature of your dissertation.
- To help you write an abstract, use the following abstract template as an *aide-mémoire*:

Abstract

The focus of this research is in the area of . . . *Such a study is important in order to* . . . The *research approach adopted* in this dissertation includes . . . *The findings from this research* provide evidence that . . . *The main conclusions drawn* from this study are . . . *This dissertation recommends that* . . .

Keywords: a, b, c, d, e

9

Practical issues

Presenting your work and preparing for a viva • The marking scheme • Good grammar • A word of warning: plagiarism

Presenting your work and preparing for a viva

If you are lucky, once you write and hand in your dissertation to be marked, your part in the dissertation process will be over. On the other hand, some institutions also require their students to present their work and submit to an oral examination. Presenting your work usually involves standing up, making use of a data projector, explaining your work to your examiner(s) and then, once you have completed your presentation, answering questions on your dissertation. Alternatively, you may be subjected to an oral examination without the need to make a presentation. In either case a common mistake by students is not to prepare properly. In fact, many students often seem taken aback when asked even the most simple of questions, such as 'Tell me, Linda, why did you pick this topic?' or 'Joseph, in one sentence – what is your research about?' This sub-section will guide you on how to prepare yourself for either scenario.

Presenting your work: common mistakes

We will now go through the common mistakes made by students who have to stand up and talk about their dissertation, including advice on how to avoid these mistakes. Student unfamiliarity with presentation equipment, resulting in embarrassing fumbling and awkward silences, is an elementary mishap that is avoidable. If you are using a traditional projector, with overhead transparencies, then try them out beforehand, so that you know how to do the simple things like turn on the projector, position the slides properly, and manipulate the size of the image on the wall/board. Similarly, floundering with a data projector, laptop or USB pen will not impress your audience. Whatever equipment you are using to support your presentation, carry out a dry run beforehand to ensure a confident, smooth start. In other words, do not get caught fiddling while your presentation burns!

The next type of mistake is a simple one. Students sometimes forget to introduce themselves and thank their audience for attending. They assume that because the examiner, who may also be their tutor, is attending, that there is no need to introduce themselves. It is a matter of politeness to introduce yourself. An introduction also allows you to take control of proceedings: 'Good morning. Thank you for coming. My name is John Brown, a postgraduate student on the MSc E-Business programme, and the title of my dissertation is "E-security in the Digital Age", which I will now present to you, beginning with . . .'

Rushing the presentation is another problem. This tends to be the result of a lack of confidence in dwelling over your own work. Take your time. Try and breathe! Explain, in simple terms, an identifiable section of your dissertation, then move on to the next meaningful section, and so on, each time setting out your work carefully and deliberately, explaining any issues. Eschew the other extreme, whereby you spend too much time discussing the early stages of your work and run out of time to present, for instance, your research findings. This is perceived as a lack of preparation on your part and will be penalized. Students new to presenting their work really ought to rehearse their 'talk' beforehand, just to make sure that they can stick to their allotted time. Experienced speakers, e.g. your tutors, can estimate with reasonable accuracy the number of (PowerPoint) slides that they will need to meet a certain time-slot. Despite meticulous preparation, though, even the best of talks can exceed the allocated time limit, but try and avoid over-stepping the mark to such an extent that your examiners ask you to wind up your talk.

Unstructured presentations give a bad impression. This is easily solved. Have a slide, or two, devoted to what you consider to be the main stages of your work, with the first slide giving your name and title of your dissertation and other identifying details as you see fit. For example, if your name was Pat Houston, a student at Barra University, and your dissertation was entitled 'Barriers to e-Learning' – created using PowerPoint – then your first slide could be as shown in Figure 9.1.

Your next slide should outline the structure of your talk, so that your audience have an idea of what to expect (Figure 9.2).

In that way your presentation will have a clear, logical structure and will be easy to follow for both you and your audience. The number of slides you use is personal choice, but try and refrain from *slide overload*.

Typical of student presentations is the tendency to fill each slide with copious amounts of text. Once again, this tends to occur because of a lack of confidence: students panic that they might not remember what they want to say, and so err on the side of caution by cramming their slides with text. This is

Figure 9.1 Example introductory presentation slide

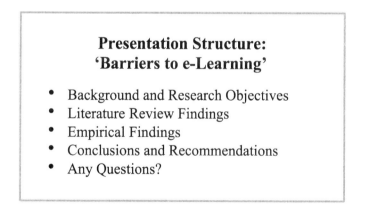

Figure 9.2 Example presentation structure

a mistake, from two perspectives. In the first instance you will find yourself laboriously reading your slides, word for word – in which case you will be talking to the wall, not your audience. Second, a screen full of text is aesthetically unappealing. Your audience will either be bored very quickly or be forced to work hard and read the text in order to fathom your research.

The trick to avoid *text overload*, is to have simple headings, followed by a reasonable number of bullet points. That way, your screen becomes uncluttered, focused and easy on the eye. Also, inserting diagrams and/or pictures is a good way to make your presentation more interesting, although do not be too clever with the technology, e.g. spinning shapes and strange noises – that can be irritating and hide what you are trying to say. Figure 9.3 illustrates a bad PowerPoint presentation, whereas Figure 9.4 shows the same information, but in a simpler, more appealing way, making use of indented bullet points and minimal text, resulting in a clearer, accessible slide.

Reading from your notes in your hand, verbatim, is equally depressing to witness. You lose eye contact with your audience and all they will see is the top of your head and hear an inaudible mumble as you try and make head or tail of your own notes. There is nothing wrong with having notes, but use them sparingly. What you can do is use Post-it notes, which can be stuck to the side of your transparencies, or if you are using a data projector and PowerPoint, create little reminders on the slides, which you can keep hidden from the audience, but which you can see (PowerPoint has this facility). That way you can face the audience and, if you are having difficulty recalling a point, then you can look down at your hidden reminder. For example, you can have notes that say 'at this point talk about such-and-such a case study' or have pertinent facts and figures written down. Also, try and avoid looking down *all the time* at your slides, whether they are on a traditional projector or appear on a data projector. It is much better to face your audience, and refer your audience to aspects of your slides as they appear on the screen on the wall. You should be alternating between looking at your audience and looking at your presentation as it is reflected on a screen, talking to your audience and indicating key points

---

    –   Universities are clearly under pressure to find ways to meet government expectations (increased student numbers, exploitation of ICT, lifelong learning, etc.) within tight budgetary constraints.

    –   Other factors, such as student and employer demands for flexibility, improvements in technology (including reduced costs), public familiarity with the Internet, and market forces (competing with other universities, collaboration with the private sector, and the need to seek other markets), all combine to present powerful, and perhaps irresistible, strategic drivers for universities to explore the concept of e-Learning.

    –   But what are the barriers to e-Learning?

Figure 9.3 Example of a cluttered slide

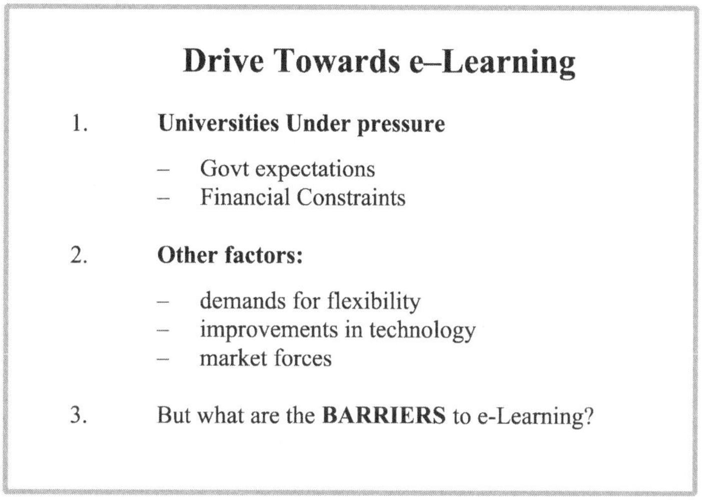

Figure 9.4 Improved slide

on the projected screen. You should not be constantly staring down at a computer screen/transparency or reading long passages from notes in your hand: it looks shabby and is bad form. And avoid standing in front of the projector – it is a particularly stupid thing to do, yet it is easily done. All you are doing is blocking your carefully prepared slides from view. Get in the habit of standing to the side of your projector.

Be confident. Look upon the presentation as an opportunity to accumulate extra marks, and the best way to do that is to prepare yourself, and to practise your presentation. An occasional joke goes down well. It displays a certain level of confidence on your part, offers some light relief, and creates a nice atmosphere. If you want to, you can power dress, thus adding to your professional demeanour and showing your audience that you are taking this presentation, and their presence, seriously.

The following books provide useful information on presentational skills:

Bradbury, A. (2006). *Successful Presentational Skills*, London: Kogan Page.
Ehrenborg, J. (2004). *Powerful Presentations: Great Ideas for Making a Great Impact*, London: Kogan Page.
Hall, R. (2007). *Brilliant Presentations: What the Best Presenters Know, Say and Do*, Harlow: Pearson Education Ltd.

An important part of your preparation is the need to anticipate questions from your examiner(s). This aspect will be covered in the context of a viva, because whether you are presenting your work first and then receiving questions from your examiner(s) or are subjected to an oral examination immediately (without a presentation), the type of issues that you have to deal with can be the same.

Preparing for a viva

A *viva* is an oral examination. Students have many a sleepless night worrying about their viva. There are things that you can do to improve your performance and increase the chances of a successful viva:

- Find out who your examiners will be. If they are external examiners, look them up on the Internet to see what their research interests are, and get hold of their recent publications. That way you will get an idea of their views about your research area (they are your examiners because they have expertise in your field of research). For example, if your research is in e-Learning and you have argued in your dissertation that there are many barriers to e-Learning but one of your examiners, in his publications, takes a different stance, then you will at least be forewarned and better able to prepare a response to a possible difference of opinion.
- Long before your viva, summarize your own work into manageable chunks. Take each of your dissertation sections, from your Introduction right through to your Conclusion and summarize them, using one A4 sheet of paper for each chapter. This will make it easier for you to revise.
- Write down who you think are the main players in your research area, identifying in what respect they are important (make use of one or two particularly memorable quotations). You will look incompetent if you are unable to talk about authors whom you have cited in your dissertation as key players. One postgraduate student, who referred frequently to a book by one particular author, was asked at an oral examination to name the colour of the book cover!
- Anticipate questions and prepare your answers. Do not panic, because most of the questions will be straightforward. The examiners are not your enemy – they are genuinely interested in what you have to say. It is generally not difficult to anticipate the type of questions you will be asked, although there will always be one or two from 'left field'! The questions tend to follow the structure of your dissertation. Examples of typical questions that crop up again and again are:
  - In one sentence, what is your work about?
  - What led you to do this research?
  - Why is this work worth reading?
  - Can you explain your research objectives to us?
  - You say so-and-so has such-and-such a view. Are you sure about that?
  - Who would you say are the main players in your field?
  - I don't agree with your interpretation of so-and-so's model . . .
  - Your references are pretty old. Why haven't you used more up-to-date sources?

- Explain your procedure for ensuring that your survey was random.
- You cannot claim that your case study is representative, can you?
- Why should we rely on your research?
- You know the people you interviewed, so surely your work is biased?
- Are you really saying that your approach to empirical research is the only way to do research? No other way counts?
- Can you explain to us how you analysed your empirical data?
- Do you think you achieved your research objectives?
- I'm not sure that your conclusions follow from your empirical work . . .
- What would you say are the practical implications of your research?
- Can you elaborate on your recommendations, particularly on how you see them being implemented?
- What's good about your work?
- If you had to do this research work again, what would you do differently?
- Why do you think this work deserves a pass?
- So, what would you say is your contribution to knowledge?
- Why should we award you an MSc/MPhil etc.?

- Do not interrupt the examiner when he is asking a question! Let him finish his question. In fact, as he is asking his question, write it down. That gives you time to think about what you are being asked and shows the examiners that you are treating their questions seriously. Take your time answering a question. Once you have written down the question, take a long, deep breath, then begin your answer. In a viva, patience is a virtue. Interrupting examiners and rushing answers will do you no favours.
- If there is a question that you do not understand, then say so. Ask your examiner if he could re-phrase his question or elaborate, because you are not sure what he means. It takes confidence to do this, but do not ask him to re-phrase every question! If there is a question that you find difficult to answer, then tell him 'That's a good question!' Your comment will ease the tension, and if you are lucky the examiner might offer you some clues as to how to answer it!
- On the other hand, if there is a question that you are unable to answer or you are in a situation where you are having difficulty persuading the examiner on some moot point, then admit defeat. For example, an examiner may point out a failing in your work. If you see that he is right, then you can say so, but think carefully before you concede. You are there to defend your work, and examiners are testing that you can do that. So, defend, defend, defend! If you concede points too readily then you may be vulnerable to the accusation that although your work was well written and persuasive, your oral defence of the work was feeble. Concede where you genuinely agree with the examiner. Put up a robust defence of your work, but if things are getting hostile, and you do not want to give in, then agree to disagree. [One colleague can recall defending his own thesis, again and again, at his viva, but towards the end, the examiners hung on one point of disagreement.

The colleague stood his ground, obstinately refusing to budge. Eventually he conceded, with some humour, because he genuinely 'saw the light' where he was wrong and they were right. He thanked them for pointing out an omission in his thesis. It was not a serious omission but including it did enhance his work.]

- The examiners will have read your work in detail before the viva. They will have recorded their initial impressions, including whether or not your work is deserving of a pass (you do not see these comments). They will also have written down specific points that they will examine you on. As you enter the room, your examiners may already have considered your work worthy of a pass, which means that it is yours to lose! It is much worse to be in the position where your written work is initially assessed as a fail, or borderline fail: this is very difficult, though not impossible, to turn around to a pass in your viva.
- The examiners' questions might not always follow a linear path, i.e. starting with questions on the Introduction, then the Literature Review, followed by Research Methods, and so on. If they have specific issues they want to explore then it is to these issues they will direct their questions, probably in order of importance. For instance, if they decided beforehand, among themselves, that they had problems understanding aspects of your concluding chapter, then that is where their first set of questions are likely to be directed. So be prepared for different 'angles of attack'.
- Remember, the examiners are not your enemy; nor you theirs. They want you to pass, and will be the first to congratulate you, but only if your work is of an acceptable standard. They are asking you probing questions, not because they do not rate your work, but because it is their job as guardians of academic standards to be convinced that: (a) it is your work; (b) you can defend your work; and (c) you are a competent researcher when judged against university and national standards.

A viva can be a nerve-wracking experience, but, believe it or not, it can also be an enjoyable one. If you are well prepared beforehand, then you ought to be looking forward to the experience, nerves notwithstanding, so that you can show the examiners the fruits of your labour, something that you should take pride in and be prepared to defend. Figure 9.5 identifies the preparation that you ought to do before your viva, together with a sensible approach to adopt during the viva. In short, know your own work (through your summaries); anticipate questions related to each stage of your dissertation; develop answers to these questions; request a mock viva; and at the actual viva write down questions and take your time answering them (think about what you are being asked). Finally, defend what you wrote in your dissertation, and be polite!

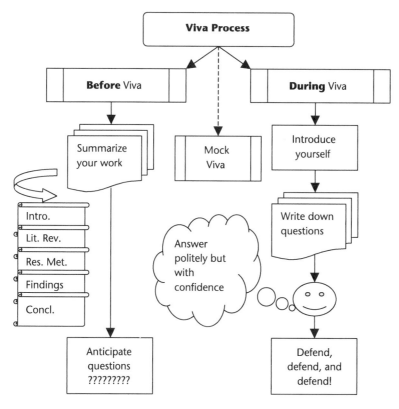

Figure 9.5 Viva advice

The marking scheme

When an examiner starts to mark your written work, she does so with reference, consciously or subconsciously, to what is called a 'marking scheme'. Marking schemes are used for a number of reasons. First, the alternative is to depend on the examiner plucking a figure out of her head – e.g. '85%' – or, worse, failing a student, but on what basis? Second, a marking scheme introduces guidelines that all staff can use and against which student dissertations can be judged, ensuring consistency of approach and fairness to students. Third, marking schemes allow institutions to keep a record of their student work, including assessment rationale, so that external auditors can see that the standard of student work and assessment is appropriate and reflects agreed university and national criteria. Finally, marking schemes are there to assist *you*, the student, in understanding how your work will be assessed.

A common mistake by students

A common mistake by students is to develop their dissertation without refer-ence to the marking scheme. This is stupid. You are being tested that your dissertation meets pre-determined criteria, so why ignore the stated criteria or pay it lip service?

What does a marking scheme look like? Dissertation marking schemes come in all shapes and sizes, but they have certain elements in common, regardless of how they are constructed. They will have a place for the student's name to be entered (usually at the top of the page), the specific areas that the student dissertation is to be marked on (together with the maximum marks achievable for each area), a space for the actual marks to be entered, including the total mark achieved, and a section for examiner comments. Appendix G is an example of a simple marking sheet. Let us look closely at the completed marking sheet in Appendix H, which is reproduced here in a smaller version (Figure 9.6).

Notice that there are two different marks: a total mark of 85% (bottom right-hand of marking sheet) as well as an 'AGREED MARK' of 87% (near the top right-hand corner of the marking sheet). Why is this? This is because it is unlikely that your dissertation will be marked by just one member of staff. To

---

STUDENT NAME: Pat Houston

1st Marker: Dr John Biggam
2nd Marker: Dr Alan Hogarth   AGREED MARK: **87%**

Aspect	Possible Mark	Actual Mark
1. Aim and Objectives	10	10
2. Literature Review	15	11
3. Research Methods	15	12
4. Findings and and Discussion	20	17
5. Conclusion(s) and Recommendations	15	12
6. Referencing	5	5
7. Abstract	10	10
8. Structure and Quality of written English	10	8
	100 TOTAL:	**85%**

Figure 9.6 Sample completed marking sheet

ensure consistency of marking it is normal practice for two members of staff to mark the same dissertation, as a means of providing checks and balances. The different marks for Pat Houston's dissertation occurs as a result of one member of staff (Dr John Biggam) giving a mark of 85% while another member of staff (in this case Dr Alan Hogarth) – looking at the same dissertation and completing a duplicate marking sheet – arrives at a different mark. They have got together to compare their marks and have come to an agreement about the final mark, 87%. The fact that the student's mark has been increased from 85% to 87% suggests that the mark given by Dr Alan Hogarth was greater than Dr John Biggam's mark, although not significantly so, and that they have come to an agreement on what mark to award the student. A significant difference of opinion (e.g. one marker giving 25%, while another awards a mark of, say, 90%) suggests that at least one of the markers has not understood the marking criteria (or, equally problematic, is not a specialist in the subject area). If the markers cannot work out their differences, then a third marker may be called in to adjudicate or an external examiner may be asked to offer a view.

An alternative approach to marking dissertations involves the use of qualitative terms – *Poor, OK, Good, Very Good, Excellent* – which are then, in turn, converted into quantitative marks. This approach is based on the marking of final year 'honours' dissertations where, typically, a dissertation mark between 40–49 equates to a 3:3 classification; a mark between 50–59 equates to a 2:2 classification; a mark between 60–69 equates to a 2:1 classification; and 70+ equates to a first class classification. If the pass mark for your dissertation is 40, then each of these qualitative terms would equate to the bandings shown in Table 9.1.

Table 9.1 Relationship between *qualitative* terms and *quantitative* banding

Qualitative term	Quantitative banding
Poor	<40
OK	Between 40 and 49
Good	Between 50 and 59
Very Good	Between 60 and 69
Excellent	70+

If the pass mark for the dissertation was 50 instead of 40, then the qualitative bandings would move up correspondingly: Poor < 50; OK equates to between 50 and 60; Good, between 60 and 69; Very Good, between 70 and 79; and Excellent, 70+.

When your dissertation marker reads your dissertation he may, in the first instance, rate the various key chapters – Introduction, Literature Review, Research Methods, etc. – using the aforementioned qualitative terms: 'The

Intro is *OK* . . . The Literature Review is *very good* . . . the chapter on Research Methods is *excellent* . . .' His next step might then be to translate his qualitative views into marks. So if he rates your dissertation 'sections' as shown in Table 9.2 then he has come to the conclusion that your overall dissertation is OK because most of the sections in your dissertation are OK (the *good* Literature Review and the *poor* Conclusion also average out to an OK) and so you merit a basic pass ranging from 40 to 49 (Table 9.2). For this grading system, if you wanted to secure a mark of between 60 and 69 then you would need to ensure that each of the sections in your dissertation were *very good*. Similarly, if you are seeking a mark of 70+, then you need to aim for excellence in each major section of your dissertation. The problem with qualitative marking is that where parts of the dissertation are weighted, for example, if the Literature Review was worth twice the marks awarded to the Introduction, it can be difficult to fit such a relationship into the qualitative ↔ quantitative model. Nonetheless, it is a simple approach that staff and students can use to gauge the overall worth of a dissertation.

When students submit their final dissertation, they ought to ask themselves what mark they would give to their own dissertation. When you are reviewing your work, either individual sections, or the final submission, it is a worthwhile exercise to consider what mark *you* believe your work merits, using either the straight-forward quantitative approach ('I think this is worth a 65') or using the qualitative model ('This is *good* so I reckon I deserve between 50 and 59'). In that way, you will begin to think like a marker, checking your efforts against the set criteria. You can even have some fun by getting your friends to 'mark' yours, while you reciprocate for them, each giving the other a completed marking sheet with marks, including comments.

Getting good marks is not rocket science. It requires hard work and an understanding of what is expected of you. There are easy marks to pick up for your *abstract*, *referencing* and *aims and objectives*. If you have grasped how to write an abstract, follow a style of referencing and know how to clarify your overall aim and related objectives, then you really ought to be securing top

Table 9.2 Example of converting qualitative terms

Dissertation sections	Qualitative 'mark'	Quantitative banding
Abstract	OK	Between 40 and 49
Introduction	OK	Between 40 and 49
Literature Review	Good	Between 50 and 59
Research Methods	OK	Between 40 and 49
Findings	OK	Between 40 and 49
Conclusion and Recommendation	Poor	< 49
Referencing and quality of writing	OK	Between 40 and 49

marks in each of these tasks, as did Pat Houston in the sample marking sheet. Students who lose marks for each of the aforementioned areas to do so because they do not know what they are doing and are reduced to guessing about how to complete each of the tasks. For the *Literature Review* you are essentially getting your marks for the breadth and depth of literature studied, relevant to your overall aim and research objectives, in a way that is not merely descriptive, but exhibits critical evaluation of pertinent literature. For the *Research Methods* you gain marks for explaining and justifying your design decisions, that they are appropriate for your study. Marks for the *Findings and Discussion* concentrate on your ability to analyse the results of your empirical research in relation to your Literature Review and to your declared research objectives. Your *Conclusion* needs to provide cyclical closure, i.e. that you summarize your results, provide final comments, make recommendations, and review your own work (either from a critical perspective or lessons learned, or both).

When you start your dissertation get hold of the marking scheme that will be used by your tutors, as well as any accompanying explanatory notes. Make sure that you understand it and use it as a checklist to ensure that, as you develop your dissertation, you are ticking all the right boxes ('Have I justified the need for my research?', 'Are my research objectives clear and achievable?', 'Is my review of literature extensive, showing critical evaluation?', and so on). When you attend meetings with your supervisor, ask your supervisor the same questions ('Are you convinced that I have justified the need for my research?', 'In your view, are my research objectives clear and achievable?', and so on). Prior to submitting your completed dissertation, go over the marking scheme again to check that you have made no damaging omissions (one colleague's dissertation student failed to notice that he had absent-mindedly forgotten to include his list of references).

One last point on dissertation marking schemes: if there is no marking scheme, or set of marking guidelines, then you can legitimately ask your institution how they – markers – arrive at a mark for your work and, at the same time, ensure consistency of approach? They may be leaving themselves open to the claim that their approach to dissertation marking is subjective and unfair.

Good grammar

Marks for your dissertation under the banner *Structure and Quality of Written English*, or the more generic heading *Standards*, refers to how well you have structured your dissertation (logical structure, appropriate numbering of sub-sections within chapters, use of appendices, figures, inclusion of glossary of terms, correct page format, style of referencing, etc.) and how well you have expressed yourself in written English.

In terms of the quality of English evidenced in student dissertations, two common mistakes recur frequently: poor student attention to spelling and a failure to understand the basic linguistic rules associated with good grammar. Sadly, both problems are on the increase. Such was the importance of grammar in medieval times that special schools were created – *grammar schools* – to educate the English middle classes on Latin and Greek grammar. Unfortunately, schooling in the rules of good grammar, even in one's own natural language, has dissipated down through the ages. As a result, many of today's students lack even a basic understanding of what constitutes good grammar.

One student, on being berated by her dissertation supervisor about the excessive grammatical errors and spelling mistakes found in her draft submission, emailed her tutor to reassure him that, in future, she would pay particular attention to her grammar and spelling. Her supervisor replied: 'It's gramm*ar*, not gramm*er*.' Spelling mistakes can be eradicated by using a spell checker, making friends with an authoritative dictionary and getting someone else to check over your work. The issue of sloppy grammar is more deep-rooted and so advice is given in this section on the common grammatical errors committed by dissertation students. Most of the grammatical errors witnessed by dissertation supervisors seem to involve: (a) confusion between *its* and *it's*; (b) general misuse of the apostrophe; (c) split infinitives; and (d) inappropriate application of the colon and semi-colon.

(A) Confusion between *its* and *it's*

It's is a contraction of *it is*, whereas *its* is one of seven possessive pronouns in the English language (the others being *mine, yours, his, hers, ours* and *theirs*). A correct use of *it's* is:

> It's only fair that we share the shopping.

If you expand *it's* to *it is* and the sentence still makes sense then you are using the contraction *it's* correctly. We can see that if we expand the contraction *it's* in the example above that the sentence retains its meaning:

> **It is** only fair that we share the shopping.

A proper use of *its* is:

> Jealousy rears its ugly head.

If you tried to expand that example with *it is* then it would not make sense, showing that *it's* (the contracted form of *it is*) would be inappropriate in this case:

> Jealousy rears **it is** ugly head.

'It's a lovely cat' is correct because if we expand *it's* to *it is* the sentence still makes sense ('**It is** a lovely cat'); whereas 'That dog is so big! It's head is as big as a lion's!' does not make sense because if we expand *it's* to *it is* in this example then the sentence reads 'That dog is so big! **It is** head is as big as a lion's!', which is obviously nonsense. The correct term to use in this case is the possessive pronoun *its* ('That dog is so big! **Its** head is as big as a lion's!').

So, read *it's* as an abbreviation of *it is* and *its* as a substitute term for a previously referred to noun ('Jealousy', 'Dog', etc.). Some supervisors might prefer that you shun the use of the contraction *it's* altogether and use the fuller form *it is* instead, minimizing any drift towards colloquialism.

It's can also be viewed as an abbreviation of 'it has', as in 'It's been established that people are living longer'. This abbreviation is quite rare these days, but it is an acceptable use of *it's*.

(B) General misuse of the apostrophe

An apostrophe can denote a missing letter, as in 'What's life all about?' (= 'What *is* life all about?') or 'You're not dressed for the occasion' (= 'You *are* not dressed for the occasion'), but it is when an apostrophe is used to denote possession that students tend to get it wrong, particularly when dealing with *plurals*.

When we wish to convey that an object (such as a car) is owned by a subject (such as John) then we usually do so by placing an apostrophe at the end of the subject followed by an *s* (e.g. John's), as in 'John's car is red'. Other examples include: 'Alan's notes are illegible'; 'Robert's exam results are excellent'; 'Thomas's hair is soaking wet'; and 'Kay's eyes are lovely!' As you can see, it is normal practice to add an apostrophe s ('s) to someone's name, even if it ends in '–s' (e.g. 'What is Collins's response to this criticism?'), although it is still convention in some quarters to place an apostrophe after the possessive 'Moses' and with Greek names ending in 'es' (Moses' beliefs, Sophocles' writings, Xerxes' battles).

When you connect two or more names together with an 'and', you put the apostrophe s ('s) after the last name: Kennedy and Smith's opposition to free speech is difficult to comprehend.

If the subject is plural to begin with (e.g. Boys) then you place an apostrophe after the *s* (e.g. Boys'), as in 'The boys' clothes were covered in mud'. If you were to write 'The boy's clothes were covered in mud', then you are referring to one boy, which is fine if that is your intention. Similarly, the sentence 'Politicians' views are often contradictory' means that you are referring to more than one politician. As an alternative to placing the apostrophe after a subject when it is plural, you can use 'of' and the noun, as in 'The clothes of the boys were covered in mud' and 'The views of the politicians are often contradictory', but this is a clumsy way of expressing oneself and ought to be avoided. If the subject is plural but does not end in an s (e.g. Women), then place the apostrophe s at the end of the subject, as in 'Women's struggle for equal pay is an endless fight', or 'The children's games are fun'.

(C) Split infinitives

Some tutors have bugbears about *split infinitives*. Here is the technical bit . . . a split infinitive occurs when a word or phrase – usually an adverb – appears between *to* and the *base form* (infinitive) of a verb. Let us put this into simple English. Imagine that you have written the following sentence (the pronoun *to* and the verb *convince* are highlighted for discussion purposes):

> Those in favour of building a new community centre need **to convince** the local populace of the merits of their case.

Suppose further that you decide to separate (i.e. split) the words *to* and *convince* with the adverb *fully* so that your sentence now reads:

> Those in favour of building a new community centre need **to fully convince** the local populace of the merits of their case.

We have now split the infinitive, i.e. placed a word between the base form 'to' and the infinitive 'convince', which some grammarians would argue is sloppy English. A grammatically 'correct' version is:

> Those in favour of building a new community centre need **fully to convince** the local populace of the merits of their case.

Some grammarians hold to the belief that an infinitive should never be split. However, this is a rule that was introduced in the nineteenth century which is now considered by others to be outdated and misplaced as split infinitives are part of everyday language. A famous split infinitive appears at the start of the TV series *Star Trek*, where the aim of the *Starship Enterprise* is '**to boldly go** where no man has gone before', splitting *to* and *go* with *boldly* (instead of the grammatically correct '**to go boldly** . . .'). The original *Star Trek* version ('to boldly go') has a natural rhythm to it, which is lost in the grammatically correct version ('to go boldly'). Indeed, trying to deliberately avoid split infinitives can make for odd reading (did you spot the split infinitive in this sentence?). The *Concise Oxford Dictionary* (1998) – 'the foremost authority on current English' – cautions against strict adherence to avoiding split infinitives, citing its own example: 'this is an artificial rule and can produce clumsy or ambiguous sentences. In many cases a split infinitive sounds more natural than its avoidance, e.g. *'What is it like to actually live in France?'* (splitting *to* and *live* with *actually*). Grammatically correct alternatives such as 'What is it like to live actually in France?' or 'What is it like to live in France actually?', although maintaining the infinitive, sound disjointed and awkward.

The rationale for not having split infinitives seems to stem from the days when those of education and high culture, who were fluent in Latin, a language where split infinitives are not in evidence, believed that the English language would benefit by mimicking aspects of Latin grammar. Unfortunately, the split infinitive is one grammatical imposition that has proved an odd custom, based on a misunderstanding between Latin and English. Verbs in Latin consist of one (infinitive) word (e.g. *amare*, to love), whereas the English equivalent can have two parts (e.g. *to* and *love*). Thus, while it is impossible to split an infinitive in Latin (because it consists of only one word anyway, the infinitive part), it is possible, indeed highly likely if not inevitable, that split infinitives will occur in the English language. Table 9.3 provides further examples of split infinitives and their allegedly grammatically improved alternatives.

Table 9.3 Examples of split infinitives

'To' + verb	With split infinitive	Grammatically correct alternatives
To desire	**To** always **desire**	**To desire** always / Always **to desire**
To increase	**To** slowly **increase**	**To increase** slowly / Slowly **to increase**
To love	**To** intensely **love**	**To love** intensely / Intensely **to love**
To consider	**To** carefully **consider**	**To consider** carefully / Carefully **to consider**
To argue	**To** aggressively **argue**	**To argue** aggressively / Aggressively **to argue**
To evaluate	**To** critically **evaluate**	**To evaluate** critically / Critically **to evaluate**

Having split infinitives is not automatically wrong: if it sounds right then it probably is, for instance 'to critically evaluate' sounds and reads more natural than the stunted and clumsy, but grammatically acceptable, 'to evaluate critically'. The world will not stop spinning if you have split infinitives but it is better to play safe in your dissertation and avoid them where possible.

On the other hand, if you are comfortable with the subtleties and nuances of the English language, there are occasions when you can make the deliberate decision to split your infinitives: where you consider that the alternative hinders the flow of what you are trying to say. This book, for example, contains a number of split infinitives, a conscious decision on the part of the author after dismissing the grammatically correct alternatives as stiff and artificial. If you decide to split your infinitives then you are in good company: Raymond Chandler, the famous detective writer, often complained vigorously about overzealous proofreaders 'correcting' his split infinitives, commenting on one occasion that

By the way, would you convey my compliments to the purist who reads your proofs and tell him or her that I write in a sort of broken-down patois which is something like the way a Swiss-waiter talks, and that when I split an infinitive,

God damn it, I split it so it will remain split . . . The method may not be perfect but it is all I have (Hiney and MacShane 2000: 77).

(D) Inappropriate use of the colon and semi-colon

The use of the colon and semi-colon is often so erratic in student dissertations that many supervisors are of the view that their students *guess* rather than *know* how to use this type of punctuation. A colon, in the context of writing, is not the greater part of a large intestine but a punctuation mark that is used typically in the following circumstances:

1 when introducing a quotation;
2 when presenting a list;
3 When separating distinct parts of a sentence (clauses) where the second part builds on or illustrates the first part.

Examples of each of the aforementioned uses are now given.

---

1. **When introducing a quotation** (or referring to a quotation).
    E.g. 1 Johnson (2006: 7) introduced his guests as follows: 'My dear friends! Please leave your sorrows at the door, for tonight will be a night to remember!'
    E.g. 2 To paraphrase Dylan Thomas: do not go gently into a fight!
2. **When presenting a list.**
    E.g. 1 Kay's chocolate cake had many wonderful ingredients: flour, white sugar, baking soda, ground cinnamon, butter, cocoa powder, egg, vanilla extract, chopped walnuts, and water.
    E.g. 2 A good life contains three elements: a healthy body, an educated mind, and a moral spirit.
3. **When separating distinct parts of a sentence where the second part builds on or illustrates the first part.**
    E.g. 1 Jim is a bad boy: he is always in trouble.
    E.g. 2 Pearson (2007) has a strange definition of e-Learning: he neither relates it to learning nor does he mention technology.
    E.g. 3 There are two main conclusions that can be drawn from this research: small businesses lack the means to operate in a global environment and they are reluctant to seek advice from consultants.

A semi-colon can be used in the following cases:

1 to separate a list of items; and
2 to separate closely related, but independent, parts of a sentence.

Examples:

---

1. **To separate a list of items,** where the list is not simple.
    E.g. 1 Proficiency in a martial art requires the development of a number of traits: technical ability in both hand and foot techniques; flexibility and balance when initiating an attack and defending against an aggressive opponent; a fit body, built around cardiovascular exercises, and capable of short 'fighting' bursts; and, not least, a fighting spirit.
    If you are dealing with a simple list then use commas instead of semi-colons.
    Example:
    Edward failed three of his subjects: History, Art, and Geography.
    However, where the list is simple and already contains commas then you need to revert back to using semi-colons. Example:
    We travelled to Paris, France; Rome, Italy; Vienna, Austria; and Amsterdam, Holland.
2. **To separate closely related, but independent, parts of a sentence.**
    E.g. 1 The soldiers were on leave; they were exhausted from fighting on the front.
    E.g. 2 I love ice-cream; eating too much makes me sick, though.
    E.g. 3 Ten runners started the race; only two failed to cross the finishing line.

The opening lines of W.H. Auden's poem *Musée des Beaux Arts* demonstrates perfectly the combined use of the colon and the semi-colon:

About suffering they were never wrong,
The Old Master's: how well they understood
Its human position; how it takes place
While someone else is eating or opening a window or just walking dully
   along;
How when the aged are reverently, passionately waiting
For the miraculous birth, there always must be
Children who did not specially want it to happen, skating . . .

The colon is used in line 2 as an indication that what will follow will be an expansion of Auden's thoughts on the 'human position'; the semi-colons are employed to separate his observations on what he sees as the 'human condition'. Shortly after, Auden repeats his uses of the colon and semi-colon:

In Breughel's *Icarus,* for instance: how everything turns away
Quite leisurely from the disaster; the ploughman may

Have heard the splash, the forsaken cry,
But for him it was not an important failure; the sun shone
As it had to on the white legs disappearing into the green . . .

The colon in the first line lets the reader know that the poem will now look at the human condition as it is depicted in Breughel's painting of Icarus, in which Icarus falls from the sky into the sea and drowns; the semi-colons are used as a way to list aspects of the painting that reflect examples of nature's indifference towards seemingly tragic events suffered by humans.

Students can also fall prey to writing incomplete sentences. Refrain from writing sentences that do not make sense (as in 'During when Napster trading and sharing music files for free') or truncating sentences, leaving them hanging (e.g. 'The transformation to a successful business'). There is not much to be said regarding incomplete sentences, other than it is something that is avoidable. Read your work out aloud and you will soon spot sentences that do not make sense, either because they are garbled or because they are incomplete. If uncorrected, you will lose marks on two counts: the standard of English employed is inadequate and you have failed to communicate fully your ideas.

Getting marks is not just about what you write in your dissertation but also *how* you write. Make an effort to expunge trivial spelling mistakes and slovenly grammar from your final dissertation. An excellent book that will help you get to grips with elementary grammar is *Eats, Shoots and Leaves* by Lynne Truss (2003). Another educational, and entertaining, book on grammar is *Fumblerules: A Lighthearted Guide to Grammar and Good Usage* by William Safire (2002). Careless grammar and slapdash spelling could prove costly in terms of lost marks, so take time to iron out such errors. In other words, watch your language!

A word of warning: plagiarism

In the world of education, technology is ubiquitous. Understandably, student use of the Internet in support of their academic studies is common in universities; indeed, it is to be encouraged. A student interested in Renaissance Art can be transported, with a few clicks of the keyboard, to a virtual gallery depicting works by Michelangelo, Leonardo Da Vinci, and Raphael. The same student can also access expert opinion on these artists. However, with a similar paucity of keyboard clicks, students can effortlessly cut and paste material found on the Internet, insert it into their assignments (e.g. essays, reports, papers, etc.) and submit it as their own work. Therein lies the danger with coursework and easy access to the Internet: that avenues and opportunities exist that may encourage you to cheat.

Plagiarism is clearly a growing problem in the world of education. School pupils reared on the Internet, and the move towards continuous assessment, have contributed towards a 'cut and paste' generation. You may be guilty of this practice yourself. Given the seriousness of this issue, this is a topic that is worth looking at in some depth.

What counts as plagiarism?

It requires to be emphasized that it is your institution's view of what counts as plagiarism that matters most, not the one that is given in this book. Marshall and Garry (2006) raise the point that many students themselves appear to be unaware of what constitutes plagiarism. Find out what your institution has to say on the issue of plagiarism, including the consequences of such cheating if you are caught. If you are not sure what counts as plagiarism then be proactive and ask your dissertation supervisor to give you examples of what is and is not plagiarism and how to avoid it.

Defining plagiarism is not an abstract, academic exercise: how an institution views what counts and does not count as plagiarism can impact not only on a student's future career – your future – but also on an institution's reputation. A simple definition of plagiarism is given by Northwestern University (2005: 1): 'submitting material that in part or whole is not entirely one's own work without attributing those same portions to their correct source'. An obvious example of plagiarism that would meet this definition is where a student takes a complete chapter from a book, changes the authorship, and then submits it as his own work. What if a student 'stole' a paragraph (not a whole chapter) from another source, copied it into his essay, word for word, and failed to cite the source. Is that plagiarism? For example, the following paragraph was submitted by a student:

> Cryptography may seem to be a black art requiring extremely complex mathematics and access to supercomputers. This may be the case for professional cryptanalysts (codebreakers). But for ordinary people who need to protect data, cryptography can be a strong, often simple to use, and sometimes freely available tool.

The actual source of the text was found on the web. The student neither acknowledged the source nor placed the verbatim text in quotation marks, implying that these were her own words. Even though it may only have formed a small part of her essay, it is still plagiarism ('submitting material . . . in part . . .'). By the same logic, even if a student copies a sentence verbatim without acknowledgement, that is still plagiarism. It is a simple fact: taking someone else's text, word for word, without due acknowledgement, is straightforward plagiarism.

The types of plagiarism that students get up to, based on ideas developed at Indiana University of Bloomington's School of Education (www.indiana.edu/~istd/examples.html), with real-life examples of plagiarism italicized, include:

Copying whole paragraphs verbatim, e.g.:

There is no easy or perfect solution, no silver bullet to eliminate the security risks involved in operating online. Threats and vulnerabilities are constantly evolving. Moreover, a network is as weak as its weakest point: if one component is compromised, whether deliberately or by accident, everyone connected to the network is potentially exposed.

Copying whole sentences verbatim, e.g.:

Cryptography, when used properly, should increase security in a computing environment.

Copying part of a sentence verbatim, e.g.:

Conflicting goals appear to be in operation too: *security is based on limiting access, while collaborative computing requires that access to certain information be shared.*

Copying text verbatim – paragraph/sentence/part sentence – and citing the author, but failing to use quotation marks, e.g.:

Digital signatures can be a significant tool in reducing online fraud and can thereby increase consumer confidence in online transactions (Kontogeorgou and Alexiou, 2002). *Digital signatures should enable enforceable online transactions since any specific transaction is tightly if not irrevocably tied to a specific person. Businesses utilising digital signatures should be more efficient – since online transaction processes will be streamlined – and consequently highly competitive again thereby increasing their appeal to consumers.*

Copying text verbatim without sufficient acknowledgement of the actual source(s) is plagiarism, irrespective of whether it occurs in part of a sentence, a complete sentence or a full paragraph. *Sufficient acknowledgement* means that when you are using someone else's ideas then you have to cite the author, and that when you are using another author's words then you do two things: cite the author and place the verbatim text in quotation marks. If someone retorts that 'surely copying part of a sentence, or even a complete sentence, can't be treated as plagiarism?', they are confusing an act of plagiarism with how a university intends to respond to such an act. If an institution chooses to ignore it, then fine, but the institution's action cannot be justified on the basis that it is not plagiarism, but on the grounds that it does not view it seriously. If verbatim text has been copied and is insufficiently acknowledged, then plagiarism has occurred, pure and simple. That is different from deciding how an institution reacts to such incidences, and that depends on the extent of the plagiarism unearthed in a student's assessment.

When institutions define plagiarism as occurring if '*substantial* unacknowledged incorporation . . .' has taken place, they are in fact implying that a certain level of plagiarism is acceptable. In one sense this is understandable: do you instigate formal proceedings against a student for plagiarizing a sentence? Clearly not, but you ought to educate the student that this is careless and bad academic practice. But it does beg the question as to what is an acceptable or unacceptable level of plagiarism.

There is another variant on the plagiarism classification types above, and that is when a student paraphrases – rewords – an author's passage, but embeds too much of the author's original text, including sentence/paragraph structure, and fails to provide sufficient acknowledgement. This is more problematic to detect (and punish) for staff and not easy for students to do successfully. For example, let us take the sentence 'The same article reported that in May 2003, after 1,800 essays were tested by plagiarism-catching software, 120 students (6%) at the University of Virginia were suspected of plagiarism' – this was written, by this author, after reading a Times Online article (McLennan 2003), the original of which read: 'Last May 120 students at the University of Virginia were accused of cheating on their physics coursework when a computer programme checked 1,800 essays and found up to 60 incidences of copying'. Is this plagiarism? Similarly, from the same article, the sentence 'In 2002, a study of six universities in Australia reported that approximately 8% of student essays revealed plagiarism to varying degrees' was derived from the original sentence: 'A study carried out by the six universities in Victoria, Australia, last September, found that 1 in 12 essays contained some copied material'. Is this plagiarism?

Both the examples mentioned illustrate the difficulty of translating simple statements from a discovered source. How *can* you write that 'as a result of 1,800 essays being inspected at the University of Virginia, 120 students were charged with plagiarism' and, at the same time, achieve dissimilarity from the original text? In the second example it is difficult to use the pertinent facts – the year 2002, the figure of six universities, and the statistic 1 in 12 – without the two sources appearing similar. What you can do is: (1) cite the source; and (2) either quote the original source verbatim – McLennan (2003) states that '120 students at the University of Virginia . . .' – or make a genuine attempt to use the same facts but rewrite the sentence. Falling into lazy habits when dealing with sources, even where it is only one sentence, is bad academic practice and may lead you to engage in extensive plagiarism in the future.

One must accept, though, that it can sometimes be difficult to rewrite sentences and to paraphrase in a way that does not lose the gist of what the original passage is saying and at the same time does not cross the boundary into plagiarism. This is the problem with paraphrasing: you can unknowingly wander across the divide between receiving praise for skilful interpretation of an author's work and finding yourself accused of plagiarism. Nonetheless, poor paraphrasing can result in plagiarism and ought not to be encouraged. Glasgow Caledonian University (GCU) identifies that this type of plagiarism – patchwork plagiarism or *paraplagiarism* – occurs where there is 'too much direct borrowing in sentence structure and wording [i.e. poor paraphrasing]' regardless of whether or not the author is cited (http://www.gcal.ac.uk/ coursework/writing/plagiarism.html).

Plagiarism can still occur even where there is 'good paraphrasing of wording and sentence structure' but the author's original ideas are not cited. GCU, in the same article, defines 'borderline plagiarism' as occurring when the text, after paraphrasing, 'borrows too much language', once again even when the author is cited. Bone (2003: 1) emphasizes that students 'need a very clear understanding of . . . where to draw the line between copying and paraphrasing'. Biggs (1999), cited in Bone (2003), uses the term *plagiphrasing* as a substitute term for patchwork plagiarism.

Another facet of plagiarism that needs to be confronted is the notion that only *deliberate* plagiarism counts as plagiarism, for reasons that will be made clear. The *Concise Oxford Dictionary* (1998) records that the word *plagiarize* has its roots in the Latin word *plagiarius*, meaning 'kidnapper', and goes on to define the verb plagiarize as the attempt to 'take and use (the thoughts, writings, inventions, etc. of another person) as one's own'. Given that you cannot kidnap someone accidentally, this definition, in effect, implies that when a student commits plagiarism he is engaging in a *deliberate* attempt to kidnap the work of another and pass it off as his own. The Council of Writing Program Administrators (2003: 2) concur with this interpretation when they define plagiarism as occurring when 'a writer deliberately uses someone else's language, ideas, or other original (not common-knowledge) material without acknowledgement'.

However, to include student intentions in a definition of plagiarism is to conflate the act of plagiarism with student motivation. If a student copies pages of text verbatim and neither cites the author(s) nor uses quotation marks, then plagiarism has occurred, regardless of the student's intentions. When determining incidents of plagiarism, universities need to separate a student's intentions from the act of plagiarism. Student intent should only come in to play when determining punishment, not when making the initial judgement. A work is either plagiarized or it is not: the motivation of the student is irrelevant. The UK Centre for Legal Education (Bone 2003: 1) supports this position when it concludes that the 'general view however is that intention is irrelevant – and that leniency should relate to the penalty and not to the definition', warning that 'otherwise serious cases of plagiarism in the final year may be defended by statements such as "I didn't know" or "I must have accidentally pasted those three pages across" '. In addition, if a university decides that student intention should be an important factor in deciding whether to accuse a student of plagiarism, then there is the potential for staff to be influenced by whether or not they like the student or perceive the student to be a 'good' student or consider it unlikely that such a student could behave in this manner. Such extraneous influences may expose universities to the criticism that students are being treated differently, based on staff perceptions of student personality traits rather than on evidence of plagiarism.

The Council of Writing Program Administrators (2003: 2) makes the valid point that one should distinguish between plagiarism and a student's incompetent attempt at citation, and that the latter is not plagiarism:

> *A student who attempts (even if clumsily) to identify and credit his or her source, but who misuses a specific citation format or incorrectly uses quotation marks, or other forms of identifying material taken from other sources, has not plagiarized. Instead such a student should be considered to have failed to cite and document sources appropriately.*

Students who mix and match referencing styles in the body of their work or slightly misplace quotation marks or, at the back of their essays, when collating sources, italicize the wrong part of a journal citation or are unsure on how to cite a Web source are guilty of incompetence, not plagiarism.

Figure 9.7 based on sensible ideas suggested by Joyce (2006) may help you grasp what you have to do to avoid plagiarizing someone else's work.

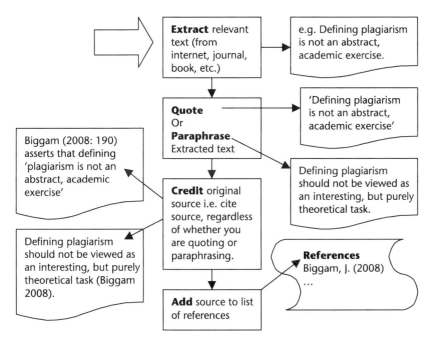

Figure 9.7 Mechanism for avoiding plagiarism

Just remember the general approach, *viz.*: *extract* the text that you are interested in; *quote* or *paraphrase* the text; *credit* the source; then *add* the source to your list of references. By following this procedure you ought to avoid inadvertently plagiarizing someone else's words or ideas.

On the other hand, if you decide to 'cut and paste' work from the Internet but stop short of crediting your sources then you are inviting the charge of plagiarism, as illustrated by the top half of Figure 9.8. It is an easy matter, and good academic practice, to go that bit further and quote or paraphrase your borrowed text, cite your sources and update your reference list (the bottom half of Figure 9.8).

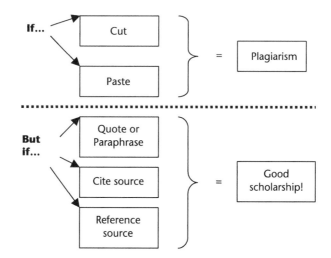

Figure 9.8 From plagiarism to good scholarship

Identifying what counts as plagiarism is not as difficult, or as daunting, as it may appear. Although there are degrees of plagiarism, essentially copying text verbatim without sufficient acknowledgement is plagiarism. What is more problematic is determining when *paraplagiarism* has occurred (i.e. patchwork plagiarism). Although it should be discouraged, it is a lesser form of plagiarism, particularly when the original source is cited; and it probably requires education on your part rather than initial punishment.

Although plagiarism is easy to do, it is also easy to detect. You should be aware that many universities are now turning to the use of plagiarism-catching software such as Turnitin (www.turnitin.com). Staff submit a student's essay to the Turnitin facility and within minutes an Originality Report is produced, providing a 'similarity index' of matching text (e.g. 80%), with colour-coding of text that was found elsewhere. The software does not accuse the student of plagiarizing. That is left to the institution. Turnitin is proving a useful resource in the efficient detection of incidences of plagiarism.

It may be that if you are more aware that your institution is using software to detect incidences of plagiarism then you might pay more attention to the correct citing of sources! That is not to argue that technology is the solution to the thorny problem of plagiarism – the problem is far more complex than that, involving student education, ethics, cultural issues, law, staff training, what it means to learn, concepts of ownership, and so on. Staff can also set up the Turnitin system to allow students to submit their own work for checking, allowing students to view such software as a useful facility rather than an attempt by their university to 'catch them at it'. Turnitin's database is impressive: over 10 million papers and 4.5 billion Internet pages.

What if you are accused of plagiarism?

If you are accused of plagiarism, the first thing you should do is obtain a copy of your institution's plagiarism procedures. In that way you will be better placed to understand, and prepare yourself, for what lies ahead.

To defend yourself against the accusation of plagiarism you need to ascertain how your institution defines the term plagiarism. If the definition refers to '*deliberate* copying' then you may be able to argue that what you did was accidental and therefore, in your institution's eyes, not plagiarism. More often than not, when students are formally accused of plagiarism it is because they have copied too much text verbatim and omitted to credit the original authors in the body of the text. Perhaps you intended to include the references at a later date, but simply forgot. If that was the case then say so. Too many omitted references in the body of your text will weaken your position. As for copying too much text verbatim – was it ever explained to you that this practice is unacceptable, i.e. did you receive instruction on what counts as plagiarism and how to avoid it? Of course, if you were aware of your institution's regulations and decided to cheat anyway, then arguing from a position of ignorance would be untenable. Even if what you did was a deliberate act of plagiarism then there may have been extenuating circumstances which you wish to emphasize, such as stress, domestic problems, ill health, etc.

Next, satisfy yourself that you have a fair hearing. Jones (2006) stresses that universities need to ensure that students accused of plagiarism have a fair hearing, one that does not contravene natural justice. Unfairness may be evidenced, for example, in the composition of the disciplinary panel or where a student has not been made aware of the stages of the disciplinary process and their rights. Jones points to the model adopted by Edinburgh University as an exemplar which could be adopted by other institutions, where the disciplinary panel consists of a pool of academics from a variety of discipline areas and departments, none of whom are in the same subject area as the accused student, so removing a potential complaint from a student that someone on the panel is in his own subject area and may therefore know him and, as a result of that knowledge, be biased. What should not happen is that the supervisor who first spots the alleged plagiarism also appears on a formal disciplinary panel, at whatever level, in effect acting as judge and jury, which would clearly conflict with natural justice. So make sure that whoever is accusing you of plagiarism is not on the disciplinary panel judging your case.

Baroness Ruth Deech is in charge of an independent student complaints scheme called the Office of the Independent Adjudicator for Higher Education (OIAHE), a service which is free to UK students (www.oiahe.org.uk). If a student writes to her office, complaining that he is the victim of a false accusation of plagiarism or that he has been treated unfairly (e.g. too severe a punishment), her office will in turn communicate directly with the student's institution, requesting the following information (Deech 2006):

• How is plagiarism explained to students?
• How were disciplinary procedures brought to the student's attention?
• Were mitigating circumstances considered (e.g. bereavement, ill health, disability, plagiarism not explained to student, cultural issues, financial problems, computer failure)?
• Minutes of disciplinary hearing (to ascertain if student was treated fairly)
• Reasons for decision (are they reasonable, based on evidence and communicated to student)?
• Penalties applied to other offenders in the past (to find out if punishment is consistent and not arbitrary).

The reason behind this request is to assist in determining if the student has been treated fairly and in line with natural justice (no bias, charge explained and both sides allowed to argue their case) and that the institution has applied its regulations properly and that its decision was reasonable.

Interestingly, when Dordoy (2002) surveyed 600 new graduates from Northumbria University (about 22% response rate) on the reasons why they plagiarized, top of the list came 'to get a better grade', next on the list was 'laziness or bad management', followed by 'easy access to Internet material'. Students *unclear about university regulations on plagiarism* and *accidental plagiarism* – the reasons attributed by some staff for students plagiarizing work – came a distant fourth and fifth, respectively, on the list. Hart and Friesner (2003: 191) with reference to these results – particularly the top two reasons given by students – observed that 'the pressure to plagiarise may increase if students leave their academic writing until the last moment'.

Hopefully this discussion has added to your understanding of plagiarism, at different levels. At the root of all this is the simple fact that you need to give credit where credit is due!

10

Summary of good practice to adopt and bad practice to avoid

Forewarned is forearmed • Dissertation writing: summary of good practice to adopt and bad practice to avoid • Practical issues: summary of good practice to adopt and bad practice to avoid

Forewarned is forearmed

This book has taken you through the things that you need to do to complete a dissertation. In doing so, it has also highlighted the common mistakes that tutors observe their dissertation students making, again and again, year in, year out. As a memory aid, this information is summarized for easy reference in four tables:

- Table 10.1 Dissertation writing – summary of *good* practice to adopt
- Table 10.2 Dissertation writing – summary of *bad* practice to avoid
- Table 10.3 Practical issues – summary of *good* practice to adopt
- Table 10.4 Practical issues – summary of *bad* practice to avoid

Tables 10.1 and 10.2 concentrate on, respectively, the good and bad things that occur in the typical phases that go to make up the written dissertation (Research Proposal, Abstract, Introduction, Literature Review, Research Methods, Findings and Discussion, and Conclusion). Tables 10.3 and 10.4

summarize, respectively, the good and bad things that happen in the presentation of the dissertation and in the Viva. In addition, Tables 10.3 and 10.4 make reference to the dissertation marking scheme and the problem of plagiarism.

There are other matters that you need to consider when completing your dissertation, from picking a topic that is of genuine interest to you, to creating a dissertation template at the start (to give you an idea of what lies ahead), to making the most of meetings with your supervisor, to keeping an eye on your word count. Above all, doing a dissertation ought to be an enjoyable experience, an opportunity to show what you can do, but it requires serious effort on your part. It is an intellectual journey that demands your active participation: passengers rarely pass. Being forewarned about the common pitfalls to avoid, together with the skills required to get through the dissertation process, will allow you to start off on your dissertation odyssey with confidence.

Dissertation writing: summary of good practice to adopt and bad practice to avoid

Table 10.1 Dissertation writing – summary of *good* practice to adopt

Phase	Summary of good practice to adopt
Dissertation Proposal	– Provide background information on research topic – Justify the need for your study – Identify overall research aim and specific research objectives – Outline your research methods – Estimate duration of dissertation phases
Abstract	– Write it last! – Identify the problem/issue that you investigated – Outline how you did your research (i.e. your research methods) – State your main findings/conclusion(s) – Indicate your recommendations – Include keywords – Keep to one paragraph (it is not an essay!) – Apply the abstract template!
Introduction	– As in Dissertation Proposal, and: – Show initiative (in sourcing information) – Produce clear, achievable research objectives – Emphasize the value of/ need for your research
Literature Review	– Remind the reader of your research objectives – Let the reader know about the topics you intend covering

Table 10.1 Continued

Phase	Summary of good practice to adopt
	– Develop meaningful discussions, providing evidence of critical evaluation (offer views, support views)
	– Use wide variety of sources (websites, journals, books, reports, etc.)
	– Reference sources properly
	– Avoid dissertation *drift* – keep focused on your research objectives
	– Summarize main Lit. Rev. findings and highlight emerging issues
	– Provide link (and justification) for empirical research
Research Methods	– Identify your research strategy (case study, survey, grounded theory, experimental research, etc.)
	– Justify why your chosen research strategy meets your research needs
	– Describe your data collection techniques (interviews, questionnaires, documents, observation, types of experiments, etc.)
	– Explain where you will get your data, and state your sample size
	– Summarize the above, using diagrams where possible
	– Explain how you will analyse your collected data (framework for data analysis)
	– Outline limitations/potential problems (but explain why your work is valid and reliable)
Findings and Discussion	– Keep it simple: describe the data, compare/contrast with Lit. Rev. findings
	– Stick to your framework for analysis (if you have one!)
	– Keep focused on relevant research objective(s), thus avoiding *drift*
	– Summarize main empirical findings
	– Place evidence of (non-confidential) empirical research in appendices (questionnaires, interview transcripts/notes, experiment results, etc.)
Conclusion	– Remind reader of your initial research objectives
	– Summarize Lit. Rev. and Empirical Research findings (related to research objectives)
	– Elicit main conclusions from your findings
	– Offer recommendations (specific to your research objectives), including ideas about implementation
	– Include self-reflection (limitations of study, lessons learnt, advice to others)

Table 10.2 Disertation writing – summary of *bad* practice to avoid

Phase	Summary of bad practice to avoid
Dissertation Proposal	– Lack of subject focus
	– Vague research objectives
	– Over-ambitious
	– Unrealistic timescales
	– Not justifying need for research
Abstract	– Write it without having a clue what you are supposed to be doing!
	– Engage in mini Literature Review (not the place for that)
	– Fail to provide basic information about your work
	– Write an essay (it is an *abstract*, not an essay)

Introduction	– Paying scant attention to Background reading
	– Too dependent on supervisor for research ideas
	– Devoting too much attention to Background reading!
	– Lack of continuity between sub-sections
	– Unconvincing rationale (or no rationale!) on the value of the work
Literature Review	– Ill-structured
	– Superficial, skeletal sub-sections (lists, simple descriptions, lack of discussion)
	– Concentrating almost exclusively on web sources
	– Not offering, or justifying, your own views (i.e. devoid of critical evaluation)
	– Lack of development of ideas
	– Inconsistent referencing styles
	– Plagiarizing work
	– No sense of direction
	– No obvious relevance to research objectives
	– No evidence of need for empirical research
	– Ends abruptly with no obvious link to next section (Research Methods)
Research Methods	– Spending the bulk of your time describing a whole realm of research strategies (case studies, ethnography, experimental research, surveys, etc.)
	– Not justifying your chosen research strategy
	– Misunderstanding the nature of qualitative/quantitative research
	– Introducing unexplained philosophical terms!
	– Producing a long descriptive monologue on the different ways that data can be collected (questionnaires, interviews, etc.) but:
	– Lack of detail on how and where *you* will collect data or what *you* intend doing with the data once you get it
Findings and Discussion	– Having an unstructured, confusing approach to analysing your collected data or using inappropriate analysis techniques, or using appropriate techniques incorrectly!
	– Coming to conclusions without any evidence of meaningful discussion
	– Not relating your findings/discussion to your research objectives/Lit. Rev.
Conclusion	– Not revising your research objectives to check on whether or not you have achieved them (as a result of your Lit. Rev. and Empirical Research)
	– Not linking your conclusions, if you have any, to your Lit. Rev. or Empirical Research findings
	– Not summarizing your work
	– Offering no recommendations on the way forward
	– Treating your Conclusion as if it were another Literature Review!
	– Ending abruptly!

Practical issues: summary of good practice to adopt and bad practice to avoid

Table 10.3 Practical issues – summary of *good* practice to adopt

Practical issues	Summary of good practice to adopt
Presenting your work	– Prepare and practise for your presentation – Give out handouts of your (e.g. PowerPoint) presentation at the start – Have a logical structure: → who you are → what you are going to talk about → your research objectives → how you did your research → what you found . . . Literature Review . . . Empirical Research → your recommendations – Invite questions
The Viva	– Prior to your viva, summarize, for revision purposes, your different dissertation chapters – Anticipate questions (and prepare answers): → on preliminary issues (e.g. research focus, need for your research, etc.) → aspects of your Lit. Rev. (scope, depth, focus, range of sources, relevance, your interpretation of what other people are saying, etc.) → your research methods and data collection techniques (relevant, justified, clearly explained?) → how you analysed your empirical work → your conclusions (justified?) and associated recommendations – Have a mock Viva – Write examiner questions down – Take your time answering questions – Defend your work!
The marking scheme	– Get hold of how your dissertation will be marked – Use it as a checklist as you do the work (are your research objectives clear, do you show evidence of critical evaluation? Etc.) – Pick up easy marks (for abstract, dissertation structure, referencing, research objectives) – Make sure that you know what you are getting the big marks for in your dissertation – Before submission, have a go at marking it yourself!
Grammar	– Watch your language! – Know the difference between *it's* and *its* – Apply the apostrophe correctly – Keep your infinitives intact – Use the colon and semi-colon properly
Plagiarism	– Understand your institution's rules and regulations on plagiarism – Give credit where credit is due!

Table 10.4 Practical issues – summary of *bad* practice to avoid

Practical issues	Summary of bad practice to avoid
Presenting your work	– Fumbling with the equipment – Rushing through your presentation at break-neck speed! – Cluttering your screen with text – Standing in front of your projector (blocking your presentation!) – Reading directly from your notes
The Viva	– Not anticipating obvious questions – Rushing your answers – Arguing with the examiners (there is a difference between having a professional disagreement and rudeness) – Giving monosyllabic answers – Not referring to your dissertation when answering questions (you are being tested on the work that you have submitted, so it is to your work that you refer when giving answers)
The marking scheme	– Ignoring the things that you are getting marked on
Grammar	– Confusing *it's* with *its* – Misplacing the apostrophe – Unnecessarily splitting infinitives – Inappropriate use of the colon and semi-colon
Plagiarism	– Copying the work of others without due acknowledgement

Appendix A: Sample Introduction

Background • Research Focus • Overall Research Aim and Individual Research Objectives

Background

The traditional approach to teaching and learning has, for millennia, rested on the central premise that for instruction to take place, the tutor and student co-exist in the same place at the same time. Aristotle's lectures, preserved in the writings of Plato, are examples of such an approach, where the student is educated on particular topics through the mechanism of illuminating conversations – *dialogues* – between tutor and student (Taylor 1955). However, few universities have the generous resources required to support one-to-one tuition as the prevailing mode of educational delivery; rather, the common method consists of a combination of lectures, seminars/tutorials and, where appropriate, laboratory work; where each of the aforementioned ways of imparting knowledge involves face-to-face instruction and discussion.

At a simple level, the use of Information and Communication Technologies (ICT) are used frequently to support the traditional teaching and learning paradigm. Academic staff regularly use presentational software, such as PowerPoint, to facilitate lectures; during laboratory sessions, university networked computer systems are used by students to access applications software and print to a common printer; and e-mail systems are used by students to send messages to one another and receive advice from tutors. Haywood *et al.* (2004) believe that most students about to enter university own a PC with Internet access, and that they use ICT regularly, for a variety of activities, ranging from recreational purposes, such as browsing online music stores or e-mailing friends, to more complex activities, such as media downloads or shopping; and that as a result, their expectations of ICT-usage at university are high.

Universities not only use ICT at a simple level – for e-mailing, printing documents, student access to common application software – but have moved rapidly into acquiring advanced software and hardware technologies. In particular, use of the Internet coupled with dedicated software platforms that enable independent learning, such as Blackboard and WebCT, provide institutions with the opportunity to offer educational programmes free from the shackles of time and place (Farrell 2001). It is estimated that over 80% of the use of WebCT, a course authoring software platform, is to support classroom teaching (Bates 2001). There is also much interest from universities to exploit ICT in distance learning, with Moe and Blodget (2000: 104) emphasizing that 'the next big killer application for the Internet is going to be education'.

Online learning, networked learning, distributed learning, flexible learning, virtual learning, are some of the terms used to describe learning that uses technology as a vehicle for educational delivery (Salmon 1998; Jung 2000; Rosenberg 2001; Collis and Moonen 2001; Britain and Liber 2002). Another, more commonly used term is *e-Learning* (Ryan 2001; Sloman and Rolph 2003). Tearle *et al.* (1999: 14) caution universities that they need to engage e-Learning, particularly for distance learning, and that 'it is no longer possible to opt out.' In the UK, the Dearing Report (1997) foresaw benefits of using ICT in higher education:

> . . . we believe that the innovative application of . . . C&IT holds out much promise for improving the quality, flexibility and effectiveness of higher education. The potential benefits will extend to, and affect the practice of, learning and teaching and research. (13.1)

The Higher Education Funding Council for England (HEFCE 2000) in an online press release, reinforced the promise of e-Learning as outlined in the Dearing Report, when it enthuses that e-Learning will be a 'dynamic new way of delivering high quality higher education'.

It is not difficult to find examples of universities responding to the call to develop e-Learning initiatives. The International Virtual Medical School (IVMeDS) is a worldwide partnership of 36 leading edge medical schools and institutions, including Trinity College Dublin (Ireland), James Cook University (Australia) and the University Cattolica del Sacro Cuore (Italy). IVMeDS uses e-Learning to aid medical education. Partnership institutions have access to the online digital learning resources (Figure A1). The Centre for Instructional Technologies, a unit of the Division of Instructional Innovation and Assessment at The University of Texas at Austin have embraced enthusiastically the concept of e-learning by creating an online 'World Lecture Hall', whereby online course materials are provided free to any interested parties who, in turn, can also contribute new material if they wish.

However, is this push for e-Learning, whether on-campus or off-campus, problem-free, leading to an educational utopia, where university staff and students can seamlessly exploit e-Learning to enhance teaching and learning? Technological advances increasingly present a serious and genuine challenge to the traditional teaching and learning model (Collis and Moonen 2001; Laurillard 2002). Tomei (2004), for example, highlights the impact of online teaching on academic staff 'load', warning that the ideal class size for online

Figure A1 IVMeDS

Source: (www.ivimeds.org/).
Reproduced with kind permission of IVIMEDS.

teaching ought to be 12 students. Jones *et al.* (2004) highlight that e-Learning students expect staff to respond expediently to their online queries, and no later than 48 hours. And Hodges (2004) argues that e-Learning tutors need to incorporate techniques to motivate students involved in subjects that are delivered through e-Learning. Increased staff workload, response times and online motivational techniques are some of the issues that academic tutors involved in e-Learning ought to be trained to cope with, particularly if they are new to making the transition from teaching and learning in the traditional environment to one where e-Learning technologies are to be used.

E-Learning environments are changing the role of the university tutor, where tutors need to learn to become guides and facilitators, rather than the main source of knowledge, as in the traditional teaching and learning environment (Collins and Berge 1996), with Salmon (2000) underlining that such a transition requires new skills, including time management skills, ability to monitor the student learning process, and the skill to change teaching methods to meet the needs of e-Learning students.

Research focus

There is some confusion about the benefits of e-Learning. Serious issues are being raised concerning possible impediments to the successful adoption of e-Learning. For example, there have been concerns over student drop-out rates (Flood 2002), inadequate IT infrastructures to support e-Learning (Cowan 2004), and the need to ensure that e-Learning software facilities can accommodate students with disabilities (UK eUniversities Worldwide 2003). Massy (2002), in a European survey on quality and e-Learning, lamented that only 1% of respondents – a mixture of Higher Education (HE) teachers, Further Education (FE) Teachers, HE and FE managers, and private trainers – rated the quality of e-Learning courses as excellent, with 61% of all respondents rating the overall quality of e-Learning negatively.

E-Learning commentators are also warning that academic staff in universities require to be prepared to cope with e-Learning, to make the shift from *sage on the stage* to *guide on the side*. As early as 1997, Dearing highlighted in his report (1997: 36) that 'many academics have had no training and little experience in the use of communications and information technology as an educational tool.' Laurillard (2001) argues that e-Learning requires new skills to deal with new pedagogy. Straub (2002), the director of eLearning Solutions and chairman of the European eLearning Industry Group, complains that 'e-learning [is not] taking off [in Europe] in our daily lives – in schools, companies and universities', concluding that key reasons for this include, *inter alia*, the lack of 'professional development of educators' and a failure to engage 'new pedagogy'.

Clearly, academic staff support is crucial for the success of e-Learning, and a major factor in gaining academic support is the need to prepare them to be able to meet the challenge of e-Learning (Bates 2000; Epic 2002; Gerrard 2002). Given that the traditional model for teaching and learning in the university environment is one that has prevailed for centuries, and that e-Learning (theoretically) encourages a different, more collaborative relationship in the learning process between the principle teaching and learning stakeholders – staff and students – then it would be unwise to assume that such a significant shift in educational practices will occur naturally in the university environment. Critical to the value and logic of the research in this study is an understanding of the type of support that is required to prepare academic staff from making the change from *sage on the stage* to *guide on the side*, the type of support that is available to prepare staff for e-Learning, and what recommendations can be made to help improve existing support frameworks. Understanding how academic staff are being prepared for e-Learning, and their views on their preparation experiences is therefore an area worthy of study and one that would contribute knowledge to the e-Learning research community. The importance of research in this field of e-Learning becomes even more apparent when other researchers mourn the lack of research in this area. Vermeer (2000: 329) complains of too little research of staff experiences in e-Learning and that much commentary is anecdotal in nature, mainly coming from 'the enthusiasm of the recently converted', while Coppola *et al.* (2001: 96) urge that 'there is a critical need for study of faculty experiences'; and as far afield as New Zealand there is a national priority for 'more research into the effectiveness and theoretical base of e-learning' as a result of practitioners 'finding their progress restricted by the lack of available research into e-Learning' (Ministry of Education 2004: 1).

A major focus of this research will concentrate on university academic staff preparation issues related to e-Learning, including barriers to the successful implementation of e-Learning. What training are they receiving to prepare them for e-Learning? What advice is available to help staff better understand the pedagogical shift from traditional teaching and learning paradigms to e-Learning environments? Are there guidance models or frameworks to help prepare staff for e-Learning? What motivates staff to become involved in e-Learning? What demotivates them to become involved? What barriers can hinder staff involvement in e-Learning? To gain a deeper understanding of these issues related to academic staff preparation, two main activities will need to be tackled: a review of relevant literature to ascertain current research findings on e-Learning preparation issues, including potential barriers; and empirical data collection on academic staff experiences of preparing for e-Learning.

Further, to gain a meaningful picture of how academic staff are being prepared for e-Learning, including personal drivers and barriers, it is important to place academic staff preparation issues in the context of the wider e-Learning picture in universities. Thus, the literature review will examine the forces that are driving universities to engage e-Learning, and the potential barriers to successful e-Learning innovations. Similarly, the empirical data – although concentrating on academic staff experiences and perspectives – will seek the views of those who are directing e-Learning (mainly senior staff) to place the views of academic staff in a wider university context.

One could argue that e-Learning is a subset of learning, and that a study of e-Learning is actually a study of learning, and that, as such, the 'e' in e-Learning is, if not superfluous, then over-emphasized. To adopt this approach would be to introduce unnecessary artificial barriers between learning and e-Learning. The traditional approach to teaching and learning is based on an instructional model, where teachers are the providers of knowledge and students the receivers; e-Learning underlines a constructionist model, one which requires participation between teacher and student, where the student plays a more active role in the learning process, and the tutor a more passive role in the teaching process (Papert 1998). In other words, e-Learning is a different approach to learning (and teaching) in terms of *emphasis* placed on staff and student roles: it is not different from learning. This may be a subtle point, but it is an important one. The move away from the traditional teaching paradigm to a constructivist model impacts on staff and students and thus makes the study of e-Learning – a vehicle for a constructivist paradigm – an area worthy of study.

Overall research aim and individual research objectives

The overall aim of this research is to advance an understanding of the impact of e-Learning in the university environment in relation to academic staff training preparation. However, in order to understand staff preparation issues it is felt necessary to gain an insight into the forces driving e-Learning and to explore the barriers to the implementation of e-Learning programmes. It would be difficult to comprehend how staff ought to meet the challenge of e-Learning without knowing the drivers behind e-Learning or the potential barriers, both strategic and personal. And given the confusion between those who predict an exponential e-Learning utopia and those who raise some concerns, it is all the more important to try and clarify e-Learning drivers and barriers. Further, this research will assess existing guidelines supporting staff and student needs (teaching staff need to understand what support a student requires to be in a position to help the student) and explore the experiences and views of staff involved in e-Learning preparation. In turn, two main research vehicles will be exploited to facilitate this study: an in-depth review of relevant literature and the collection and analysis of empirical data. The section entitled Research Methods contains the details of both the research strategy and the data collection techniques to be used to obtain the empirical data.

Specifically, within the context of higher education, the objectives of this research are to:

1 *Identify* the forces driving e-Learning and the barriers to the successful delivery of e-Learning programmes.
2 *Evaluate critically* models and frameworks relevant to supporting academic staff in coping with e-Learning.
3 *Explore* staff stakeholder views and practices related to e-Learning preparation, including drivers and barriers to e-Learning.
4 *Formulate* recommendations on staff preparation issues.

At the risk of oversimplification of the purpose and value of each of the above objectives, objectives 1 and 2 focus on reasons and emerging issues, whereas it is in objectives 3 and 4 where this research will make key contributions to the field of e-Learning. It would be a mistake for the reader to view each of the stated research objectives as separate, unrelated activities. The listed objectives are necessarily interlinked. The first objective – on e-Learning drivers/barriers – will cover initially both strategic and personal drivers, each of which will be of relevance to universities preparing for e-Learning. For example, it will, in effect, attempt to answer the question 'are there forces pushing universities towards e-Learning and, if so, what are they?' An example of such a driver could be perceived saving in teaching time, which, if the case, may act as a driver to encourage staff to participate in university e-Learning initiatives. Objective 1 will also reflect on impediments to e-Learning preparation: an example of a barrier might be perceived threats to job security for academic staff, thus impacting on staff motivation to become involved in e-Learning. Objective 2 – on structured approaches to help staff and universities tackle e-Learning – is of obvious relevance to e-Learning preparation. And objective 3 – on stakeholder views – provides an opportunity to gain meaningful insight into the views of academic staff, and management, on what would encourage them to become involved in e-Learning (drivers), what would discourage them (barriers) and how are they actually preparing for e-Learning as well as their views on their institution's approach. Finally, objective 4 – formulating recommendations – will, as a result of both a review of literature and the collection and discussion of empirical data, make recommendations. The objectives are not to be seen as independent of each other, but rather as all linked to issues surrounding e-Learning preparation in higher education.

This research work will contribute to the development to the discipline of e-Learning in a number of important ways: firstly, by providing a critical review of issues pertinent to the implementation of e-Learning (what is driving e-Learning and what can act as a barrier); secondly, by critically examining existing models and frameworks to support academic staff; thirdly, by obtaining the views of a variety of staff stakeholders on existing practices in e-Learning a rich picture of e-Learning can emerge, allowing a meaningful comparison between theory and practice, from which an improved understanding of e-Learning issues in higher education can be derived, particularly with regard to academic staff training and support in preparing for e-Learning.

The next chapter – Issues and review of related literature – examines literature pertinent to the objectives of this research, beginning with an investigation of what is meant by the term *e-Learning*.

Appendix B: Sample chapter outline

Outline Structure

Chapter 1: Introduction

This chapter provides the reader with *background* information on the impact of e-Learning on the traditional paradigm for teaching and learning in the University environment, including an illustration of some drivers and barriers, and the need for an understanding on how staff are being prepared for e-Learning, to make the switch from *sage on the stage* to *guide on the side*. The *focus* of this research is discussed and justified and the *overall research aim* and *individual research objectives* are identified.

Chapter 2: Issues and review of related literature

This chapter *defines* the term e-Learning, discusses *distance learning* (a driver for e-Learning), clarifies the *drivers* for e-Learning (including major reports, strategic forces, and the benefits of e-Learning to different stakeholders), explores *barriers* to e-Learning, evaluates *guidelines and models* on e-Learning support infrastructures in relation to providing support for academic staff preparation and *justifies the need for empirical data* on academic staff preparation issues.

Chapter 3: Research methods

This chapter discusses and justifies the *research strategy* (a case study) and *data collection techniques* (centred on structured interviews) to be adopted in the empirical collection of data for this study. Details on the *site and sample* are provided, together with a *framework for analysis* of the qualitative data. In addition, the *limitations* of the adopted approach to this research are discussed, in terms of validity and reliability, as well as *potential problems* related to implementing a case study at Inverclyde University.

Chapter 4: Case study results: academic staff; elite staff

This chapter reports on the findings from the case study. In the first instance, the results of the *interviews with academic staff* are discussed (under the themes: Drivers, Barriers, Preparation, IT Infrastructure, Academic Staff Motivation, and Reflections and Future Directions); next, the empirical findings from the *interviews with elite staff* – university staff with an influence on the shape and direction of e-Learning in the institution under study (mainly senior management) – are discussed (with an added theme: e-Learning Strategy). It is in the section on the elite staff findings that *analysis and synthesis takes place*, in terms of not only comparing and contrasting the empirical findings from both stakeholder groups – academic staff and elite staff – against each other, but also where the empirical findings are compared and contrasted against the findings in the literature review. Thus, this chapter describes, discusses, analyzes and synthesizes the empirical findings and the findings from the literature review.

Chapter 5: Conclusion

This chapter revisits the overall aim and specific objectives of this research study. The *findings are summarized* and related to the specific research objectives: forces driving e-Learning; barriers to e-Learning; guidelines and models/ frameworks to support e-Learning implementation (in terms of preparing academic staff for e-Learning). *Conclusions* from this research work are derived and linked to the research objectives, and based on these conclusions, *recommendations* are made. The *limitations* of this work are also highlighted. Importantly, the issue of *managing* the implementation of the recommendations is addressed. The *contribution of this research to knowledge* is clarified. Lastly, a section on *Self-reflection* is included, providing the reader with a personal reflection on the process that has been undertaken to complete this work.

Chapter 6: References

This chapter contains an alphabetical listing of the sources referred to in this work. The Harvard system of referencing (author-date system) is used.

Appendix C: Sample Literature Review Introduction

Sample Introduction to a Literature Review

Sample Introduction to a Literature Review

This Literature Review will examine the main issues surrounding the drive for e-Learning environments within the university sector, impediments to the successful implementation of e-Learning, and guidelines that are available to assist academic staff in tackling identified issues. The study within this review of literature focuses on objectives 1 and 2 as set out in sub-section 1.3 of the introductory chapter (the third objective will be met through the vehicle of empirical data collection and analysis, while the final objective – objective 4 – is derived as a result of the findings from objectives 1, 2 and 3):

1 *Investigate the forces driving e-Learning and the barriers to the successful delivery of e-Learning programmes.*
2 *Evaluate critically models and frameworks relevant to supporting academic staff in coping with e-Learning.*
3 Explore staff stakeholder views and practices related to e-Learning preparation, including drivers and barriers to e-Learning.
4 Formulate recommendations on staff preparation issues.

By exploring the above areas of literature, a significant contribution will be made to this research. The strategic forces pushing universities to engage e-Learning, together with the benefits to staff and students, will be evaluated. Similarly, barriers to e-Learning involvement in universities will be examined, such as individual and social barriers, opposition to globalization, inadequate student infrastructures and the need for academic staff support. Importantly, guidelines to support academic staff will be assessed in terms of their relevance to preparing academic staff for e-Learning. In effect, the value of studying the aforementioned literature areas will be to provide a meaningful discussion and analysis of e-Learning, in a structured way, to facilitate a critical understanding of academic staff preparation issues.

At the end of this major section it is hoped that a critical understanding of key issues is exhibited, that the reader will be better informed in these areas and that there will emerge a clear focus, and justification, for empirical research in the field of e-Learning in higher education. In the first instance, a sensible starting point is to investigate what is meant by the term *e-Learning*. Additionally, the educational phenomenon referred to as *distance learning* – seen by many as an obvious use of e-Learning – will be explored to help place in context drivers and barriers to e-Learning.

Appendix D: Sample Literature Review Conclusion

Emerging issues and need for empirical research

Emerging issues and need for empirical research

The study of relevant e-Learning literature revealed that e-Learning is a complex and moving landscape. To begin with, there is no agreed definition of e-Learning. One was produced, highlighting connectivity, support infrastructures, and flexibility of access and delivery. Similarly, although there were many strategic drivers (perceived reduced costs, access to global markets, increased students, etc.) and potential educational benefits to staff and students (such as: flexibility of delivery and access, independent learning, job opportunities, etc.), there were also many barriers that were identified that could impact on universities and staff contemplating involvement in e-Learning (staff resistance, concerns over student drop-out rates, student inability to cope with independent learning, opposition to globalization, access to support facilities, inadequate student support infrastructures; and, crucially, lack of staff preparation to cope with e-Learning).

The review of literature stressed the need to have in place an infrastructure to support academic staff (Hara and Kling 1999; Farrell 2001; Ryan 2001). With the emphasis on greater student independence and responsibility in e-Learning, the tutor encounters a pedagogical shift from 'sage on the stage' to 'guide on the side'. To accommodate this new paradigm shift in teaching approach, staff, as well as students, require support mechanisms. The main support mechanism highlighted by research was the provision of training (both pedagogical and skills-based) to prepare staff to meet the needs of students engaging with e-Learning. There was concern that universities may not train their staff, or have available for reference, guidelines on how to support their staff in the development and management of e-Learning. Guidelines and Models on e-Learning support infrastructures were reviewed. Meaningful guidelines were identified as a necessary prerequisite to preparing academic staff for e-Learning environments. However, the guidelines and models, although useful in part, tended to concentrate on the needs of students or, where advice on preparing staff for e-Learning was given, were mainly skeletal and general in nature with relatively little advice based on academic staff experiences. That is not to say that useful advice on key skills is not available (e.g. Jones *et al.* (2004a) identifies key skills needed by staff preparing for e-Learning, as does Salmon (2001b)); but there is a need to understand how staff are being prepared for e-Learning and if they are being trained on the pedagogical skills highlighted in the Literature Review. Also, do staff have an understanding of the benefits of e-Learning and the impediments to successful e-Learning?

A crucial issue for the development of e-Learning in universities is that recommendations on future directions ought to be based on research. There exist various means by which universities keen on preparing staff for e-Learning can obtain guidance and advice: e-Learning web sites; consultants; e-Learning courses (at a price); attendance at conferences. However, for meaningful debate and academic credibility, e-Learning guidance and recommendations ought to be based on research findings, using valid and reliable methods of data collection. Unfortunately, empirical data on university approaches to staff training are few and far between; for example, when Britain and Liber (1999: 8) surveyed 100 HE institutions in the UK to determine use of VLEs in these institutions, only eleven responses were returned: 'too low to warrant detailed analysis of results.' E-Learning is moving slowly and in a piecemeal fashion in the HE sector, with little strategic guidance and direction. The Department for Education and Skills (2003: 25), as a result of a low uptake of e-Learning in Higher Education, urged universities to participate and contribute to the principles of 'pedagogy and practice for e-Learning', particularly through a practice-based research environment. In other words, there is a continuing need for empirical data on how academic staff are preparing for e-Learning, and the aforementioned review of literature supports this claim.

To arrive at a deeper understanding of how universities are meeting the challenge of e-Learning, empirical research will be implemented. Specifically, such research will attempt to find out how academic staff are preparing for e-Learning, what motivates them to do so, and, from a wider perspective, the drivers and barriers acting on the university environment in relation to developing e-Learning programmes. The next stage of this research will detail the Research Methods to be used to capture the empirical data, including details on the research strategy to be adopted, data collection techniques, sample selection and management of the researcher's role.

Appendix E: Sample Research Methods

Sample introduction to research methods • Research strategy • Data collection: site and sample selection • Data collection techniques • Framework for data analysis • Limitations and potential problems

Sample introduction to research methods

This research study has a number of inter-related objectives set within the context of Higher Education:

1 *Identify* the forces driving e-Learning and the barriers to the successful delivery of e-Learning programmes.
2 *Evaluate critically* models and frameworks relevant to supporting academic staff in coping with e-Learning.
3 *Explore* staff stakeholder views and practices related to e-Learning preparation, including drivers and barriers to e-Learning.
4 *Formulate* recommendations on staff preparation issues.

A valuable aspect to this research work relates to Objective 3: the opportunity to study e-learning strategy and implementation in practice in a subject that, although generating much discussion and demand, is in terms of usage and research within the wider university community, in its embryonic stages (Farrell 2001; Straub 2002). The slow advancement of e-Learning in practice was acknowledged by The Commission of the European Communities (2002: 5) when it stated that 'the transition may not be as quick or as smooth as originally expected . . . e-learning is proving to be a major evolution rather than a revolution . . .' The opportunity, therefore, to gain a variety of stakeholder views ought to contribute significantly not only to the study of e-learning in general, but to a richer understanding of staff training issues in particular.

Chapter 2 ('Issues and Review of Related Literature') identified a gap in existing research in that there was ample evidence on the need for academic staff to be provided with guidance and training on how to prepare for e-Learning and that such guidance, to gain academic credibility, ought to be based on research. An important contribution of this research work will be the study and analysis of empirical data on how university academic staff prepare for an e-learning environment and the lessons to be learned from such preparation. Objectives 1 and 2 were initially addressed in the previous section, in the form of a review of literature in the field of e-Learning; Objective 3 takes this research one step further through the collection and analysis of empirical data obtained from a university setting. Importantly, although a focus of the empirical work will be to gather data on academic staff training to cope with e-Learning, data will also be collected on stakeholder views on perceived drivers and barriers to e-Learning within a university setting, thus providing the opportunity to explore why a university is becoming involved in e-Learning and what a variety of university stakeholders consider to be impediments to e-Learning. By comparing theory with practice – i.e. comparing the Literature Review findings with the 'real world' – the researcher will gain a fuller understanding of the issues surrounding the implementation of e-Learning and so be better placed to contribute useful knowledge in relation to e-Learning in the university environment.

This section – Research Methods – will provide the details of the research strategy adopted to address the research issues identified above, together with the means of collecting data for analysis, including site and sample selection, and the analysis approach to be adopted. In addition, the reader will be directed towards the thorny issue of potential limitations and problems with the chosen research strategy and its implementation.

Research strategy

Saunders *et al.* (2000: 92) summarizes the use of research strategies thus: 'what matters is not the label that is attached to a particular strategy, but whether it is appropriate for your particular research . . .' Objective 3 of this research sets out to 'explore staff stakeholder views and practices related to e-Learning preparation, including drivers and barriers to e-Learning', and this will be implemented through the collection and analysis of empirical data. But what research strategy should be adopted to meet Objective 3?

The empirical research in this study is interested in an in-depth study ('*explore* staff stakeholder views . . .') within a real university environment, of a number of inter-related objectives: how are academic staff being prepared for e-Learning, staff views on their university's approach to e-Learning (including training, drivers, barriers, IT infrastructure, and motivational issues) and – to place academic staff views in a wider context – the views of senior staff on the same issues? The primary focus, in terms of stakeholders, will be a single research unit, a postgraduate programme team of academic staff involved in preparing for e-Learning. Other stakeholder perspectives, those in positions of authority, will also be collected and analysed, to place e-Learning within the institution in context. Which type of research strategy is best suited to facilitate an in-depth study of a contemporary issue, that promotes focus, and supports the concept of obtaining different stakeholder perspectives to gain a richer understanding of a phenomenon (in this case e-Learning) in a complex setting (a university environment)?

Historical research, as a strategy, is not appropriate to this research work as it is normally associated with looking at non-contemporary phenomena (this research is interested in a contemporary phenomenon, e-Learning). *Experimental* research is also inappropriate, as it concentrates on causal relationships and, in attempting to achieve objectivity, separates phenomena from its social context (this empirical research centres on e-Learning *within* the context of a university environment). Similarly, *survey-based* research, using postal or e-mail surveys, fails to address the researcher's aim of dealing with a variety of e-Learning issues (preparation, drivers, barriers, motivation, IT infrastructures) in depth. *Action* research has appeal in that it involves in-depth analysis of a problem that is current and can best be solved by close collaboration between the researcher and those involved in the problem area. Such an approach is iterative in nature, whereby data is collected, analysed, the problem is revisited, more data is collected, analysed further, the problem is revisited again, and so on, until an agreed solution to the problem is achieved. However, this research work is not concerned with one specific practical problem that can be tackled in this way: the researcher is interested in exploring a number of e-Learning issues related to preparation, not in solving a clearly defined practical problem, hence the emphasis on securing a variety of stakeholder perspectives, not on testing a theory iteratively to find a solution to a specific problem.

In essence, this research is primarily qualitative in nature, not quantitative, where the former relates to studying 'things in their natural settings, attempting to make sense of, or interpret, phenomena in terms of the meanings people bring to them' (Denzin and Lincoln 1994: 2), whereas the latter tends to be used in the natural sciences (such as physics) to study natural phenomena, using methods such as laboratory experiments and mathematical modeling, although quantitative research can often employ survey techniques within social settings and be used in conjunction with qualitative methods (Myers 1997).

Mertens (1998) holds that a researcher's philosophical views of the world will impact on the type of qualitative research strategy that she will adopt for her research. Orlikowski and Baroudi (1991) proposed three categories underlying qualitative research epistemology: positivist, critical and interpretive. A researcher with a *positivist* view of the world, i.e. someone who believes that reality is objective and independent of the observer and so can be measured and predicted, would be interested in testing theories and drawing inferences from a tested sample. This researcher does not hold to a positivist view of the world, nor is he trying to test theories and make generalizations from a sample population. A researcher with a *critical* perspective of the world, views that reality is historically based and that people are influenced consciously and subconsciously by social, cultural and political circumstances, and that it is the researcher's task to focus on such constraining conflicts and so assist in removing the 'causes of alienation and domination' (Myers 1997). This researcher accepts that the world has much conflict and restricting forces that are historically based, and that aspects of his research work may overlap with such sentiments (e.g. drivers and barriers to e-Learning), but that the main focus of his research is not on freeing staff from any feeling of alienation or domination, so that they become better citizens, but instead to understand better e-Learning and contribute knowledge in this field to the e-Learning community. *Interpretative* researchers believe that an understanding of the world can only be accessed through social interaction, and that such interaction in turn is understood in terms of the context of the interaction (time and place). If a researcher chooses to accept 'the ontological assumption associated with interpretative/constructivism that multiple realities exist that are time and context dependent, they will choose to carry out the study using qualitative methods so that they can gain an understanding of the constructions held by people in that context' (Mertens 1998: 161). The interpretative perspective of the world fits in with this researcher's view of the world and his aim of gathering different stakeholder perspectives to 'gain an understanding of the constructions held by people [related to e-Learning] in [the] context' of a university environment.

The research strategy that will be used to implement the empirical research is a case study. What is a case study approach and why is it suitable for this research? Cohen and Manion (1995: 106) describe a case study thus:

> '. . . the case study researcher typically observes the characteristics of an individual unit – a child, a class, a school or a community. The purpose of such observation is to probe deeply and to analyse intensively the multifarious phenomena that constitute the life cycle of the unit.'

According to this definition, a case study is therefore concerned with close observation of how a particular population group behave in a particular context. A case study approach facilitates this researcher's drive to probe deeply into a university's response to e-Learning by devoting time and energy concentrating on specific aspects of e-Learning in one higher education institution. However, there is some disagreement about what constitutes a case study. Yin (2003: 13), for example, defines a case study in a different way:

> 'A case study is an empirical inquiry that
>
> - *Investigates a contemporary phenomenon within its real-life context, especially when*
> - *The boundaries between phenomenon and context are not clearly evident'*

Yin, with the above definition, is trying to distinguish a case study from other research strategies. An *experiment*, he argues, intentionally separates phenomenon from context; *historical* research, although integrating phenomenon and context, normally deals with non-contemporary events; *surveys* can investigate phenomena and context together, but lack the in-depth investigation of a case study approach. That a case study is an in-depth study of a phenomenon is not evident from Yin's definition (Cohen and Manion's definition makes the depth of study clear – *probe deeply and analyse intensely*), although his book *Case Study Research* makes it obvious that he knows that case study research is a detailed and time-consuming undertaking. This research is concerned with an in-depth study of the phenomenon e-Learning in a contemporary context – a university environment – where the boundaries between e-Learning and a university environment are not obvious. For example, the review of literature showed clearly that there is confusion over what is meant by the term e-Learning; further, it is difficult to compartmentalize e-Learning in a teaching and learning institution; also, the boundaries, if there are any, between e-Learning and learning, a university's primary focus, whether it be through teaching or research, are not *clearly evident.*

Although this research meets Yin's second condition – *the boundaries between phenomenon and context are not clearly evident* – it seems likely that Yin's second condition has more to do with emphasizing the interpretative/constructivism view of the world than insisting that complexity of environment is a necessary condition that needs to be satisfied to justify the use of a case study as a research strategy (in any case, the university environment is a complex environment and one that encompasses different stakeholder perspectives and interest groups). Thus, either definition of a case study, whether it be Cohen and Manion's simple, but helpful, description of a case study, or Yin's conditional definition, meets this researcher's aim of delving deeply into a contemporary phenomenon, e-Learning, within the context of a university environment.

The U.S. General Accounting Office (1990: 14), also provides a definition of a case study, one that ties in aspects of Cohen and Manion's definition and that provided by Yin: 'A case study is a method for learning about a complex instance, based on a comprehensive understanding of that instance obtained by extensive descriptions and analysis of that instance taken as a whole and in its context'. This definition is useful in that it captures Cohen and Manion's emphasis on depth of study and focus on a particular phenomenon, while recognizing Yin's view that an understanding of a phenomenon in a particular setting is done in a complex context that requires 'extensive description and analysis' to arrive at meaningful interpretations.

Given the nature of this research – in-depth study of a contemporary phenomenon (e-Learning), in a complex environment (a university), where a variety of stakeholder perspectives are sought (with a specific focus on academic staff preparing for e-Learning, but where other staff will form part of the study to place the study in the context of a complex environment), and where the underlying research philosophy is based on an interpretive understanding of the world – a strategy that meets the needs of this research is a case study. As discussed previously, the case study approach provides the focus that is required, emphasizes depth of study, is based on the assumption that reality can only be understood through social constructions and interactions, and that the context in which the phenomena under study is situated is complex. These facets of case study strategy fit perfectly with the aim of Objective 3 of this research: to implement an in-depth exploratory study of staff stakeholder views and practices related to e-Learning preparation, including drivers and barriers, focusing on a specific unit of analysis (a team of academic staff preparing for e-Learning for a particular programme), but obtaining other stakeholder views in recognition that a university is a complex environment and academic staff views need to be placed in context.

This research is also interested in comparing what was discovered in the Literature Review with the results of a case study. Saunders *et al.* (2000: 92) believe that a case study approach meets that objective: 'we would argue that case study [*sic*] can be a very worthwhile way of exploring existing theory and also provide a source of new hypotheses.' Although the intended output of this research is not a set of 'new hypotheses' it is nevertheless worthwhile in that existing theory (found in the Literature Review) will be compared against the behaviour of one institution and, as a result, an improved understanding – rather than 'new hypotheses' – will be developed to aid universities in their quest to address e-Learning. Specifically, the findings of the case study will be compared and contrasted with the Literature Review findings in terms of views on the drivers and barriers to e-Learning and staff preparation to deal with e-Learning.

A case study strategy is not without its critics and there are limitations in adopting this approach that require to be addressed. In the first place, the researcher is aware of the difficulty of making generalizations as a result of one case study (Adelman *et al.* 1977; Borg 1981), in this case selecting one university in which to study aspects of e-Learning. Bell (2005: 11) comments that 'critics of the case-study approach draw attention . . . that generalization is not always possible . . .' This researcher also holds that view. For example, there are many types of universities in the world of higher education. Within Scotland alone there exist the 'new' universities (e.g. Glasgow Caledonian University), 'red-brick' universities (e.g. University of Strathclyde) and the 'ancient' universities (e.g. Glasgow University). There is also the University of the Highlands and Islands. Selecting one university, however random, will not ensure, it could be argued, that it is any more representative of the population of universities in Scotland, not to mention the rest of the world, where the variety is even richer.

This researcher, instead, is attempting to shed light on what is happening in a particular setting (Saunders *et al.* 2000), thereby adding knowledge to the rich picture of e-Learning research. The case study approach facilitates this aim. Aspirations to adopt e-Learning are not confined to a particular type of university: Gerrard's web-based survey of 110 HE institutions in the UK show that they are all involved with, to some extent, or interested in developing, e-Learning (2002). E-Learning can catch the interest of, and be adopted by, any type of university: research universities, teaching universities, distance-learning universities, public universities, private universities, large universities, small universities, rural universities, urban universities, etc. In other words, the findings from a [case] study of e-Learning, regardless of the type of university, may be of interest and benefit to any type of university keen on using e-Learning as a new mode of educational delivery.

The use of a case study in this research thus exploits the concept of *relatability*, where other institutions in relating to situational aspects of the case study and recognizing similar issues and problems described in this research work can learn from the findings. Bassey (1981: 85), for example, is a strong supporter of the concept of relatability and believes that 'relatability of a case study is more important than its generalisability'. The contribution of this research work to the e-Learning knowledge pool will be developed from a synthesis of the case study analysis and the findings of the Literature Review. It is not expected that the fruits of this research will be representative of all universities undertaking e-Learning. It is expected that, in the fullness of time, as more case studies are implemented by other researchers then the contribution to the e-learning academic community will be progressively amended and developed accordingly. This view of the contribution of case studies to the research community is one held by Nunes and McPherson (2002: 24) who, in their revealing case study of an MA programme in IT Management, accept that it is difficult to make generalizations from one case study – 'it is important to reflect whether theory can be generalized from a single case study' – but who also believe that such a view does not minimize their findings or their contribution to knowledge, for, as further studies are implemented, the body of knowledge in their field of interest will progressively increase and they, in turn, will have contributed. In addition, when the results of a case study are related to a large body of work such as a review of relevant literature, then the contribution to knowledge can prove meaningful and worthwhile to the wider research community.

Yin believes that the criticism against case study research on the basis of an inability to generalize is harsh. He argues that the same type of criticism can be directed towards other types of research. For example he writes (2003: 10), 'However, consider for a moment that the same question [how can you generalize from a single case?] had been asked about an experiment: "How can you generalize from a single experiment?" ' He concludes that generalization is typically arrived at through repeated experiments, and that generalizations from a case study are similarly arrived at through repeated case studies. This is the intention and expectation of this researcher: that the results of this research is used to contribute incrementally to the body of knowledge in the e-Learning community and that, as other research is implemented, then so generalizations can be made in time.

Another criticism of case study research is its validity as a research approach in the research community. Conole *et al.* (2004), although recognizing the need for research on e-Learning guidelines for staff, complain that research into e-Learning is often ill-defined and lacking in theoretical underpinning, lumping case study research with anecdotal activities. They favour research that yields results which allow generalization and so, in their view, are 'more authentic'. Inherent in their interpretation of case study research, is that it lacks academic rigour and is only marginally better than anecdotal evidence. This is to misunderstand the nature of case study research and to ignore the wide uses of case study strategy in the world of, for example, education research. Yin believes that such critics confuse case study research with case study teaching. The latter is used by academics to illustrate a particular point, and though useful in serving a purpose in highlighting specific contextual issues to students, is not subject to the same rigour applied to the former and are open to the accusation of bias. In the end, Yin puts this misunderstanding of what case study research is down to two factors: it is not easy to understand and it is not easy to do. To understand case study research requires an attempt to appreciate the factors that constitute a case study, together with its philosophical underpinning (as discussed earlier). To do case study research, he argues, can be time-consuming, and so not an easy option for a researcher. Hoaglin *et al.* (1982: 134) – five statisticians – accept the benefits of a Case Study approach to their research, but recognize that it is not easy to understand or implement and that as a result it receives criticism that is undeserved:

> *'Most people feel that they can prepare a case study, and nearly all of us believe we can understand one. Since neither view is well founded, the case study receives a good deal of approbation it does not deserve.'*

To remove any accusation of (a) not understanding the nature of case study research and (b) sloppy or ill-defined approaches in designing and applying case study strategy for this research, this researcher has done four things. First, the nature and philosophical underpinning of case study research has been discussed openly and related to the nature of this work; second, well-established data collection methods will be used to collect the empirical data; third, a structured, disciplined, approach to data analysis will be adopted; and fourth, precise details of data collection and data analysis techniques applied to this empirical research will be described in detail, be transparent and available for scrutiny.

Data collection: site and sample selection

The case study is generally considered to be a qualitative study. Bell (2005: 6) states that researchers 'adopting a qualitative perspective are more concerned to understand individuals' perceptions of the world. They seek insights rather than statistical' interpretations of the world. This is the central ambition of the empirical aspect of this project: to understand what is happening in an institution in e-Learning, why a university has reacted to the challenge of e-Learning, and, above all, to seek individual perspectives from those academic staff involved in preparing for e-Learning delivery. To understand instances of e-Learning activity and to seek explanations requires an in-depth probing that is more than simply the gathering of facts and figures. In the process of collecting qualitative data, attempts will be made to collect quantitative data. Examples of this include the number of e-Learning initiatives in the university, the number of staff involved, the number of students involved, types of training programmes on offer, number of staff on these programmes, and so on. It is then hoped that such an approach, combining both quantitative and qualitative methods, will assist in understanding the issues developed in the section on 'Issues and Review of Related Literature' by providing a 'thick description' (Geertz, 1973) of the e-Learning matters encountered in the Case Study. Nonetheless, the primary focus of this research strategy is the gathering of qualitative data.

Convenience sampling was used to select both the university and the postgraduate program. It is convenient because the researcher works at the university. This means that the subjects under study have not been chosen at random and that therefore there can be no claim to achieving representative views related to the broader university community. Instead, this research has as its focus the aim of achieving an in-depth and qualitative insight into e-Learning preparation issues. The review of relevant literature established that e-Learning is an area of increasing interest in the wider university community and so the results of this study will be of interest to those grappling with similar staff preparation issues. Convenience sampling is also used because of time issues and easy access to research subjects. How will this data be collected? The case study data will rely on two data collection techniques: interviews and documentary secondary data (e.g. University Strategic Plan), with the former the main source of data. The main data collection technique will be structured interviews (detailed in section 3.3 Site and Sample Selection). Interviews are an appropriate means of collecting qualitative data, and commonly used in case studies. Indeed, Yin (2003, p. 89) believes that 'interviews are essential sources of case study information', principally because most case studies are human affairs (as is this case study) and that interviews can provide insights into complex situations (an expectation of this research). This technique, although time-consuming, provides the opportunity to obtain qualitative data in a manner that has the benefit of providing an overall question framework and focus for the interviewer yet also providing the opportunity for the interviewee to express their views. Additionally, the interview is not restricted to questions that the interviewer initially intends to pose: in other words, if issues arise during the interview process, and are deemed relevant to the research issues, then these issues will be pursued. The use of interviews are therefore appropriate to this research because they allow the opportunity for in-depth discussion with a variety of pertinent stakeholders within a focused framework (this research is interested in stakeholder perspectives on aspects of e-Learning preparation, including drivers and barriers).

The interviews will be structured to ensure that the interview has a clear direction and theme but there will also be opportunities for staff to express their views, explain individual perspectives and expand on answers. The structured interview – or 'focused' interview – meets the researcher's aim of respecting 'how the participant frames and structures the responses. This, in fact, is an assumption fundamental to qualitative research – the participant's perspective on the social phenomena of interest should unfold as the participant views it, not as the researcher views it' (Marshall and Rossman, 1989, p. 82). As such, to provide an overall structure to the interview, and seek the collection of quantitative and qualitative data, a combination of closed and open questions will be utilized (Moser and Kalton, 1977; Grummitt, 1980; Robson, 1993).

The use of structured interviews and existing documentation will provide the opportunity to relate different stakeholder perspectives related to specific research objectives: university perspectives on e-Learning, on drivers, barriers and university intentions in the area of e-Learning, including plans to involve academic staff; academic support-staff perspectives on, primarily, the detail of training for academic staff, but also issues related to strategic and personal e-Learning drivers and barriers; and university documentation (from, for example, University Strategic Plans). Central to this research are the views of academic staff engaged in preparing for e-Learning. The latter may also highlight important practical issues related to the drivers and barriers to developing e-Learning material and as a guide to how the university's strategic e-Learning objective is being implemented.

This introduces the concept of *triangulation* where different accounts of the same phenomena – in this case e-Learning – can be compared and contrasted. At a simple level triangulation is said to occur 'as the use of two or more methods of data collection', e.g. interviews and documented sources, but can also be used, as intended in this case study, to 'map out, or explain more fully, the richness and complexity of human behaviour by studying it from more than one standpoint' (Cohen and Manion, 1995, p. 106).

The opportunity to implement a Case Study within a university to explore staff stakeholder views and practices related to e-Learning training, including drivers and barriers to e-Learning, is an exciting one. Empirical research in e-Learning tends to take place via the mechanism of e-mailed questionnaires (examples include: Britain and Liber 1999; Rockwell *et al.* 2000; Gerrard

2002; Massey 2002), resulting in a preponderance of quantitative data (such as '61% of all respondents rated the overall quality of eLearning as fair or poor') rather than probing, qualitative data. In addition, such surveys tend to be sent to one individual or centre for response, hence lacking in different stakeholder views. This empirical research will attempt to delve deeply into an institution's approach to e-Learning by implementing a case study and by concentrating on collecting qualitative data from pertinent stakeholders. It is hoped that the results of this study will provide the reader with a three-dimensional picture of e-Learning and, through its *relatability*, add to the tapestry of knowledge that is forming around the field of e-Learning.

The site will be Inverclyde University (IU). This case study is not intended to be an exhaustive study of all the e-Learning initiatives operating in the university. Such a study would, in order to produce meaningful results, be enormously time-consuming and perhaps never-ending (e.g. as one moved the study from one School or Faculty to another School or Faculty, or indeed between departments, new blended e-Learning programmes may suddenly appear and others may just as quickly disappear). Instead, one division within the Inverclyde Business School (IBS) will form the focus of academic staff interviews. Specifically, those staff involved in preparing lecture and seminar material on the VLE software platform Blackboard for a suite of postgraduate programmes in E-Business, Knowledge Management and Management of Information Systems will receive structured interviews. This will allow a focused, achievable approach to the study, giving academic staff the opportunity to express detailed views on e-Learning preparation. Eight teaching staff who have been involved in preparing material for their modules for Blackboard usage on the China programme will be interviewed.

Blackboard will be used in a number of ways: first, all the teaching and learning material related to each module will be placed on Blackboard; administration and guidance material will also be included; the students will have access to Blackboard in order to access the teaching and learning material (lectures and seminars) including material to be used during the module leader visits. Blackboard will also be used to facilitate teaching and learning communication between China staff (academic and administrative) and Divisional staff (academic and administrative) and also between students in China and staff in the Division (academic and administrative). The stage at which this collaboration has reached is that the teaching and learning material for the first cohort of modules have been prepared by staff in the Division and incorporated into the e-Learning platform Blackboard.

Given that a major focus of this research is to gain a deeper understanding of how staff, in practice, prepare for e-Learning, in whatever form, and that these staff have prepared aspects of the e-Learning part of this blended approach, then selecting X [name of Division] as part of the case study presents an excellent opportunity to address issues surrounding staff views and experiences of e-Learning preparation. Selecting X is not a pretence that X is representative of other Divisions, or Departments, within IU and that what happens in X in this context happens, or will happen, elsewhere. Instead, it is to the concept of *relatability* – discussed earlier – that is expected to be of interest to other Departments in other universities. E-Learning is of great interest to universities and the experiences and perspectives of one department will add incrementally to the knowledge base of e-Learning research.

There are two other reasons for choosing X's postgraduate programme as the main focus for this Case Study. The UK Council for Postgraduate Education (1999), in a report – *The International Postgraduate: Challenges to British Higher Education* – raised the issue of the potential for using new technologies for teaching and learning with international postgraduate students but revealed that evidence of staff e-Learning experiences with international postgraduate students were from 'anecdotal' sources (section 7: 2). Selecting X's postgraduate programme provides an excellent opportunity to obtain empirical data on how X's staff prepare for e-Learning and how they prepare for the challenge of dealing with students (and staff) from a different culture. Secondly, The Commission of the European Communities (2002: 5) lamented that the 'most successful players [in e-Learning initiatives] to-date, however, remain the well-established and prestigious institutions'. The Literature Review section appears to support that assertion, with many of the e-Learning initiatives coming from leading academic institutions, examples of which include: Cambridge University negotiating with educational technology companies to offer a Cambridge E-MBA (www.geteducated.com/vubd/vubdjan2001.pdf); Oxford University's Diploma in Computing and an Advanced Diploma in Local History via the Internet (www.tall.ox.acuk); the development of a 'World Lecture Hall' by the University of Texas (www.utexas.edu/world/lecture/); MIT's Open Knowledge Initiative (http://web.mit.edu/oki); and the establishment of an e-university by the University of Southern Queensland (www.usq.edu.au). IU is one of the 'new' Universities in Scotland, known for its social inclusion policy. Researching their e-Learning strategies and implementation issues, particularly related to staff involvement and preparation, offers a chance to capture important data from a university that is neither an 'ancient' university nor a 'redbrick' university, but one that has been created in relatively recent times as a result of the removal of the binary divide in higher education.

The overall aim of this empirical study is to gain a rich, three-dimensional picture of e-Learning and to do so necessarily means involving a variety of stakeholders. As well as academic staff involved in the preparation of teaching and learning material for the China initiative, the Head of X will also form part of the research. It is important to ascertain his views of e-Learning, how he has prepared his staff, how he has motivated staff to participate, what he considers to be the benefits of e-Learning, the barriers, what are his views on IT support, and on issues of staff motivation.

If Division X is viewed as central to this Case Study, then, in order to achieve a three-dimensional perspective of e-Learning at IU, other stakeholders need to form part of this research. To concentrate solely on staff from Division X would produce, at best, a two-dimensional perspective: experiences and views of academic staff and Head of Department. To gain a fuller perspective, the research needs to be widened to include staff outwith Division X. Those who have a part in training academic staff to cope with e-Learning ought to form part of the study. Similarly, *elite* staff – staff with influence, and who are well-informed in the organization (Marshall and Rossman 1989) – need to be included. Figure E1 illustrates an outline model of the research units under study, emphasizing that, although the views of elite staff are important, central to this research are the views of academic staff.

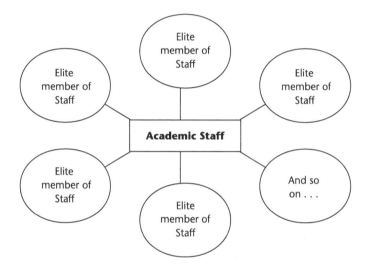

Figure E1 Case study: outline model of Inverclyde University (IU) research units

To capture a School/Faculty view of e-Learning issues, the Dean of the Inverclyde Business School (IBS) will be included in the Case Study; similarly, the Principal and Vice-Chancellor is included to give a strategic perspective on e-Learning. The Pro Vice-Chancellor of Learning and Information Services will be part of this study, for his over-arching role in achieving strategic objectives related to the use of ICT. And because Division X is located in IBS, the C&IT Fellow located in IBS (someone with direct responsibility for encouraging and supporting e-Learning initiatives in the IBS) will also be interviewed.

This thick view of e-Learning will be enhanced further by including members of those who have a role in best teaching practices within IU: the Head of the Academic Practice Unit (APU), and a member of the Teaching and Learning Team (LTAS). In effect, empirical data will be obtained from academic staff involved in the field of e-Learning preparation, from staff in the e-Learning

Innovation Support Unit, as well as staff with a specific role in offering guidance and strategy on teaching practice; and, for a wider management perspective, data will be captured from the Head of X, the Dean of IBS and the Principal and Vice-Chancellor. Figure E2 illustrates the stakeholder groups that will form the units of research for this IU Case Study on e-Learning.

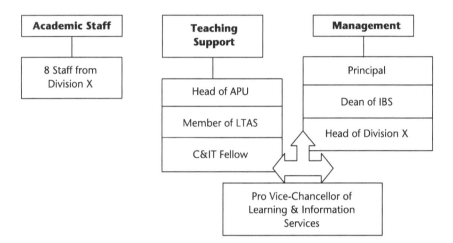

Figure E2 Inverclyde University (IU) Research Units

Data collection techniques

Selecting the means by which to collect empirical data is just as important as choosing an appropriate research strategy. This research is interested in capturing qualitative data. As such, the use of postal or e-mail question-naires, although useful in gathering quantitative data, would not satisfy the researcher's desire for detailed input from staff on their experience of and views on e-Learning. That, in turn, would make it difficult for the researcher to compare and contrast his findings in any meaningful way with the findings from the literature review. Any advice or strategy on a way forward, with regard to preparing academic staff for e-Learning, would be significantly weak-ened by the lack of qualitative data from a Case Study.

Qualitative data will be obtained primarily through the vehicle of inter-views. This will open the opportunity to discuss, with the various stakeholders, e-Learning issues in depth. However, in order to establish a framework around the interviews, and to focus on specific issues with different interviewees, the interviews will be structured with questions prepared beforehand, but the interviewer will be open to new issues and follow different, associated leads depending on the responses and willingness of the interviewee. Qualitative interviewing, using structured questions, makes use of open-ended questions – such as, for example, 'What do you consider to be the benefits, if any, of e-Learning?' – to encourage meaningful responses (Patton 1990).

Interviewing different staff (e.g. Principal, academic staff, member of LTAS, etc.) will allow for cross-comparisons of responses, encouraging different perspectives of similar e-Learning issues to emerge (e.g. rationale for involvement, perceived barriers, staff support required, etc.). For example, the Vice-Chancellor and Dean of IBS will be questioned mainly on strategic issues related to e-Learning, whereas the Head of X, although receiving questions on strategic issues, will be questioned mainly on implementation issues linked to strategic objectives, including support for staff training. The interviews will be recorded, where possible, for two reasons: to ensure that the analysis of data is based upon an accurate record (e.g. transcript) and to allow the interviewer to concentrate on the interview.

The following staff will be interviewed:

1 Principal and Vice-Chancellor of Inverclyde University (IU)
2 Pro Vice-Chancellor of Learning and Information Services
3 Member of e-LISU
4 Head of Academic Practice Unit (APU)
5 The Dean of the Inverclyde Business School (IBS)
6 The Head of the Division X
7 Member of Learning and Teaching Strategy (LTAS) Team
8 C&IT Fellow
9 Academic Staff from Division X: module teaching team involved in development of teaching and learning material, using Blackboard, for the delivery of an MSc E-Business to students in China.

By selecting a variety of e-learning stakeholders, from those involved in strategic decision-making (1, 2, 4 and 5), those charged with providing training to academic staff (2 and 3), those involved in providing IT Support (2 and 5) and learning and teaching advice (3, 4, 7 and 8), and by selecting a Division that has recent experience of implementing e-learning strategy (6 and 9), it is expected that an enriched understanding of e-learning will emerge, one that will better inform the e-learning process and assist in the development of, for instance, the ingredients for improved guidance to support those faced with implementing e-Learning: academic staff.

Secondary data, in the form of university documents and academic staff teaching and learning material, will also be collected to form part of the analysis. The secondary data will come from a variety of documented sources:

• University Strategic Plan
• IBS Plan for 2002/03–2005/06
• Division X's Strategic Plan

- Learning, Teaching and Assessment Strategy (LTAS) 2000–2004
- APU E-Learning Strategy

The secondary data, coupled with the interview data, will assist in providing a rich picture of e-Learning in the university by facilitating a comparison of the stated university, Business School, and Divisional objectives against staff perceptions, at various levels within the institution.

Appendix A contains the collection of structured questions to be used for the academic staff; Appendix B contains the actual interview transcripts of interviews with academic staff; and Appendix C contains the questions and transcripts of interviews with elite staff.

Framework for data analysis

To help focus the interviews in terms of reflecting the main objectives of this research and ease the analysis of the qualitative data, the interviews will be structured according to themes. These themes reflect the overall aim and objectives in this research and also echo main areas arising from the review of literature: *University Drivers for e-Learning, Barriers, Preparation, IT Infrastructure, Academic Staff Motivation* and, to conclude, *Reflections and Future Directions*. It is important not to view these themes as separate topics: they are inter-related. All of the topics could have been placed under the heading 'Preparing for e-Learning'. For example, questions on academic staff motivation relate specifically to what motivates/demotivates staff to become involved in e-Learning; similarly, IT Infrastructure concerns the IT support suitable for an e-Learning environment. The themes are there to help the interviewer and interviewees focus, and as an aid to the analysis of the transcripts. Further, as an indication to the quest for depth as well as focus to this research, academic staff will be asked 4 questions on Drivers, 5 questions on Barriers, 2 questions on IT Infrastructure, 5 questions on Motivation, 3 questions on Reflections and Future Directions, and over 30 questions (including sub-questions) on Preparation. Table E1 reveals the breakdown of questions (including sub-questions) under each theme, for academic staff and elite staff. An additional theme – e-Learning Strategy – is included for elite staff, to reflect their role in the strategic shaping and delivery of e-Learning.

Under each theme, staff will receive a combination of open and closed questions. For example, under the initial theme *University Drivers for e-Learning*, academic staff will be questioned on their knowledge of the University's Strategic Planning Document, the IBS's plan for 2002/03–2005/06, their views on why they think management wish academic staff to become involved in

Table E1 Case study: breakdown of themes and questions

Theme	Academic staff questions	Elite staff questions
X. e-Learning Strategy	–	10
A. Drivers	5	4
B. Barriers	5	6
C. Preparation	33	12
D. IT Infrastructure	2	6
E. Academic Staff Motivation	6	3
F. Reflections and Future Directions	3	4

e-Learning, what advantages they think e-Learning will have for students, and on the advantages e-Learning will have for academic staff.

Figure E3 illustrates graphically the approach that will be adopted to analyse data from the case study, based on the iterative process of *description*, *analysis* and *interpretation* (Wolcott 1994) of the collected data, particularly with regard to extracting and understanding emerging themes. However, analysis of qualitative data is not a linear activity and requires an iterative

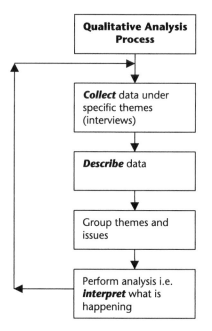

Figure E3 Qualitative data analysis process for Inverclyde University case study

approach to capturing and understanding themes and patterns (Miles and Huberman 1984; Creswell 1997).

The question of how to record the interviews is one that has been given much consideration in this case study. Taking notes as respondents talk is one simple alternative. However, the disadvantage of having to write as respondents are talking, and so failing to give respondents your full attention and, in turn, perhaps omitting crucial comments and nuances, together with the problem of having to interpret summary comments some time after the event, in the end made this mode of recording unsuitable. Instead, all interviews will be recorded on tape and transcribed. Such an activity will prove time-consuming, but the resulting data will aid in the researchers aim of gathering enriching, qualitative data. Over-riding advantages include the freedom to concentrate on the interview process and, crucially, the capture of everything said by the respondents. As each interview will be structured under the themes mentioned earlier (Drivers, Barriers, etc.), the transcriptions for each interview will not form one mass of oral text, but rather be categorized under pre-determined topics and sub-topics, in turn aiding the analysis phase. One last point on transcribing: all the interviews will be transcribed. As Strauss and Corbin (1990: 31) recommend: 'better more than less'. The researcher has decided to err on the side of caution and have all interviews transcribed.

An important part of this research is to analyze the case study data, comparing and contrasting different stakeholder perspectives (as above), and to reflect on the Case Study results with respect to the findings in the Literature Review. Figure E3 is updated (Figure E4) to show this over-arching reflective process.

In terms of analysis, there will be a two-pronged approach: first, academic staff case study findings will be described and analysed; second, elite staff case study findings will be described and analysed, not only comparing elite staff findings against each other, but also comparing elite staff findings against academic staff findings. However, it is in the second phase that, as well as comparing elite staff findings against academic staff findings, relevant literature review findings will also be compared and contrasted against the case study findings (this is to avoid repetition of comment with reference to the findings in the literature review). The essence of this qualitative analysis paradigm reflects accepted practice in dealing with qualitative data, and is perhaps more succinctly described by Bogdan and Biklen (1982:145) as 'working with data, organizing it, breaking it into manageable units, synthesizing it, searching for patterns, discovering what is important and what is to be learned, and deciding what you will tell others'.

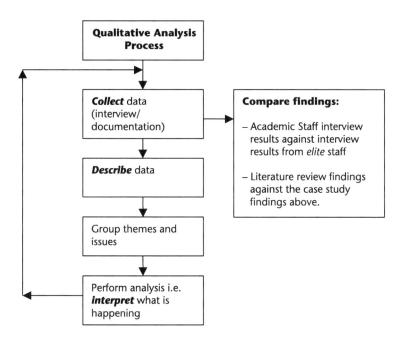

Figure E4 Qualitative data analysis process for Inverclyde University case study [updated]

Limitations and potential problems

There are limitations to this research, as well as issues related to implementing a case study in an environment where one is employed. The results of this study cannot be generalized to the wider research community. Indeed, the results of this research cannot even be generalized to represent the university under study: although key elite staff will be interviewed, and strategic documentation will be referred to, the study of a different programme team in the institution, preparing for e-Learning, may lead to different results. The question of the validity of case study research, in the sense that generalizations cannot normally be made, has already been discussed and addressed. This researcher is using a tried and tested research strategy, appealing to the concept of *relatability* rather than *generalizability*, although it was also argued that generalization, although not immediate, can take place over a period of time – incremental generalizability – as more empirical research case studies are implemented. This researcher is sacrificing immediate generalizability for depth of study.

Nonetheless, there is also the question of the *reliability* of using such a strategy, particularly when interviews are used as the main means of data collection. In the first place, there is the matter of studying one instance of one phenomenon, the results of which are not open to immediate generaliza- tion. Next, there is the question of depending on a data collection technique – interviews – that relies on personal opinion, and so open to bias and inaccur- acy. Even more problematic, how can the researcher maintain *objectivity* when he interviews colleagues in an environment wherein he works!

In terms of the reliability of case study research, Yin (2003: 38) states that the way to deal with reliability in a case study is to 'make as many steps as oper- ational as possible and to conduct the research as if someone were looking over your shoulder'. This research work met this test of reliability by providing details of the appropriateness of the case study strategy to this research, as well as the data collection techniques to be used, the site selected, the type of staff to be interviewed, their roles, the specific themes that will be addressed, the actual interview questions, and the method of data analysis. In addition, full transcripts are provided. Reliability is sought through a highly structured, transparent and detailed approach to this study, using a research strategy and data collection techniques that have validity in the research community.

The issue of depending on interviews as the main source of data, when interviewees can exhibit bias or poor memory recall, was dealt with by ensur- ing that the researcher was not depending on his results from one or two respondents, but on a number of sources. To begin with, a team of academics preparing for a new suite of programmes will be interviewed. A number of views are collected on the same issues, from staff working on the same programmes, ensuring that the researcher is not dependent on one or two respondents for key data. Second, staff from outwith this programme will be interviewed, further removing the dependence on opinion that may be factually wrong or skewed and to place academic staff views in a wider context, lessening the opportunity for bias or misinformation. Third, the interview questions are extensive and detailed, where some of the same issues are tackled in different themes (e.g. barriers to e-Learning), which presents an opportunity for staff to consider some topics in different contexts and acts as a check on the consistency of staff views. Fourth, documentation will be used as a means of understanding the university's e-Learning objectives and imple- mentation issues, and also used to compare against interview answers. It must also be accepted that people are not robots and that to err is human, both in terms of expressing occasional bias and making honest errors of recollec- tion; but that for the most part respondents will answer interview questions in a professional, competent manner. Nonetheless, by adopting the afore- mentioned procedures, it is expected that any bias or misinformation will be minimized.

Interviewing one's colleagues raises the issue of objectivity. Implementing a case study within one's place of employment has the comforting advantage of access to subjects. However, such a scenario brings with it problems that, if not managed properly, may hinder the research and endanger relationships between the researcher and the participants in the research project. There may be the concern expressed that 'how can a colleague, albeit one engaging in research, not be influenced by his prior knowledge of his fellow colleagues' views and bring such knowledge to bear when interpreting transcripts of interviews?' This indeed was a concern expressed by a colleague, and relates to the objectivity of the researcher. To minimize such an influence, the researcher adopted the following strategy: until he had secured all staff interviews and completed the transcripts, the researcher would refrain from attending any e-Learning seminars within Division X (to avoid directly or indirectly presenting his views of e-Learning or acquiring the views of his research subjects); after the transcription of interviews, staff names would be replaced by codes (Lecturer A, Lecturer B, Senior Member of Staff A, and so on); and a deliberate and significant time-gap created between the transcriptions and transcription analysis to further minimize the possibility of bias when interpreting staff views. Furthermore, as far as is practical, staff transcriptions will be edited to remove identifying comments. This may help allay any concerns that staff may have concerning their transcriptions, with the added benefit that they may speak more freely.

Another important issue relates to interviewing staff within Division X. These staff are also the researcher's colleagues and, although access to such staff for interview purposes is almost guaranteed, nevertheless access to one's colleagues to facilitate research brings with it responsibilities on the part of the researcher. The researcher now has to view his fellow colleagues, not as colleagues, but as research subjects and this role change needs to be communicated to staff. Linked to this role change is the need for the researcher to gain the trust of his research subjects (in terms of how the research data will be used). It is the intention that interviews be recorded, where allowed, to facilitate accurate analysis. Staff may understandably be nervous about expressing their views openly and so to encourage open and honest discussion, anonymity for academic staff will be guaranteed where requested.

The transcribing of interviews, in particular, is a sensitive matter. To avoid quotations that may embarrass respondents, if identified, or worse, cause concern or internal strife, quotations will not be attributed to specific named individuals, unless prior permission has been sought and given. As stated earlier, when analysing transcriptions, academic staff will be identified as Lecturer A, B and so on; and elite staff will be identified as Senior Member of Staff A, B, and so on.

Another issue, connected to objectivity, is that it may prove more difficult for colleagues to view the researcher other than a colleague than it may be for the researcher to view current colleagues as research subjects. This is a danger that the researcher is aware of and will attempt to minimize by clarifying the researcher's role and by informing participants of the purpose of the research, the uses of the collected data and the manner in which participants could assist in the research. The fact that the researcher is recognized within Division

X as a researcher with publications in the field may go some way to gaining the respect and trust of colleagues.

This chapter has provided the rationale and operational details of the research strategy used in this research. It has also addressed the limitations of this research and illustrated the approaches used to minimize potential criticisms. The next chapter – Case Study Results – initially places the study within the context of IU, and then discusses and analyses the results of the case study.

Appendix F: Sample Questionnaire

Data Collection Technique: Structured Interview (Academic Staff)

Data Collection Technique: Structured Interview (Academic Staff)

Interviewer:
Interviewee reference:
Date:
Time:
Place:

Thank you for agreeing to this meeting. This interview forms part of my dissertation research into e-Learning in universities. The purpose of this interview is to obtain your views on a number of aspects related to e-Learning within Inverclyde University.

A. THEME: University Drivers for e-Learning

Question 1A
The university's Strategic Planning Document makes reference to e-Learning targets and objectives.
Do you know what these are?

Question 2A
The Inverclyde Business School's (IBS) plan for 2002/3 to 2005/6 also makes reference to e-Learning targets and objectives.
Do you know what these are?

Question 3A
Why do you think university management wish academic staff to become involved in e-Learning?

Question 4A
What advantages do you think e-Learning will have for students?

Question 5A
What advantages do you think e-Learning will have for academic staff?

B. THEME: Barriers

Question 1B
Which of the following terms best describes your reaction to e-Learning?

- *Enthusiastic*
- *Interested*
- *Indifferent*
- *Not interested*
- *Concerned*

Could you elaborate, please?

Question 2B
Do you think that e-Learning will have any disadvantages for students? If so, what?

Question 3B
Do you think that e-Learning will have any disadvantages for academic staff? If so, what?

Question 4B
Overall, do you have any concerns or fears about implementing e-Learning in your department? (impact on pass rates, social exclusion, dependence on technology, job security, diminuition of power). If yes, what are your main concerns?

Question 5B
Are there any barriers to hinder you becoming involved in e-Learning and, if so, what would you suggest are ways to overcome such barriers (if they exist)?

C. THEME: Preparation

Question 1C
Do you think that you are adequately prepared to cope with e-Learning?

If not, why not?

Question 2C
Do you think that academic staff need any special skills or aptitude to be able to cope with e-Learning? (if so, what?)

Question 3C
Do you think that students need any special skills or aptitude to be able to cope with e-Learning? (if so, what?)

Question 4C
Do you know how students are being prepared for e-Learning?

Question 5C
How do you think IU students will cope/ are coping with e-Learning? What impact do you think e-Learning will have for IU on-campus students?

Question 6C
The e-Learning environment Blackboard was used as the vehicle to prepare the postgraduate E-Business programme for the China market. Using the suite of post-grad programmes prepared for the China market as a case study of a blended approach to e-Learning:

(a) *What will encourage you to place your material on Blackboard?*
(b) *What will discourage you?*
(c) *Will you place your material on Blackboard? (and why?)*
     If yes:

     How do you envisage that your material (content and presentation) will differ from that given to traditional IU students for the same module?

Question 7C

(i) *Your department invited several guest speakers to talk about e-Learning:*

     (a) *Were these seminars compulsory or optional?*
     (b) *Did you attend these seminars? If not, why not and what would encourage you to attend?*
          If yes,

          – *why did you attend?*
          – *how long were the seminars?*
          – *what did you think of the seminars (specifically what did you learn)?*
          – *did the seminars differentiate between on-campus e-Learning and distance learning?*
          – *what models of good practice, if any, were you encouraged to adopt? What did you think of these models?*

(ii) *The university offers courses in e-Learning:*

     (a) *Are these courses compulsory or optional?*
     (b) *Have you attended any of these courses? If not, why not and what would encourage you to attend?*
          If yes,

          – *what courses did you attend (and why)?*

- *what did you think of them (specifically what did you learn)?*
- *did these courses differentiate between on-campus e-Learning and distance learning?*
- *what models of good practice, if any, were you encouraged to adopt? What did you think of these models?*
- *and do you now feel confident about implementing an e-Learning environment?*

Question 8C
Is there an e-Learning guidance framework to assist academic staff in preparing for e-Learning?

D. THEME: IT Infrastructure

Question 1D
What do you think of the current system of IT support in IBS? (happy/unhappy with it?)

Question 2D
Are you confident that the existing IT support system is good enough to facilitate e-Learning environments? (if not, why not?)

E. THEME: Academic Staff Motivation

Question 1E
Do you think that academic staff should be rewarded for developing e-Learning environments?
If yes:
- *What sort of rewards do you think would be appropriate?*
- *What incentives are currently on offer to develop e-Learning initiatives, if any?*

Question 2E
Are you expected to develop e-Learning initiatives in addition to your existing duties?

Question 3E
What would encourage you to become/continue to be involved? What would discourage you?

Question 4E
Would you consider the university's approach to involving staff in e-Learning encouraging or discouraging? (Why?)

Question 5E
Do you think academic staff need to be motivated to become involved in e-Learning?
If yes, what should be done to motivate staff to participate in e-Learning?

F. THEME: Reflections and Future Directions

Question 1F
How would you rate the progress of e-Learning initiatives within your department as a whole?

Question 2F
What factors do you consider to be crucial to the successful implementation of e-Learning?

Question 3F
In what way do you envisage e-Learning changing your role as a university teacher? Is this good or bad (this change)?

Appendix G: Sample marking sheet

MSc. BUSINESS MANAGEMENT
(UNIVERSITY OF BARRA)

MARKING SCHEME

STUDENT NAME: _____

1st marker: _____
2nd marker: _____   AGREED MARK: ____

Aspect	Possible Mark	Actual Mark
1. Aims and Objectives	10	__
2. Literature Review	15	__
3. Research Methods	15	__
4. Findings and Discussion	20	__
5. Conclusion(s) and Recommendation(s)	15	__
6. Referencing	5	__
7. Abstract	10	__
8. Structure and Quality of written English	10	__
	100	**Total Mark:**

Comments:

Appendix H: Sample completed marking sheet

MSc. BUSINESS MANAGEMENT
(UNIVERSITY OF BARRA)

MARKING SCHEME

STUDENT NAME: Pat Houston

1st marker: Dr John Biggam
2nd marker: Dr Alan Hogarth   AGREED MARK: 87%

Aspect	Possible Mark	Actual Mark
1. Aim and Objectives	10	10
2. Literature Review	15	11
3. Research Methods	15	12
4. Findings and Discussion	20	17
5. Conclusion(s) and Recommendation(s)	15	12
6. Referencing	5	5
7. Abstract	10	10
8. Structure and Quality of written English	10	8
	100	Total Mark: 85%

Comments:

This is an excellent dissertation, showing a clear grasp of both theory and practice. In particular:

 – the aims and objectives are crystal clear, as well as being realistic
 – the abstract is faultless, as is the student's use of the Harvard system of referencing
 – the research methods used for his empirical work are appropriate, lucidly explained and justified
 – the discussion follows a clearly mapped-out frame of analysis, eliciting interesting comparisons between theory and practice

– the concluding chapter admirably summarizes the work, revisiting the initial research objectives, and provides logical conclusions, as well as making sensible recommendations on the way forward

In terms of room for improvement, the Literature Review concentrates too much time and effort on definitions, and he has omitted some recently published surveys that are particularly pertinent to his Literature Review. That said, this is a very impressive effort, for which the student is to be applauded.

Appendix I: Comprehensive set of useful verbs

Accepts
Acknowledges
Acquiesces
Adduces
Admits
Adopts
Advances
Advises
Advocates
Agrees
Alludes
Appears
Argues
Arrives at
Articulates
Asserts
Assumes
Attempts
Bombasts
Bores
Builds
Cajoles
Calculates
Captures
Cautions
Challenges
Clarifies
Clings
Clutches
Comments
Compares
Compiles
Complains
Concludes
Concocts

Concurs
Confirms
Confuses
Considers
Conspires
Constructs
Contemplates
Contends
Contrives
Conveys
Convinces
Cultivates
Dabbles
Debates
Debunks
Declares
Deduces
Defends
Delves
Demonstrates
Denounces
Denies
Derides
Derives
Desists
Determines
Develops
Digresses
Dilutes
Disagrees
Discloses
Discovers
Discusses
Dismisses
Dispels

Dispenses
Displays
Disputes
Dissects
Dissents
Distils
Distinguishes
Distorts
Diverges
Diverts
Dodges
Drags
Drifts
Earns
Eases
Echoes
Effaces
Effects
Effuses
Elaborates
Elucidates
Embarks
Embellishes
Embraces
Emphasizes
Employs
Enables
Enchants
Endears
Endorses
Engages
Engineers
Enlightens
Enthrals
Entices

Enunciates
Epitomizes
Equates
Erects
Errs
Eschews
Espouses
Establishes
Evaluates
Evangelizes
Evokes
Exaggerates
Excels
Exhibits
Expands
Explains
Explores
Expresses
Expunges
Extricates
Fabricates
Faces
Fails
Falters
Favours
Fawns
Feigns
Ferments
Fiddles
Fields
Finds
Fluctuates
Forges
Forms
Formulates

Fortifies
Frees
Fulfils
Fusses
Gambles
Gathers
Gauges
Generates
Gets
Gilds
Gives
Glides
Glorifies
Grafts
Grapples
Grasps
Grates
Grinds
Gropes
Guesses
Hampers
Handles
Hankers
Has
Hatches
Hedges
Helps
Heralds
Hesitates
Highlights
Hijacks
Hikes
Hinders
Holds
Identifies

Ignores
Illuminates
Illustrates
Imagines
Imbues
Imparts
Impedes
Impels
Impinges
Implants
Implicates
Implies
Implores
Imposes
Impregnates
Impresses
Improves
Impugns
Imputes
Incites
Inclines
Includes
Inculcates
Indicates
Induces
Indulges
Infers
Infests
Inflames
Inflates
Inflicts
Influences
Informs
Infringes
Inhibits
Injects
Inquires
Insinuates
Insists
Inspects
Inspires
Instigates
Instructs
Insults
Integrates

Intends
Interferes
Interjects
Interprets
Intertwines
Interweaves
Intimates
Introduces
Intrudes
Inundates
Invalidates
Inveighs
Invents
Investigates
Invigorates
Invites
Involves
Irritates
Iterates
Joins
Jostles
Jumps
Justifies
Juxtaposes
Knows
Kowtows
Labours
Lacerates
Lags
Laments
Lampoons
Lances
Lapses
Lauds
Launches
Lays
Leads
Leans
Learns
Lectures
Lends
Lets
Likes
Limps
Lingers

Links
Lists
Litters
Livens
Loads
Lobs
Locates
Loiters
Looks
Lurches
Magnifies
Maintains
Makes
Maligns
Maltreats
Manages
Manifests
Marks
Marvels
Massages
Master's
Mauls
Means
Measures
Meddles
Mediates
Mentions
Merges
Merits
Militates
Milks
Minces
Miscalculates
Misfires
Misinforms
Misinterprets
Misjudges
Misleads
Misrepresents
Misses
Mistakes
Misunderstands
Misuses
Mitigates
Mixes

Moans
Mocks
Models
Modifies
Modulates
Motivates
Moulds
Mounts
Moves
Muddles
Mulls
Muses
Musters
Nags
Names
Narrates
Needs
Negates
Neglects
Negotiates
Niggles
Notes
Notices
Nullifies
Nurtures
Obeys
Obfuscates
Objects
Obliges
Obliterates
Obscures
Observes
Obsesses
Obstructs
Obtains
Occupies
Offends
Offers
Omits
Oozes
Operates
Opposes
Oppresses
Opts
Ordains

Organizes
Oscillates
Ostracizes
Outlines
Outwits
Overawes
Overcomes
Overindulges
Overlooks
Overreaches
Overreacts
Overworks
Pads
Paints
Panders
Panics
Papers
Parables
Paraphrases
Participates
Peddles
Pens
Penetrates
Peppers
Perceives
Percolates
Perfects
Performs
Permeates
Permits
Perpetrates
Perpetuates
Perseveres
Persists
Personifies
Persuades
Pervades
Perverts
Pierces
Pilfers
Pillories
Pinions
Pioneers
Placates
Places

Plans	Professes	Reassures	Repels	Scrambles
Plods	Proffers	Rebels	Repents	Scrapes
Plucks	Profiles	Rebuffs	Replies	Scrutinizes
Plugs	Profits	Rebukes	Reports	Searches
Plummets	Profligates	Rebuts	Represents	Secures
Plunders	Progresses	Recants	Reprimands	Seems
Plunges	Proliferates	Receives	Reproaches	Sees
Poaches	Promotes	Reciprocates	Repudiates	Seizes
Points	Prompts	Recites	Repulses	Selects
Pollutes	Pronounces	Reckons	Requests	Sacrifices
Ponders	Propagates	Recognizes	Requires	Sends
Pontificates	Proposes	Recommends	Rescinds	Senses
Populates	Propounds	Reconciles	Rescues	Separates
Portends	Proscribes	Reconsiders	Researches	Serves
Portrays	Prostrates	Reconstructs	Resembles	Sets
Poses	Protests	Records	Resents	Settles
Positions	Provides	Recreates	Resists	Shapes
Possess	Provokes	Rectifies	Resolves	Shares
Postures	Publishes	Redeems	Resorts	Shifts
Praises	Puffs	Redresses	Respects	Shines
Prances	Pulverizes	Reduces	Responds	Shirks
Prattles	Pursues	Refers	Restricts	Shocks
Preaches	Pushes	Reflects	Retains	Shoulders
Precedes	Postulates	Reforms	Retracts	Shows
Precipitates	Puts	Refrains	Retreats	Shrinks
Predicts	Qualifies	Refuses	Retrieves	Shrouds
Pre-empts	Quantifies	Regales	Reveals	Shuns
Prefers	Quarrels	Regards	Reviews	Shuts
Prejudices	Queries	Regrets	Revises	Shies
Prepares	Questions	Reinforces	Revokes	Signals
Prescribes	Quibbles	Reiterates	Resolves	Signifies
Presents	Quotes	Rejects	Rids	Simplifies
Preserves	Radiates	Relapses	Ridicules	Simulates
Presses	Rages	Relates	Rues	Sinks
Presumes	Raises	Relents	Ruminates	Sketches
Pretends	Rallies	Relies	Sabotages	Skims
Prevails	Rambles	Relishes	Salvages	Skips
Prevaricates	Rants	Remains	Samples	Skirts
Prevents	Rates	Remarks	Sanctions	Slams
Probes	Rationalizes	Remedies	Satirizes	Slanders
Processes	Raves	Reminds	Satisfies	Slants
Proclaims	Reaches	Removes	Savages	Slays
Procures	Reacts	Renders	Schemes	Slights
Prods	Realizes	Repairs	Scintillates	Slings
Produces	Reasons	Repeats	Scorns	Slips

Slots	Struts	Teeters	Undermines	Wallows
Smears	Studies	Tempers	Underrates	Wanders
Smothers	Stumbles	Tempts	Understands	Wants
Snubs	Subjects	Tends	Understates	Warms
Softens	Submits	Terminates	Undertakes	Warrants
Solicits	Subscribes	Tests	Undervalues	Wastes
Solidifies	Substantiates	Testifies	Unearths	Wavers
Solves	Subverts	Thanks	Unfolds	Waxes
Sorts	Succeeds	Theorizes	Unifies	Weaves
Sources	Succumbs	Thrives	Unites	Welcomes
Sparks	Suffers	Thrusts	Unloads	Wheedles
Spearheads	Suffices	Tirades	Unlocks	Whines
Speculates	Suggests	Toils	Unravels	Whittles
Spends	Summarizes	Tolerates	Untangles	Wills
Spins	Supplants	Touches	Unties	Winds
Spoils	Supplies	Traces	Unveils	Wishes
Spots	Supports	Tracks	Unwinds	Withdraws
Spouts	Supposes	Transcends	Upholds	Withers
Spreads	Suppresses	Transforms	Upsets	Withstands
Squabbles	Surmises	Transgresses	Urges	Witnesses
Squanders	Surmounts	Transmits	Uses	Wobbles
Squares	Surpasses	Traverses	Utilizes	Wonders
Stands	Surrounds	Treats	Validates	Works
Starts	Surveys	Tricks	Values	Wrenches
States	Suspects	Trifles	Vents	Wrestles
Stiffens	Sustains	Triumphs	Ventures	Wriggles
Stimulates	Sways	Trivializes	Verges	Wrings
Stirs	Symbolizes	Trumps	Views	Writes
Stops	Sympathizes	Trumpets	Vilifies	Yanks
Strafes	Synthesizes	Tries	Vindicates	Yearns
Strains	Tabulates	Tweaks	Violates	Yields
Strays	Taints	Typifies	Vituperates	Zaps
Strengthens	Takes	Unburdens	Vocalizes	Zings
Stresses	Talks	Undercuts	Voices	Zips
Stretches	Tarnishes	Underestimates	Volunteers	
Strives	Taunts	Undergoes	Wades	
Structures	Teases	Underlines	Waffles	

Appendix J: List of research objective **keywords**

Analyse
Appraise
Assess
Calculate
Categorize
Clarify
Classify
Collate
Compare
Contrast
Construct
Create
Demonstrate
Derive
Detect
Describe
Design
Develop

Devise
Diagnose
Differentiate
Discern
Discover
Distinguish
Establish
Estimate
Evaluate
Examine
Execute
Expand
Experiment
Explain
Explore
Fix
Formulate
Generate

Highlight
Identify
Illuminate
Illustrate
Implement
Improve
Indicate
Integrate
Invent
Investigate
Itemize
Judge
List
Locate
Measure
Modify
Organize
Outline

Prescribe
Prioritize
Probe
Process
Produce
Progress
Prove
Quantify
Query
Recommend
Reconstruct
Refine
Reform
Reveal
Review
Scrutinize
Show
Simplify

Solve
Sort
Specify
Standardize
Streamline
Study
Synthesize
Tabulate
Test
Trace
Transform
Translate
Underline
Understand
Unite
Use
Validate
Verify

References

Adelman, C., Jenkins, D. and Kemmis, S. (1977). 'Re-Thinking case study: notes from the second Cambridge conference', *Cambridge Journal of Education*, 6: 139–50.

Akister, J., Williams, I. and Maynard, A. (2006). 'Innovations in the supervision of social work undergraduate dissertations: group and individual supervision', in *Proceedings of the Higher Education Academy Annual Conference*, July, Harrogate, UK.

Anderson, L. W. and Krathwohl, D. R. (2001). *A Taxonomy for Learning, Teaching and Assessment: A Revision of Bloom's Taxonomy of Educational Objectives*, New York: Longman.

Australian National Training Authority (2003). 'Definition of key terms used in e-Learning', *Australian Flexible Learning Framework Quick Guide Series*, 1:3.

Bassey, M. (1981). 'Pedagogical Research: on the relative merits of search for generalization and study in single events', *Oxford Review of Education*, 7(1): 73–93.

Bates, A. (2000). *Managing Technological Change. Strategies for Colleges and University Leaders*, San Francisco: Jossy-Bass.

Bates, T. (2001). 'The Continuing Evolution of ICT Capacity: the Implications for Education' [Online], in *The Changing Faces of Education*, Vancouver, Canada: The Commonwealth of Learning. Available at: www.col.org. Last accessed: 15th April 2004.

Bell, J. (1993). *Doing Your Research Project*, Buckingham: Open University Press.

Bell, J. (2005). *Doing Your Research Project: A Guide for First-Time Researchers in Education, Health and Social Science*, Berkshire: Open University Press.

Biggam, J. (2007a). 'Re-thinking dissertation supervision practices: collaborative learning through learner circles', in *Proceedings of the International Association for Technology, Education and Development (INTED)*, Valencia, Spain.

Biggam, J. (2007b). 'Give credit where credit is due: e-plagiarism and universities', in *Proceedings of the International Association for Technology, Education and Development (INTED)*, Valencia, Spain.

Biggs, J. (1999). *Teaching for Quality Learning at University*, Oxford: Society for Research into Higher Education and OUP.

Bloom, B. S. (1956). *Taxonomy of Educational Objectives: The Classification of Educational Goals Handbook I: Cognitive Domain*, New York: McKay.

Bogdan, R. C. and Biklen, S. K. (1982). *Qualitative Research for Education: An Introduction to Theory and Methods*, Boston: Allyn and Bacon.

Bone, A. (2003). 'Plagiarism: a guide for law lectures' [Online], The UK Centre for Legal Education. Available at: http://www.ukcle.ac.uk/resources/trns/plagiarism/index.html. Last accessed: 12 May 2006.

Borg, W. R. (1981). *Applying Educational Research: A Practical Guide for Teachers*, New York: Longman.

Bradbury, A. (2006). *Successful Presentational Skills*, London: Kogan Page.

Britain, S. and Liber, O. (1999). 'A Framework for Pedagogical Evaluation of Virtual Learning Environments' [Online], Joint Information Systems Committee (JISC)

Technology Applications (JTAP) Report 41. Available at: www.jtap.ac.uk/reports/htm/jtap-041.htm . Last accessed: 30th October 2003.

Buglear, J. (2001). *Stats Means Business*, Oxford: Butterworth-Heinemann.

Buglear, J. (2004). *Quantitative Methods for Business: The A to Z of QM*, Oxford: Elsevier.

Burns, E. (1994). 'Information Assets, Technology and Organization', *Management Science*, 40 (12): 645–662.

Burns, J. (2005). Jerry Burns' Classes [Online]. Available at: http://cw.mariancollege.edu/jburns/RWAC/plagiarism%20dot%20org.html. Last accessed: 11 May 2006.

Cohen, L. and Manion, L. (1995). *Research Methods in Education*, London: Routledge.

Collins, M. and Berge, Z. (1996). 'Facilitating Interaction in Computer Mediated Online Courses', in *Proceedings of FSU/AECT Distance Education Conference*, Tallahassee, FL, June.

Collis, B. and Moonen, J. (2001). *Flexible learning in a digital world: experiences and expectations*, London: Kogan Page.

Conole, G., Oliver, M., Isroff, K. and Ravenscroft, A. (2004). 'Addressing Methodological Issues in e-Learning Research', in *Proceedings of the Networked Learning Conference 2004*, Sheffield. Available at: www.sef.ac.uk/nlc/Proceedings/Symposa4.htm. Last accessed: 2nd October 2004.

Coppola, N. W., Hiltz, S. R. and Rotter, N. (2001). 'Becoming a Virtual Professor: Pedagogical Roles and ALN', in *Proceedings of the 34th Hawaii International Conference on Systems Sciences*, Maui, Hawaii, 95–104. Available at: http://csdl2.computer.org/comp/proceedings/hicss/2001/0981/01/09811003.pdf. Last accessed: 28th December 2007.

Council of Writing Program Administrators (2003). 'Defining and avoiding plagiarism: the WPA Statement on best practices' [Online]. Available at: www.ilstu.edu/~ddhesse/wpa/positions/WPAplagiarism.pdf. Last accessed: 1 June, 2006.

Cowan, J. (2004). 'Education and Learning Wales (ELWa)'. Available at: http://www.elwa.ac.uk/ElwaWeb/portal.aspx.

Creswell, J. (1997). *Qualitative Enquiry and Research Design*, Thousand Oaks, CA: Sage Publications.

Cunningham, J. B. (1995). 'Strategic considerations in using action research for improving personnel practices', *Public Personnel Management*, 24(2): 515–29.

Davenport, T. H. and Prusak, L. (1998). *Working Knowledge*, Boston: Harvard Business School Press.

Davies, C. A. (1999). *Reflexive Ethnography: A Guide to Researching Selves and Others*, London: Routledge.

Dawson, C. (2006). *A Practical Guide to Research Methods*, Oxford: How to Books Ltd.

Dearing, R. (1997). *National Committee of Inquiry into Higher Education: Higher Education in the Learner Society*, London: HMSO.

Deech, R. (2006). 'Plagiarism and institutional risk management', in *Proceedings of 2nd International Plagiarism Conference*, The Sage, Gateshead, 19–21 June.

Denzin, N. K. and Lincoln, Y. S. (eds) (1994). *Handbook of Qualitative Research*, Thousand Oaks, CA: Sage Publications.

Denzin, N. K. and Lincoln, Y. S. (2000). *Handbook of Qualitative Research*, 2nd edn, Thousand Oaks, CA: Sage.

Department for Education and Skills (2003). *Towards a Unified e-Learning Strategy*, Consultation Document, DFES: HMSO. Available at: www.dfes.gov.uk/elarningstartegy.

Dey, I. (1999). *Grounding Grounded Theory: Guidelines for Qualitative Inquiry*, San Diego: Academic Press.

Dinwoodie, R. (2007). 'Statisticians claim neutrality is compromised by executive pressure', *The Herald*, Thursday February 1.

Dordoy, A. (2002). 'Cheating and plagiarism: staff and student perceptions at Northumbria' [Online], Northumbria Online Conference. Available at: http://www.jiscpas.ac.uk/images/bin/AD.doc. Last accessed: 12 May 2006.

Dreyfus, H. L. (2001). *On the Internet*, London: Routeledge.

Ehrenborg, J. and Mattock, J. (2004). *Powerful Presentations: Great Ideas for Making a Real Impact*, London: Kogan Page.

Epic (2002). 'Making Scotland a global e-Learning player', a final report for Scottish Enterprise.

Farrell, G. (2001). 'The Changing Faces of Virtual Education' [Online], The Commonwealth of Learning, Vancouver, Canada. Available at: http://www.col.org/colweb/site/. Last accessed: 14th November 2006.

Field, A. (2000). *Discovering Statistics Using SPSS for Windows: Advanced Techniques for Beginners*, London: Sage.

Flood, J. (2002). 'Read all about it: online learning facing 80% attrition rates', *The Turkish Online Journal of Distance Learning (TOJDE)*, 3(2): 1–4.

Fowler, F. (2001). *Survey Research Methods*, Thousand Oaks, CA: Sage.

Gavron, H. (1996). *The Captive Wife*, London: Routeledge.

Geertz, C. (1973). *Thick Description: Toward an Interpretive Theory of Culture*, New York: Basic Books.

Gerrard, W. (2002). 'The Provision of Distance Education within the HE Sector – some areas of concern', *The International Journal of Management Education*, 2(3): 45–52.

Gill, J. and Johnson, P. (1997). *Research Methods for Managers*, London: Chapman.

Glaser, B. and Strauss, A. (1967). *The Discovery of Grounded Theory*, Chicago: Aldine.

Greetham, B. (2001). *How to Write Better Essays*, New York: Palgrave Study Guides.

Grummit, J. (1980). *Interviewing Skills*, London: The Industrial Society.

Hall, R. (2007). *Brilliant Presentations: What the Best Presenters Know, Say and Do*, Harlow: Pearson Education Limited.

Hara, N. and Kling, R. (1999). 'Students' Frustrations with a Web-based Distance Education Course: a Taboo Topic in the Discourse', *First Monday*, 4(12): 1–34.

Hart, C. (2006). *Doing Your Master's Dissertation*, London: Sage.

Hart, M. and Friesner, T. (2003). 'I found it on the web' – some reflections on e-Learning, plagiarism and poor academic practice, paper presented at 2nd European Conference on e-Learning, Caledonian Business School, Glasgow Caledonian University, 6–7 November.

Haywood, J., MacLeod, H., Haywood, D., Mogey, N. and Alexander, W. (2004). 'The Student View of ICT in Education at the University of Edinburgh: skills, attitudes & expectations', in *Proceedings of the 11th International Conference of the Association for Learning Technology (ALT)*, University of Exeter, England, September. Available at: www.flp.ed.ac.uk. Last accessed: 15th October 2005.

Haywood, P. and Wragg, E. C. (1982). *Evaluating the Literature*, Rediguide 2, University of Nottingham School of Education, cited in Bell, J. (1993) *Doing Your Research Project*, Buckingham: Open University Press.

HEFCE (2000). 'HEFCE launches e-University business model' [Online], Press Release, Higher Education Funding Council for England, 10th October. Available at: http://www.hefce.ac.uk/News/HEFCE/2000/euniv2.htm. Last accessed: 20th December 2007.

Heisenberg, W. (1958). *Physics and Philosophy*, New York: Harper & Row.

Henry, G. (1990). *Practical Sampling*, Newbury Park, CA: Sage.

Hiney, T. and MacShane, F. (2000). *The Raymond Chandler Papers: Selected Letters and Nonfiction, 1909–1959*, New York: Atlantic Monthly Press.

Hoaglin, D. C., Light, R. J., McPeak, B., Mosteller, F. and Stotot, M. A. (1982). *Data for Decisions: Information Strategies for Policymakers*, Cambridge, M. A.: Abt Books.

Hodges, C. B. (2004). 'Designing to Motivate: Motivational Techniques to Incorporate in e-Learning Experiences' [Online], *The Journal of Interactive Online Learning*, 2(3): 1–7. Available at: www.ncolr.org. Last accessed: 20thNovember 2007.

Jones, M. (2006). 'Plagiarism proceedings in higher education', in *Proceedings of 2nd International Plagiarism Conference*, The Sage, Gateshead, 19–21 June.

Jones, P., Packham, G., Miller, C. and Jones, A. (2004). 'An initial valuation of student withdrawals within e-Learning: the case of e-College Wales', *Electronic Journal on e-Learning (EJEL)*, 2(1): 113–120.

Joyce, D. (2006). 'Promoting academic integrity among staff and students', in *Proceedings of 2nd International Plagiarism Conference*, The Sage, Gateshead, 19–21 June.

Jung, I. (2000). *Koreas Experiments with Virtual Education*, Education and Technology Notes Series, Washington D.C.: World Bank Human Development Network Education Group.

Laurillard, D. (2001). 'The e-University: what have we learned?', *The International Journal of Management Education*, 1(2): 3–7.

Laurillard, D. (2002). *Re-thinking University Teaching*, 2nd Edition, London: Routledge.

McCabe, D. (2006). 'Ethics in teaching, learning and assessment', in *Proceedings of 2nd International Plagiarism Conference*, The Sage, Gateshead, 19–21 June.

McLellan, L. (2003). 'Briefing: Plagiarism at Universities' [Online], Times Online. Available at: http://www.timesonline.co.uk. Last accessed: 4th June 2005.

MacLeod, A. (2007). 'SNP takes a pounding from the Chancellor', *The Times*, 7 April.

Marshall, C. and Rossman, G. B. (1989). *Designing Qualitative Research*, London: Sage Publications.

Marshall, C. and Rossman, G. B. (2006). *Designing Qualitative Research*, London: Sage Publications.

Marshall, S. and Garry, M. (2006). NESB and ESB students' attitudes and perceptions of plagiarism, *International Journal of Educational Integrity*, 2(1): 26–37.

Massey, J. (2002). 'Quality and eLearning in Europe' [Online], Summary Report for Electronic Training Village. Avaliable at: http://www2.trainingvillage.gr/etv/clearing/surveys/sureport.asp. Last accessed: 23rd June 2003.

Mertens, D. M. (1998). *Research Methods in Education and Psychology: Integrating Diversity with Quantitative and Qualitative Approaches*, Thousand Oaks, CA: Sage Publications.

Miles, M. and Huberman, A. (1984). *Qualitative Data Analysis: An Expanded Source Book*, Thousand Oaks, CA: Sage Publications.

Ministry of Education (2004). *Interim Tertiary e-Learning Framework* [Online], New Zealand: MOE. Available at: http://cms.steo.govt.nz/eLearning/Downloads/Tertiary+e-Learning+Framework/showall.htm. Last accessed: 28th December 2007.

Moe, M. and Blodget, H. (2000). *The Knowledge Web*, New York, N. Y.: Merrill Lynch.

Moser, C. A. and Kalton, G. (1971). *Survey Methods in Social Investigation*, London: Heinemann.

Myers, M. D. (1997). 'Qualitative research in information systems, *MISQ Discovery*' [Online]. Available at: www.misq.org/discovery/MISQ_isworld/. Last accessed: 23 March 2006.

Northwestern University (2005). 'How to avoid plagiarism' [Online], p.1. Available at: http://www.northwestern.edu/uacc/plagiar.html. Last accessed: 14 May 2006.

Nunes, J. M. B. and McPherson, M. A. (2002). 'Pedagogical and Implementation Models for E-Learning Continuing Professional Distance Education (CPDE) Emerging from Action Research', *The International Journal of Management Education*, 2(3): 16–26.

Ogden, S., McTavish, D. and McKean, L. (2006). 'Clearing the way for gender balance in the management of the UK financial services sector: enablers and barriers', *Women in Management Review*, 21(1): 41–53.

Oppenheim, A. N. (1992). *Questionnaire Design, Interviews and Attitude Measurements*, London: Pinter.

Orlikowski, W. J. and Baroudi, J. J. (1991). 'Studying information technology in organisations: research approaches and assumptions', *Information Systems Research*, 2: 1–28.

Papert, S. (1998). *The 11th Colin Cherry Memorial Lecture on Communication* [Given at Imperial College, London]. 2nd June. Available at: http://www.connectedfamily.com/main_alt.html. Last accessed: 31st December 2007.

Park, C. (2003). 'In other (people's) words: plagiarism by university students – literature and lessons', *Assessment and Evaluation in Higher Education*, 28(5): 471–88.

Patton, M. Q. (1990). *Qualitative Evaluation and Research Methods*, 2nd edn., Newbury Park, CA: Sage Publications Inc.

Peeke, G. (1984). 'Teacher as researcher', *Educational Research*, 26(1): 24–26.

Phillips, E. M. and Pugh, D. S. (2007). *How to Get a Ph.D.: A Handbook for Students and Their Supervisors*, Milton Keynes: Open University Press.

Proudfoot, R., Thompson, A. and Kastan, D. S. (eds) (2001). *The Arden Shakespeare Complete Works*, London: Thomson Learning.

Reason, P. and Bradbury, H. (2000). *Handbook of Action Research: Participative Inquiry and Practice*, Thousand Oaks, CA: Sage.

Remenyi, D., Williams, B., Money, A. and Swartz, E. (1998). *Doing Research in Business and Management: An Introduction to Process and Method*, London: Sage.

Riddell, P. and Webster, P. (2006). 'Support for Labour at lowest level since 1992', *The Times*, 9 May.

Roberts, B. (2007). *Getting the Most out of the Research Experience*, London: Sage Publications.

Robson, C. (1993). *Real World Research: a Resource for Social Scientists and Practitioner-Researchers*, Oxford: Blackwell.

Rockwell, K., Schauer, J., Fritz, S. M. and Marx, D. B. (2000). 'Faculty Education, Assistance and Support Needed to Deliver Education via Distance' [Online], *Online Journal of Distance Learning Administration*, 3(2). Available at: http://www.westga.edu/~distance/rockwell32.html. Last accessed: 28th December 2007.

Rosenberg, M. (2001). *E-Learning: Strategies for Delivering Knowledge in the Digital Age*, New York, NY: McGraw-Hill.

Ryan, Y. (2001). 'The Provision of Learner Support Services Online', in *The Changing Faces of Virtual Education*, Vancouver, Canada: The Commonwealth of Learning, 71–94.

Safire, W. (2002). *Fumblerules: A Lighthearted Guide to Grammar and Good Usage*, New York: Barnes & Noble.

Salmon, G. (1998). 'Developing Learning Through Effective Online Moderation', *Active Learning*, 9th December: 71–94.

Salmon, G. (2000). *E-Moderating: the key to teaching and learning online*, London: Kogan Page.

Sapsford, R. (1999). *Survey Research*, London: Sage.

Sapsford, R. and Judd, V. (1996). *Data Collection and Analysis*, London: Sage.

Saunders, M., Lewis, P. and Thornhill, A. (2000). *Research Methods for Business Students*, London: Pearson Education Limited.

Saunders, M., Lewis, P. and Thornhill, A. (2007). *Research Methods for Business Students*, 4th edn., Harlow: FT Prentice Hall.

Sennett, R. (1998). *The Corrosion of Character: The Personal Consequences of Work in the new Capitalism*, New York: W. W. Norton.

Silverman, D. (1997). *Interpreting Qualitative Data: Methods for Analysing Talk, Text and Interaction*, London: Sage.

Silverman, D. (2000). *Doing Qualitative Research: A Practical Handbook*, London: Sage.

Sloman, M. and Rolph, J. (2003). 'E-Learning. The Learning Curve. The Changing Agenda'. A report for the Chartered Institute of Personnel and Development (CIPD). Avaliable at: www.cipd.co.uk.

Straub, R. (2002). 'Hi-Tech hope will never blossom amid chaos', *The Times Higher Education Supplement*, July 26th.

Strauss, A. and Corbin, J. (1990). *Basics of Qualitative Research*, London: Sage Publications.

Taylor, A. E. (1955). *Aristotle*, New York, N. Y.: Dover Publications Inc.

Tearle, P., Dillon, P. and Davies, N. (1999). 'Use of information technology by English university teachers. Developments and trends at the time of the National Inquiry into Higher Education', *Journal of Further and Higher Education*, 23(1): 5–15.

The Commission of the European Communities (2002). 'eLearning: Designing Tomorrow's Education' [Online], Interim Report, SEC (2001) 236, Brussels. Available at: http://europa.eu.int/rapid/start/cge/. Last accessed: 12th April 2004.

The Concise Oxford Dictionary (1998). Ninth Edition, Edited by D. Thomson, London: BCA.

The Herald (2007). 'Labour leads in new poll but 50% still to decide', 6 April.

The Indian Agra News (2007). 'Carbon footprints and economic globalisation', 18th April, p.4.

The Times (2007). 'Public Agenda: Media Monitor', 13 March.

The UK Council for Postgraduate Education (1999). *The International Postgraduate: Challenges to British Higher Education*, London: UK Council for Graduate Education.

The U.S. General Accounting Office (1990). *Case Study Evaluations*, Washington D.C.: Government Printing Office.

Tomei, L. (2004). 'The Impact of Online Teaching on Faculty Load' [Online], *International Journal of Instructional Technology and Distance Learning*. Avaliable at: http://www.itdl.org/journal/Jan_04/article04.htm. Last accessed: 24th December 2007.

Truss, L. (2003). *Eats Shoots and Leaves: The Zero Tolerance Approach to Punctuation*, London: Profile Books Ltd.

UK eUniversities Worldwide (2003). 'Information Support for eLearning: Principles and Practice' [Online], UKeU Briefing Paper. Available at: www.sconul.ac.uk/pubsInformation_Support_for_eLearning_Final.pdf. Last accessed: 8th April 2004.

Vermeer, R. (2000). 'Review of Internet based learning: an introduction and framework for higher education and business', *Computers & Education*, 35(4): 327–333.

Wojtas, O. (2006). 'I've had third-year students ask: is it OK to put bullet points in an essay?', *The Times Higher Education Supplement*, 1(742), May 12.

Wolcott, H. (1994). *Transforming Qualitative Data: Description, Analysis, Interpretation*, Thousand Oaks, CA: Sage Publications.

Yin, R. K. (2003). *Case Study Research: Design and Methods*, 3rd edn. Vol. 5, Thousand Oaks, CA: Sage Publications.

Zellweger, F. (2004). 'Institutional EdTech Support for Faculty at Research Universities – Insights from a Case Study at the Massachusetts Institute of Technology (MIT)', in *Proceedings of Ed-Media 2004*, World Conference on Educational Media, Hypermedia & Telecommunications, June 21–26, Lugano, Switzerland.

Zukav, G. (1979). *The Dancing Wu Li Masters*, New York: William Morrow and Company.

index